Downtown Los Angeles (Griffith Park, Hollywood, Baldwin Hills)

West (including San Fernando Valley, Verdugo Mountains, Santa Monica Mountains)

East (including Glendale, Pasadena, San Gabriel Mountains)

Coast (Malibu, Pacific Palisades, Palos Verdes)

Orange County

Ventura Canyon area (including Simi and Antelope Valleys)

60 Hikes
within 60 MILES

LOS ANGELES

INCLUDING SAN GABRIEL, VENTURA, AND ORANGE COUNTIES

Laura Randall

MENASHA RIDGE PRESS
Birmingham, Alabama

Library of Congress Cataloging-in-Publication Data

Randall, Laura, 1967–
    60 hikes within 60 miles, Los Angeles: including San Gabriel, Ventura, and
Orange Counties/Laura Randall.—1st ed.
p.cm
ISBN 10: 0-89732-638-5
ISBN 13: 978-0-89732-638-4
1. Hiking—California—Los Angeles region—Guidebooks. 2. Los Angeles Region
(Calif.)—Guidebooks. I. Title Sixty hikes within sixty miles, Los Angeles. II. Title.

GV199.42.C22L6566 2006
917.94'940454—dc22   2005053413

Cover design by Grant M. Tatum
Text design by Karen Ocker
Cover photo © Ambient Images Inc. / Alamy
All other photos by Laura Randall
Maps by Scott McGrew and Steve Jones

Menasha Ridge Press
P.O. Box 43673
Birmingham, AL 35243
www.menasharidge.com

for Jack

TABLE OF CONTENTS

TABLE OF CONTENTS

ACKNOWLEDGMENTS

A special thanks to all the park rangers and desk receptionists who patiently provided me with condition updates during last winter's damaging rainstorms and described trails with the kind of detail and enthusiasm parents exhibit when they talk about their children. The volunteers who clean and maintain trails like Sam Merrill in Altadena and Amir's Garden in Griffith Park also deserve a singling out of gratitude for upholding the spirit of the departed nature lovers for whom the trails are named and making life on the trails better for the rest of us.

I would also like to thank my parents, Bill and Rosemarie Randall, and my in-laws, Fran, John, and James Kimble, for accompanying me on several hikes with contagious doses of enthusiasm and energy. They also, uncomplaining, pitched in with babysitting whenever I needed to sneak a few hikes in by myself or hide away with the laptop to meet a deadline.

Finally, I couldn't have completed this book without the tireless legs, companionship, and encouragement of my husband, John. A nod also needs to go to our son, Jack, who at the tender age of two months was introduced (via baby carrier) to the trails of southern California and handled it with sleepy-eyed ease. I can't wait to revisit them with him when he can walk.

—*Laura Randall*

FOREWORD

Welcome to Menasha Ridge Press's *60 Hikes within 60 Miles*, a series designed to provide hikers with information needed to find and hike the very best trails surrounding cities usually underserved by good guidebooks.

Our strategy was simple: First, find a hiker who knows the area and loves to hike. Second, ask that person to spend a year researching the most popular and very best trails around. And third, have that person describe each trail in terms of difficulty, scenery, condition, elevation change, and all other categories of information that are important to hikers. "Pretend you've just completed a hike and met up with other hikers at the trailhead," we told each author. "Imagine their questions, be clear in your answers."

An experienced hiker and writer, author Laura Randall has selected 60 of the best hikes in and around the Los Angeles metropolitan area. From casual strolls through manicured gardens to history-rich explorations of old railway routes and early twentieth-century movie sets, from birding excursions in coastal wetlands to backcountry treks through the Santa Monica Mountains, Randall provides hikers (and walkers and trail runners) with a great variety of routes—and all within roughly 60 miles of Los Angeles.

You'll get more out of this book if you take a moment to read the Introduction explaining how to read the trail listings. The "Topographic Maps" section will help you understand how useful topos will be on a hike, and will also tell you where to get them. And though this is a "where-to," not a "how-to" guide, those of you who have hiked extensively will find the Introduction of particular value.

As much for the opportunity to free the spirit as well as to free the body, let these hikes elevate you above the urban hurry.

All the best,
The Editors at Menasha Ridge Press

ABOUT THE AUTHOR

A native of suburban Philadelphia, Laura Randall lived in Washington, D.C. and San Juan, Puerto Rico, before moving to the Los Angeles area in 1999. Her byline can be found in a variety of newspapers and consumer magazines, including the *Los Angeles Times,* the *Washington Post, Sunset* magazine, and the *Christian Science Monitor.* She and her family recently moved to a neighborhood in the foothills of the San Gabriel Mountains, which she was happy to discover is within walking distance of half a dozen excellent trails.

PREFACE

When I signed on to write this book, I thought I knew most everything about hiking in Los Angeles. I lived near the Hollywood Hills and hiked the canyons regularly both for exercise and as a quick escape from the chaos of living and working in a city teeming with millions of people. Whenever we had out-of-town guests, my husband and I always tried to squeeze a hike into the sightseeing agenda, often one that included postcard-worthy coastal views, to show them there was more to L.A. than movie stars and freeway gridlock. As I started to do research for this book, however, I realized I had only tapped the surface of the Los Angeles hiking experience. I discovered fabulous trails hidden behind freeway exits, amid tract developments, and next to airports. I stumbled on treks through historic city neighborhoods I never knew existed. I clambered over boulders and across fields that once served as a backdrop for John Wayne, Henry Fonda, and other movie stars. One of my favorite discoveries—the Devil's Punchbowl Loop Trail near the San Andreas Fault—opened up a whole new side of Los Angeles County I never knew existed and offered an up-close lesson on the region's vulnerability to earthquakes. Another favorite—the Peter Strauss Trail in the Santa Monica Mountains—impressed me with its seclusion and total surrender to nature; despite its proximity to busy Mulholland Drive, I had the lovely grounds and trails all to myself during the Saturday afternoon I spent there.

I still love the busy canyon trails—Runyon Canyon remains one of my all-time favorites for its city-ocean-mountain views and people-watching opportunities. But now I know that when friends and family visit, they can choose from a long list of trails guaranteed to suit every mood and season.

▶ THE TRAILS

Most of L.A.'s public hiking trails can be found north and west of downtown.

SANTA MONICA MOUNTAINS

The Santa Monica Mountains are probably the most popular and recognizable. Comprising more than 153,000 acres, the Santa Monica Recreation Area sprawls across the Hollywood Hills, Malibu, the San Fernando Valley, and the southwestern tip of Ventura County. It is the world's largest urban national park. The trails here have it all—waterfalls, volcanic-rock formations, dense woodland, and 100-mile coastal views. Anchoring the whole system is the Backbone Trail, an unfinished 60-plus-mile

Wildflowers along the way to Parker Overlook

path that runs between Will Rogers State Park in Pacific Palisades and Point Mugu State Park in Ventura County.

ANGELES NATIONAL FOREST

Established as a national forest in 1892, the 656,000-acre forest includes much of the San Gabriel Mountains and parts of the Santa Clarita and Antelope valleys. It boasts more than 500 miles of hiking trails, 110 camping and picnic sites, and 5 lakes, and its elevations range from 1,200 to 10,064 feet. Dense chaparral and fir and pine trees blanket much of the forest; it also is home to volcanic rock formations, coastal sage scrub, and a cornucopia of spring wildflowers. More than 3.5 million people annually use the forest's recreational areas, but its trails often feel seem uncrowded and secluded.

VERDUGO MOUNTAINS

A geologically detached piece of the San Gabriel Mountains, the Verdugos encompass 9,000 acres of chaparral, coastal sage scrub, southern willow scrub, coast live oak, and waterfalls. The mountains can be accessed via Burbank and Glendale on the San Fernando Valley and Tujunga and La Tuna Canyon from La Crescenta Valley. A network of relatively new fire roads makes for excellent hiking and biking conditions.

OTHERS

Then there are the random parks that dot the city and bring their own unique scenery and style to the southern California hiking experience—parks like Deukmejian Wilderness Park in Glendale, Wildwood Park in Thousand Oaks, and the Kenneth Hahn Recreation Area in Baldwin Hills. Griffith Park, a kingdom unto itself, has some excellent off-the-beaten-path trails and shouldn't be ignored. Besides 53 miles of trails, the park boasts an observatory, a merry-go-round, zoo, outdoor amphitheater, and countless picnic areas. Another great yet

A steep section of the Sunset Ridge Trail

inexplicably unsung city park is Ernest E. Debs Regional Park, a.k.a. Debs Park, in the eastern L.A. neighborhood of Highland Park. The trails are pristine, quiet, and home to grasslands, wildflowers, more than 130 species of birds, and a bucolic hilltop pond. Angelenos drive right past this park every day via the busy Pasadena freeway, yet few outside the neighborhood even know it exists.

TIPS

A few words of advice that may help your southern California hiking experience.

Always have a backup trail in mind. With the unpredictability of the weather, trails are closed at a moment's notice, and reaching a ranger familiar with current conditions is sometimes challenging. Whenever I hiked the Santa Monica Mountains, I brought along a National Park Service (NPS) map of the entire area, just in case the trail I wanted was closed due to damage or a special event. The maps are available at the park service headquarters in Thousand Oaks. Call (818) 370-2301 to request one by mail or go online to www.nps.gov/samo.

Roam if you want to. Discovering new trails is one of the best parts of hiking in southern California. It's difficult to get impossibly lost, because many of the trails are well marked or cocooned by residential developments and freeways. Many of the parks listed in this book offer a variety of trails that cater to all levels of age and fitness. It's often easy to extend or shorten the trail described to fit your own needs.

Don't judge a trailhead by its cover. Some of the best L.A. trails begin in or near crowded residential developments or unsightly debris basins. It never ceased to amaze me how quickly I would find myself surrounded by wilderness and natural beauty after leaving my car.

Get creative with parking. Citing budget cuts and other constraints, more parks are charging visitors a day-use fee to use their parking lots. The fees range from $1 (Arroyo Verde Park in Ventura) to $8 (Crystal Cove State Park in Laguna Beach). Often, though, if you don't mind walking a bit farther to reach the trailhead, there is free parking on nearby streets. Just make sure to check signs for restrictions.

A bit tougher to get around is the Adventure Pass, a controversial fee program used by the Angeles, Cleveland, and Los Padres national forests. This requires all hikers, bikers, and other visitors to purchase a vehicle pass—either $5 a day or $30 a year—to use the forest.

PREFACE

It has been a controversial program from the start—enraged forest patrons have protested the experiment from the beginning—so be sure to check to see if it's still in existence. Passes can be purchased at forest ranger offices and local sporting goods stores such as REI, Big 5, and Sportmart. For a detailed list of vendors that sell the pass, go online to www.fs.fed.us/r5/sanbernardino/ap.vendors.php. Also accepted in lieu of an Adventure Pass are the NPS Golden Eagle, Golden Age, and Golden Access passports.

LIMITATIONS

While I was working on this book in winter 2005, Los Angeles was pummeled by its second rainiest season ever. More than 37 inches fell on the metropolis during the 2004–2005 season, causing phenomenal freeway gridlock, creating mudslides that toppled homes and decimated roads, and leaving behind millions of dollars in damage. Many hiking trails were badly battered by the storms and forced to close for days and even months as rangers assessed the damage and began plotting restoration plans. Some were still closed as this book went to press—including many in the Ojai District of the Los Padres National Forest. For updated information, go to www.fs.fed.us/r5/lospadres conditions/ or call the Ojai Ranger Station at (805) 646-4348.

I had to eliminate the inclusion of a handful of good hikes in this book due to their temporary inaccessibility and my need to meet deadlines. They include Rose Valley Falls Trail, a mile-long creekside hike that leads to the highest waterfall in the Los Padres National Forest; Big Santa Anita Canyon, a seven-mile waterfall trail in the Angeles National Forest above Arcadia; and Lake Hollywood, a picturesque loop trail in the shadow of the famous Hollywood sign. Another favorite trail, Santa Paula Canyon in Ventura County, was completely washed out by the storms, and forest rangers have expressed little hope that it will ever be restored.

At the same time, the rains left many trails more beautiful than ever. Spring wildflowers popped up everywhere, unmatched in brilliant color and abundance, and attracted record numbers of migrating painted-lady butterflies from Mexico. Chaparral-covered hills, typically more brown than green in color, were blanketed by a thousand shades of green. Waterfalls that tend to be little more than a trickle gushed with vigor. It was a season that few southern California outdoors enthusiasts will ever forget.

HIKING RECOMMENDATIONS

▶ 1 TO 3 MILES

Arroyo Sequit Trail
Charmlee Wilderness Park Loop Trail
Descanso Gardens: Chaparral Nature Trail
Devil's Punchbowl Loop
Griffith Park: Amir's Garden
Griffith Park: Bronson Caves
Millard Canyon Falls Trail
Oak Canyon Nature Center:
  Bluebird and Wren Trails
Peter Strauss Trail
Placerita Canyon: Heritage Trail and
  Botany Loop
South Coast Botanic Garden Trail

▶ 2 TO 4 MILES

Arroyo Verde Park Loop
Baldwin Hills: Walk for Health Trail
Bolsa Chica Ecological Reserve
Caballero Canyon Trail
Calabasas Peak Trail
Corriganville Park Loop Trail
Crystal Cove State Park:
  El Moro Canyon Trail
Debs Park: City View and
  Walnut Forest Trails
Deukmejian Wilderness Park: Dunsmore
  Canyon and Le Mesnager Loop Trails
Devil's Gate Trail to JPL
Duarte Recreational Trail
Eaton Canyon Stream Trail
Elysian Park: Angels Point to Bishops Canyon
Elysian Park: Wildflower Trail
Fryman Canyon Loop
Fullerton Panorama Trail
Garcia Trail to Azusa Peak
Griffith Park: Hollyridge Trail
Grotto Trail
Hacienda Hills Trail
Hummingbird Trail
La Cañada Fire Road to Gabrielino Trail
Legg Lake Loop Trail
Monrovia Canyon Park: Bill Cull Trail
Mount Washington: Jack Smith Trail
Paramount Ranch: Hacienda Trail to
  Backdrop Trail
Peters Canyon Lake View Trail
Rose Bowl Loop
Runyon Canyon Trail
San Vicente Mountain: Old Nike Missile Site
Silver Lake Reservoir Loop
Stough Canyon Nature Center Trail
Temescal Ridge Trail
Towsley Canyon View Trail
Wildwood Park: Lizard Rock Trail
Will Rogers State Park: Inspiration Point Trail

▶ 4 TO 6 MILES

Big Dalton Canyon Trail
Brand Fire Road Trail: Verdugo Mountains
Franklin Canyon: Cross Mountain and
  Hastain Trails
Gabrielino/Arroyo Seco Trail
Lower Arroyo Seco Park Trail
Millard Canyon: Sunset Ridge Trail
M*A*S*H Trail, Malibu Creek State Park
Mulholland Gateway Park:
  Hub Junction Trail
Palos Verdes: Portuguese Bend Trail
Paseo Miramar Trail to Parker Overlook
Placerita Canyon: Walker Ranch Trail
Sam Merrill Trail to Echo Mountain
Switzer Falls via Bear Canyon Trail

HIKING RECOMMENDATIONS

▶ HIKES WITH STRENUOUS CLIMBS

Brand Fire Road Trail: Verdugo Mountains
Calabasas Peak
Garcia Trail to Azusa Peak
Runyon Canyon Trail

Sam Merrill Trail to Echo Mountain
Temescal Ridge Trail
Towsley Canyon View Trail

▶ HIKES ALONG WATER

Gabrielino/Arroyo Seco Trail
Legg Lake Loop Trail
Lower Arroyo Seco Park Trail
M*A*S*H Trail, Malibu Creek State Park

Peters Canyon Lake View Trail
Placerita Canyon: Walker Ranch Trail
Silver Lake Reservoir
Switzer Falls via Bear Canyon Trail

▶ WATERFALL HIKES

Millard Falls Trail
Monrovia Canyon Park: Bill Cull Trail

Switzer Falls via Bear Canyon Trail

▶ HIKES WITH COASTAL VIEWS

Charmlee Wilderness Park
Crystal Cove State Park: El Moro Canyon
  Trail
Palos Verdes: Portuguese Bend Trail

Paseo Miramar Trail to Parker Overlook
Temescal Ridge Trail
Will Rogers State Park: Inspiration Point Trail

▶ HIKES FOR SOLITUDE

Big Dalton Canyon Trail
Griffith Park: Amir's Garden
Monrovia Canyon Park: Bill Cull Trail

Peter Strauss Trail
Stough Canyon Nature Center Trail

▶ HEAVY-TRAFFIC HIKES

Gabrielino/Arroyo Seco Trail
Paseo Miramar Trail to Parker Overlook
Rose Bowl Loop
Runyon Canyon Trail

Switzer Falls via Bear Canyon Trail
Will Rogers State Park: Inspiration Point Trail

▶ HIKES FOR BIRDING

Bolsa Chica Ecological Reserve
Devil's Gate Trail to JPL

Gabrielino/Arroyo Seco Trail
Hummingbird Trail

HIKING RECOMMENDATIONS

▶ HIKES FOR KIDS

Corriganville Park Loop

Debs Park: City View and
  Walnut Forest Trails

Descanso Gardens: Chaparral Nature Trail

Oak Canyon Nature Center: Bluebird and
  Wren Trails

Placerita Canyon: Heritage Trail and
  Botany Loop

▶ TRAILS FOR RUNNERS

Big Dalton Canyon Trail

Duarte Recreational Trail

Legg Lake Loop Trail

Peters Canyon Lake View Trail

Rose Bowl Loop

Silverlake Reservoir Loop

▶ HIKES WITH HISTORICAL INTEREST

Corriganville Park Loop

M*A*S*H Trail, Malibu Creek State Park

Mount Washington: Jack Smith Trail

Paramount Ranch: Hacienda Trail to
  Backdrop Trail

San Vicente Mountain: Old Nike Missile Site

Will Rogers State Park: Inspiration Point Trail

▶ WILDFLOWER HIKES

Arroyo Sequit Trail

Charmlee Wilderness Park Loop

Descanso Gardens: Chaparral Nature Trail

Elysian Park: Wildflower Trail

INTRODUCTION

Welcome to *60 Hikes within 60 Miles: Los Angeles*. If you're new to hiking or even if you're a seasoned trailsmith, take a few minutes to read the following introduction. We explain how this book is organized and how to use it.

▶ HIKE DESCRIPTIONS

Each hike contains eight key items: an "In Brief" description of the trail, a key at-a-glance information box, directions to the trail, UTM trailhead coordinates, a trail map, an elevation profile, a trail description, and nearby activities. Combined, the maps and information provide a clear method to assess each trail from the comfort of your favorite reading chair.

IN BRIEF

A "taste of the trail." Think of this section as a snapshot focused on the historical landmarks, beautiful vistas, and other sights you may encounter on the trail.

KEY AT-A-GLANCE INFORMATION

The information in the key at-a-glance boxes gives you a quick idea of the specifics of each hike. There are 12 basic elements covered.

LENGTH The length of the trail from start to finish. There may be options to shorten or extend the hikes, but the mileage corresponds to the described hike. Consult the hike description to help decide how to customize the hike for your ability or time constraints.

CONFIGURATION A description of what the trail might look like from overhead. Trails can be loops, out-and-backs (that is, along the same route), figure eights, or balloons.

DIFFICULTY The degree of effort an "average" hiker should expect on a given hike. For simplicity, difficulty is described as "easy," "moderate," or "difficult."

SCENERY Rates the overall environs of the hike and what to expect in terms of plant life, wildlife, streams, and historic buildings.

EXPOSURE A quick check of how much sun you can expect on your shoulders during the hike. Descriptors used are self-explanatory and include terms such as shady, exposed, and sunny.

TRAFFIC Indicates how busy the trail might be on an average day, and if you might be able to find solitude out there. Trail traffic, of course, varies from day to day and season to season.

TRAIL SURFACE Indicates whether the trail is paved, rocky, smooth dirt, or a mixture of elements.

HIKING TIME How long it takes to hike the trail. A slow but steady hiker will average 2 to 3 miles an hour depending on the terrain. Most of the estimates in this book reflect a speed of about 2 mph.

INTRODUCTION

ACCESS   Notes fees or permits needed to access the trail (if any) and whether pets and other forms of trail use are permitted.

MAPS   Notes availability of onsite trailhead maps and the appropriate USGS topo.

FACILITIES   What to expect in terms of restrooms, phones, water, and other amenities available at the trailhead or nearby.

SPECIAL COMMENTS   These comments cover little extra details that don't fit into any of the above categories. Here you'll find information on trail-hiking options and facts, or tips on how to get the most out of your hike.

DIRECTIONS TO THE TRAIL

Used with the locator map, the directions help you locate each trailhead.

TRAIL DESCRIPTIONS

The trail description is the heart of each hike. Here, the author provides a summary of the trail's essence as well as highlights any special traits the hike offers. Ultimately, the hike description will help you choose which hikes are best for you.

NEARBY ACTIVITIES

Look here for information on nearby activities or points of interest.

▶ WEATHER

The climate in Los Angeles is mild and pleasant most of the year. Though contrary to popular belief, the region does have seasons. The rainy season is between December and April. Summer brings dry, hot weather, with temperatures reaching the triple digits in the San Fernando Valley and inland areas. Late spring usually means "June gloom," a few weeks during which the skies are overcast from early morning to midafternoon, especially in the coastal areas.

AVERAGE DAILY TEMPERATURES (F°) BY MONTH

	JAN	FEB	MAR	APR	MAY	JUN
HIGH	67°	68°	68°	72°	72°	76°
LOW	47°	48°	50°	52°	56°	59°
MEAN	57°	58°	59°	62°	64°	67°

	JUL	AUG	SEP	OCT	NOV	DEC
HIGH	80°	81°	81°	77°	71°	67°
LOW	62°	63°	62°	58°	52°	47°
MEAN	71°	72°	71°	67°	61°	57°

INTRODUCTION

Choose your hiking locations wisely. The trails in the hot, shade-deprived Simi Valley are best visited in the cooler months, whereas the coastal trails of Malibu, Laguna Beach, and Rancho Palos Verdes will yield the best weather and views in the late summer and early fall.

▶ ALLOCATING TIME

On flat or lightly undulating terrain, the author averaged 2 miles per hour when hiking. That speed drops in direct proportion to the steepness of a path, and it does not reflect the many pauses and forays off trail in pursuit of yet another bird sighting, wildflower, or photograph. Give yourself plenty of time. Few people enjoy rushing through a hike, and fewer still take pleasure in bumping into trees after dark. Remember, too, that your pace may slow over the back half of a long trek.

▶ MAPS

The maps in this book have been produced with great care and, used with the hiking directions, will direct you to the trail and help you stay on course. However, you will find superior detail and valuable information in the U.S. Geological Survey's 7.5 minute series topographic maps. Topo maps are available online in many locations. Easy Web resources are located at terraserver.microsoft.com (free downloadable maps and aerial photos) and www.topozone.com. The downside to topos is that most of them are outdated, some having been created 20 to 30 years ago. But they still provide excellent topographic detail.

If you're new to hiking, you might be wondering, "What's a topographic map?" In short, a topo indicates linear distance and elevation, using contour lines. The map scale defines distance between points on the map. Contour lines spread across the map like wavy spiderwebs define the elevation. Each line represents a particular elevation, and at the base of each topo, a contour's interval designation is given. If the contour interval is 20 feet, then the distance between each contour line is 20 feet. Follow 5 contour lines up on the same map, and the elevation has increased by 100 feet.

Let's assume that the 7.5-minute series topo reads "Contour Interval 40 feet," that the short trail we'll be hiking is 2 inches in length on the map, and that it crosses 5 contour lines from beginning to end. What do we know? Because the linear scale of this series is 2,000 feet to the inch, we know our trail is 4,000 feet in length. But we also know we'll be climbing or descending 200 vertical feet (five contour lines representing 40 feet each) over that distance. And the increase or decrease in elevation printed on the index contour lines (every fifth contour line) will tell us if we're heading up or down.

In addition to outdoor shops and bike shops, you'll find topos at major universities and some public libraries, where you might try photocopying the ones you need to avoid the cost of buying them. But if you want your own and can't find them locally, visit the U.S. Geological Survey Web site at topomaps.usgs.gov.

INTRODUCTION

GPS TRAILHEAD COORDINATES

To collect accurate map data, each trail was hiked with a handheld GPS unit (Garmin Etrex Venture). Data collected was downloaded and plotted onto a digital topo map. In addition to a highly specific trail outline, this book also includes the GPS coordinates for each trailhead. More accurately known as UTM coordinates, the numbers index a specific point using a grid method. The survey datum used to arrive at the coordinates is WGS84. For readers who own a GPS unit, whether handheld or onboard a vehicle, the UTM coordinates provided on the first page of each hike may be entered into the GPS unit. Just make sure your GPS unit is set to navigate using the UTM system in conjunction with WGS84 datum. Now you can navigate directly to the trailhead.

Most trailheads that begin in parking areas can be navigated to by car. However, some hikes still require a short walk to reach the trailhead from a parking area. In those cases, a handheld unit would be necessary to continue the GPS navigation process. However, readers can easily access all trailheads in this book by using the directions, the overview map, and the trail map, which shows at least one major road leading into the area. But for those who enjoy using the latest GPS technology to navigate, the necessary data has been provided. A brief explanation of the UTM coordinates follows.

UTM COORDINATES: ZONE, EASTING, AND NORTHING

Within the UTM coordinates box on the first page of each hike, there are three numbers: zone, easting, and northing. Here is an example from the Runyon Canyon hike on page 43:

UTM Zone (WGS84)   11S

Easting   375577

Northing   3774652

The zone number (11) refers to one of the 60 longitudinal zones (vertical) of a map using the Universal Transverse Mercator (UTM) projection. Each zone is 6° wide. The zone letter (S) refers to one of the 20 latitudinal zones (horizontal) that span from 80° South to 84° North.

The easting number (375577) references in meters how far east the point is from the zero value for eastings, which runs north–south through Greenwich, England. Increasing easting coordinates on a topo map or on your GPS screen indicate you are moving east. Decreasing easting coordinates indicate you are moving west. Since lines of longitude converge at the poles, they are not parallel as lines of latitude are. This means that the distance between full easting coordinates is 1,000 meters near the Equator but becomes smaller as you travel farther north or south. The difference is small enough to be ignored, but only until you reach the polar regions.

In the Northern Hemisphere, the northing number (3774652) references in meters how far you are from the Equator. Above the Equator, northing coordinates increase by

INTRODUCTION

1,000 meters between each parallel line of latitude (east–west lines). On a topo map or GPS receiver, increasing northing numbers indicate you are traveling north.

In the Southern Hemisphere, the northing number references how far you are from a latitude line that is 10 million meters south of the Equator. Below the Equator, northing coordinates decrease by 1,000 meters between each line of latitude. On a topo map, decreasing northing coordinates indicate you are traveling south.

▶ TRAIL ETIQUETTE

Whether you're on a city, county, state, or national park trail, always remember that great care and resources (from Nature as well as from your tax dollars) have gone into creating these trails. Treat the trail, wildlife, and fellow hikers with respect.

1. Hike on open trails only. Respect trail and road closures (ask if not sure), avoid possible trespassing on private land, and obtain all permits and authorization as required. Also, leave gates as you found them or as marked.

2. Leave only footprints. Be sensitive to the ground beneath you. This also means staying on the existing trail and not blazing any new trails. Be sure to pack out what you pack in. No one likes to see the trash someone else has left behind.

3. Never spook animals. An unannounced approach, a sudden movement, or a loud noise startles most animals. A surprised snake or skunk can be dangerous to you, to others, and themselves. Give animals extra room and time to adjust to your presence.

4. Plan ahead. Know your equipment, your ability, and the area where you are hiking—and prepare accordingly. Be self-sufficient at all times; carry necessary supplies for changes in weather or other conditions. A well-executed trip is a satisfaction to you and to others.

5. Be courteous to other hikers, bikers, or equestrians you meet on the trails.

▶ WATER

"How much is enough? One bottle? Two? Three?! Well one simple physiological fact should convince you to err on the side of excess when it comes to deciding how much water to pack: A hiker working hard in 90°F heat needs approximately 10 quarts of fluid every day. That's two and a half gallons—12 large water bottles or 16 small ones. In other words, pack along one or two bottles even for short hikes.

Purifying water found along the route, though less dangerous than drinking it untreated, comes with risks. Purifiers with ceramic filters are the safest, but are also the most expensive. Many hikers pack along the slightly distasteful tetraglycine-hydroperiodide tablets (sold under the names Potable Aqua, Coughlan's, and others).

Probably the most common waterborne "bug" that hikers face is *Giardia,* which may not hit until one to four weeks after ingestion. It will have you passing noxious

INTRODUCTION

rotten-egg gas, vomiting, shivering with chills, and living in the bathroom. But there are other parasites to worry about, including *E. coli* and *Cryptosporidium* (which are harder to kill than *Giardia*).

For most people, the pleasures of hiking make carrying water a relatively minor price to pay to remain healthy. If you're tempted to drink "found water," do so only if you understand the risks involved. Better yet, hydrate prior to your hike, carry (and drink) six ounces of water for every mile you plan to hike, and hydrate after the hike.

▶ FIRST-AID KIT

A typical kit may contain more items than you might think necessary. These are just the basics:

Ace bandages or Spenco joint wraps

Antibiotic ointment (Neosporin or the generic equivalent)

Aspirin or acetaminophen

Band-Aids

Benadryl or the generic equivalent—diphenhydramine (an antihistamine, in case of allergic reactions)

Butterfly-closure bandages

Epinephrine in a prefilled syringe (for those known to have severe allergic reactions to such things as bee stings)

Gauze (one roll)

Gauze compress pads (a half dozen 4-inch by 4-inch)

Hydrogen peroxide or iodine

Insect repellent

Matches or pocket lighter

Moleskin/Spenco "Second Skin"

Snakebite kit

Sunscreen

Water-purification tablets or water filter (on longer hikes)

Whistle (more effective in signaling rescuers than your voice)

▶ SNAKES

Southern California has a variety of snakes—including gopher snakes, king snakes, and racers—most of which are benign. Rattlesnakes are the exception, and they dwell in every area of the state: mountains, foothills, valleys, and deserts. Species found in the region include the Western diamondback, sidewinder, speckled rattlesnake, red diamond rattlesnake, Southern Pacific, Great Basin rattlesnake, and the Mojave rattlesnake, according to the state Department of Fish and Game.

When hiking, stick to well-used trails and wear over-the-ankle boots and loose-fitting long pants. Rattlesnakes like to bask in the sun and won't bite unless threatened. Do not step or put your hands where you cannot see, and avoid wandering in the dark. Step on logs and rocks, never over them, and be especially careful when climbing rocks or gathering firewood. Always avoid walking through dense brush or willow thickets. Hibernation season is November through February.

Rattlesnake (left)
Copperhead (right)

▶ TICKS

Ticks are often found on brush and tall grass, waiting to hitch a ride on a warm-blooded passerby. They are most active in the Los Angeles area between April and October. Among the local varieties of ticks, the Western black-legged tick is the primary carrier of Lyme disease. You can use several strategies to reduce your chances of ticks getting under your skin. Some people choose to wear light-colored clothing, so ticks can be spotted before they make it to the skin. Most important, be sure to visually check your hair, back of neck, armpits, and socks at the end of the hike. During your posthike shower, take a moment to do a more complete body check. For ticks that are already embedded, removal with tweezers is best. Use disinfectant solution on the wound.

▶ POISON OAK

Poison oak is rampant in the shady canyons and riparian woodlands of southern California. It grows in moist areas, favoring shade trees and water sources. Recognizing and avoiding the plant is the most effective way to prevent the painful, itchy rashes associated with poison oak. Identify the plant by its three-leaf structure, with two leaves on opposite sides of the stem, and one extending from the center. Refrain from scratching because bacteria under fingernails can cause infection. Wash and dry the rash thoroughly, applying a calamine lotion to help dry out the rash. If itching or blistering is severe, seek medical attention. If you do come in contact with one of these plants, remember that oil-contaminated clothes, pets, or hiking gear can easily cause an irritating rash on you or someone else, so wash any exposed parts of your body and clothes, gear, and pets if applicable.

▶ MOSQUITOES

Although it's not common, individuals can acquire the West Nile virus from the bite of an infected mosquito. Culex mosquitoes, the primary varieties that can transmit West Nile

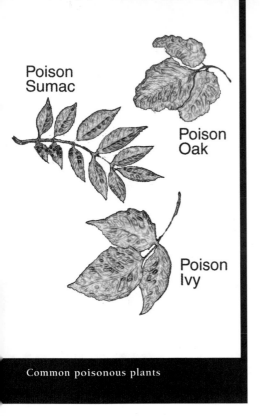

Poison
Sumac

Poison
Oak

Poison
Ivy

Common poisonous plants

virus to humans, thrive in urban rather than natural areas. They lay their eggs in stagnant water and can breed in any standing water that remains for more than five days. Most people infected with West Nile virus have no symptoms of illness, but some may become ill, usually 3 to 15 days after being bitten.

In the Los Angeles area, late February through October are likely to be the highest risk periods for mosquitoes. At this time of year, you may want to wear protective clothing such as long sleeves, long pants, and socks. Loose-fitting, light-colored clothing is best. Spray clothing with insect repellent. Remember to follow the instructions on the repellent carefully and take extra care with children.

▶ HIKING WITH CHILDREN

No one is too young for a hike in the woods or through a city park. Be careful, though. Flat, short trails are probably best when traveling with an infant. Toddlers who have not quite mastered walking can still tag along, riding on an adult's back in a child carrier. Use common sense to judge a child's capacity to hike a particular trail, and always expect that the child will tire quickly and need to be carried.

When packing for the hike, remember the child's needs as well as your own. Make sure children are adequately clothed for the weather, have proper shoes, and are protected from the sun with sunscreen. Kids dehydrate quickly, so make sure you have plenty of fluid for everyone.

A list of hike recommendations for kids is provided on page xvi. Finally, when hiking with children, remember the trip will be a compromise. A child's energy and enthusiasm alternate between bursts of speed and long stops to examine snails, sticks, dirt, and other attractions.

▶ THE BUSINESS HIKER

Whether you are in the Los Angeles area on business or are a resident, these 60 hikes offer perfect quick getaways from the busy demands of work and routine. Good hiking trails abound near LAX airport, Hollywood, and just off the exit ramps of major freeways. Instead of eating inside, pack a lunch and picnic in Griffith Park, or take a small group of your business comrades on an easy ocean-view hike at Will Rogers State Park or on one the dozens of trails in the Santa Monica Mountains Recreation Area. A brief outdoor getaway is the perfect complement to a business trip to Los Angeles.

DOWNTOWN LOS ANGELES
(Griffith Park, Hollywood, Baldwin Hills)

BALDWIN HILLS: WALK FOR HEALTH TRAIL

KEY AT-A-GLANCE INFORMATION

LENGTH: 2 miles

CONFIGURATION: Out-and-back

DIFFICULTY: Easy

SCENERY: Sagebrush, salamanders, California quail, jackrabbits, L.A. city views

EXPOSURE: Mostly sunny

TRAFFIC: Light on weekdays; moderate on weekends

TRAIL SURFACE: Packed dirt path

HIKING TIME: 1.25 hours

ACCESS: Daily sunrise to sunset; free on weekdays; $4 parking fee on weekends and holidays

MAPS: Available at kiosk at beginning of trailhead; USGS Hollywood

FACILITIES: Garbage cans at trailhead; restrooms and water fountains throughout park

SPECIAL COMMENTS: More information is available online at www.bhc.ca.gov/recreational_trails.

UTM Trailhead Coordinates for Baldwin Hills: Walk for Health Trail

UTM Zone (WGS84)   11S

Easting   373440

Northing   3764409

▶ IN BRIEF

Following a well-maintained path to great city vistas, this accessible trail near Los Angeles International Airport is dotted with coastal sagebrush and prickly pear cactus. Immaculate picnic areas, several children's playgrounds, and a lake stocked with catfish make this a nice place for an all-day family outing.

▶ DESCRIPTION

It's hard to believe that this pleasant, low-key trail was an active oil field in the first half of the twentieth century. After an earthen dam on the oil field was breached in 1968 and flooded many homes in the surrounding neighborhood, the property was turned into the Kenneth Hahn State Recreation Area, named after a longtime member of the Los Angeles County Board of Supervisors (and father of former mayor James Hahn). Little by little, conservationists and local volunteers turned it into a hillside haven that sits smack in the middle of strip malls, traffic-choked freeways, and urban sprawl. There are several picnic areas, children's playgrounds, a basketball court, and a landscaped lake that is home to dozens of ducks and catfish.

A few dozen oil pumps still operate in the weed-covered hills south of the park, but the state-funded Baldwin Hills Conservancy hopes to eliminate them eventually and expand the recreation area to about 1,200 acres from its current 370.

▶ DIRECTIONS

Take Interstate 10 to Cienega Boulevard and drive south about a mile to the Kenneth Hahn Recreation Area. Parking is plentiful on either side of the entrance kiosk and at the eastern end of the park past the police station. To access the Walk for Health path, turn left just past the guard stand at the sign for Olympic Forest and park in the lot across from the trailhead.

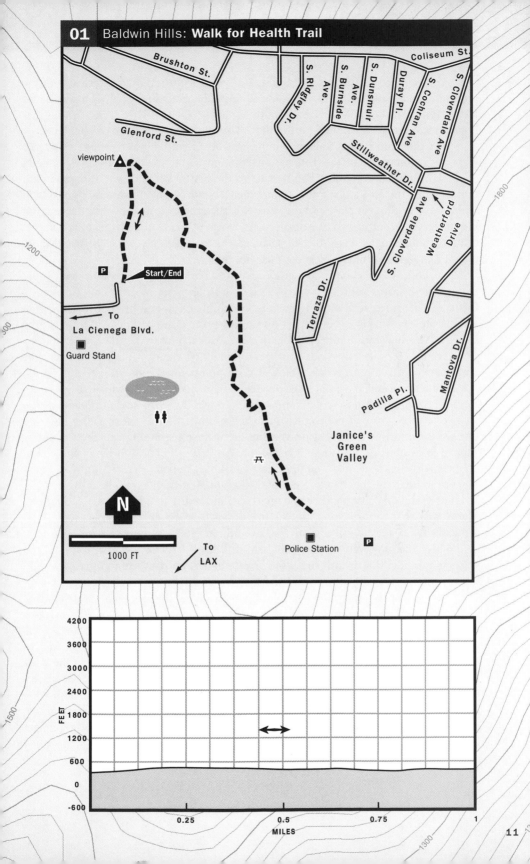

Brushton St.

Coliseum St.

S. Ridgley Dr.

S. Burnside Ave.

Ave.

S. Dunsmuir

Duray Pl.

S. Cochran Ave

S. Cloverdale Ave

Glenford St.

Stillweather Dr.

viewpoint

S. Cloverdale Ave

Weatherford Drive

P

Start/End

To
La Cienega Blvd.

Terraza Dr.

Guard Stand

Mantova Dr.

Padilla Pl.

Janice's
Green
Valley

N

1000 FT

To
LAX

Police Station

P

4200
3600
3000
2400
1800
1200
600
0
-600

FEET

0.25   0.5   0.75   1
MILES

The Walk for Health trail opened in 2003 and begins on the western side of the recreation area, near the Cienega Boulevard entrance. Look for a sign with a map and a description of the trail, then walk a dozen yards west to a large sign warning that dogs must be leashed throughout the park. This is the beginning of the trailhead.

The dirt path begins to climb south past the Olympia forest, which is covered with trees from each of the 140 nations that took part in the 1984 Los Angeles Olympics. At about 0.2 miles, you'll come to the first of several signs along the path that describe the area's plant and animal life. Despite its manmade origins, Baldwin Hills is one of the few places where coastal sage scrub and the gray fox thrive in an urban setting, according to conservationists. Western toads, prickly pear cactus, cottontail rabbits, quails, black-bellied salamanders, painted-lady butterflies, and more than 150 species of birds also make their home here.

A short, steep climb soon gives way to a landscaped viewpoint with great panoramic vistas of southwest Los Angeles and the Santa Monica Bay. Christine's Point, the first of several viewing pavilions with benches, is a brief 100-yard uphill walk to the left. This is a good spot for watching planes land and take off from nearby LAX. It's worth a stop, but keep going if you can—the next vistas are even better.

From here, the trail winds northeast, straddling views of the Hollywood Hills and downtown L.A. on the left with active oil pump–lined hills on the right. You'll see another viewing pavilion, this one called Autumn's Peak, which faces south toward LAX and the Palos Verdes Peninsula. Sit down if you'd like, but don't miss the chance to take in the view behind you to the northeast. On a clear winter day, you can see the downtown Los Angeles skyline set against a stunning backdrop of snow-capped San Gabriel Mountains—a vision that is often captured (but rarely witnessed) on souvenir-shop postcards from L.A. Lest you forget the name of the trail you're following, another sign gently lectures about the importance of eating healthy foods.

Keep walking past another unnamed pavilion as the trail heads east and follows a gray wall that used to be a part of the doomed reservoir dam. This is the least attractive leg of the trail; it's relatively flat and flanked by electric transmission towers. Where the gray wall ends and a chain-link fence begins, the path narrows and starts to meander downward; you'll see private homes on your left and the park facilities on your right.

At the 1-mile marker, the chain-link fence ends, and you'll come to a sign that marks the turnaround point for the Walk for Health Trail. From here, you can retrace your steps or continue down a flat paved path that loops around a grassy area appropriately called Janice's Green Valley and back to the parking lot at Olympic Forest. I've done both the loop and out-and-back and prefer to retrace my steps on the Walk for Health Trail. It's more scenic, and it gave me the chance to revisit the park's impressive variety of plants. I also relished another opportunity to soak up the unique views of the downtown skyline. Human contact on this trail is minimal, especially on weekdays. It seems to attract lone power walkers from surrounding neighborhoods and office buildings more than chatty groups or couples.

The entrance to Kenneth Hahn State Recreation Area is surrounded by coast live oak trees and marsh.

▶ NEARBY ACTIVITIES

Los Angeles isn't known for its barbecue restaurants, but there are a couple of exceptionally good places to get it around Baldwin Hills. JR's BBQ, at 3055 S. Cienega Boulevard, is a mile north of the recreation area's entrance and has sit-down service as well as takeout. On the other side of the park is Woody's Bar-B-Que, at 3346 Slauson Avenue. It's take-out only but has a huge loyal following, so be prepared to wait in line. Order some pulled-pork sandwiches or ribs and head to one of the recreation area's many picnic tables.

If fishing's your game, you might want to while away a couple of hours at the recreation area's manmade lake before or after a hike. It is stocked with trout and catfish, and you're allowed to catch up to five fish per day. For more information, call the park office at (323) 298-3660.

DEBS PARK: CITY VIEW AND WALNUT FOREST TRAILS

KEY AT-A-GLANCE INFORMATION

LENGTH: 2.6 miles

CONFIGURATION: Balloon

DIFFICULTY: Easy to moderate

SCENERY: Hills, city views, pond

EXPOSURE: Sunny

TRAFFIC: Light

TRAIL SURFACE: Dirt and paved path

HIKING TIME: 1.5 hours

ACCESS: Free; the park is open 5 a.m.–10:30 p.m., Wednesday–Sunday.

MAPS: Available at nature center; phone (323) 221-2255; USGS Los Angeles

FACILITIES: Restrooms, water fountains, picnic tables, benches

SPECIAL COMMENTS: Don't let the no-dogs, no-bicycles rule keep you from visiting this undiscovered 300-acre hillside in industrial east Los Angeles. The trails are pristine, quiet, and home to grasslands, wildflowers, and more than 130 species of birds.

UTM Trailhead Coordinates for Debs Park: City View and Walnut Forest Trails

UTM Zone (WGS84) **11S**

Easting   **389273**

Northing   **3773897**

▶ IN BRIEF

An array of native plants, flowers, and wildlife dominates the trails located on this 282-acre hillside between Chinatown and South Pasadena. At the trail's peak, rest at a bucolic fishing pond and take in views of downtown Los Angeles.

▶ DESCRIPTION

The official name is Ernest E. Debs Regional Park, but everyone calls it Debs Park. In an effort to raise the park's low profile and introduce more inner-city kids to nature, the Audubon Society opened a nature center on the Highland Park property in 2003, offering guided hikes, educational workshops, and other activities geared toward kids and families.

More than 130 species of native and visiting birds, including the red-tailed hawk, barn owl, blue-gray gnatcatcher, and lesser goldfinch live here, according to the Audubon Society. The park is also home to ringneck snakes, coyotes, pocket gophers, skunks, and dozens of types of butterflies, including the Western tiger swallowtail and the painted lady. It's worth grabbing a park trail guide from the nature center before embarking on your hike, but it's tough to get lost on any of the trails. Most visitors take the Walnut Forest Trail or the

▶ DIRECTIONS

From downtown Los Angeles, take the 110 Freeway north and exit at Avenue 43. Make a right onto Avenue 43 and then a left onto Griffin Avenue. The entrance is on the right across from a soccer field. There is also an entrance and parking lot off Monterey Road on the north side of the park.

Alternate Directions: From Pasadena, take the 110 Freeway south to Avenue 52. Turn left and follow Avenue 52 as it turns into Griffin Avenue. Park entrance is on the left.

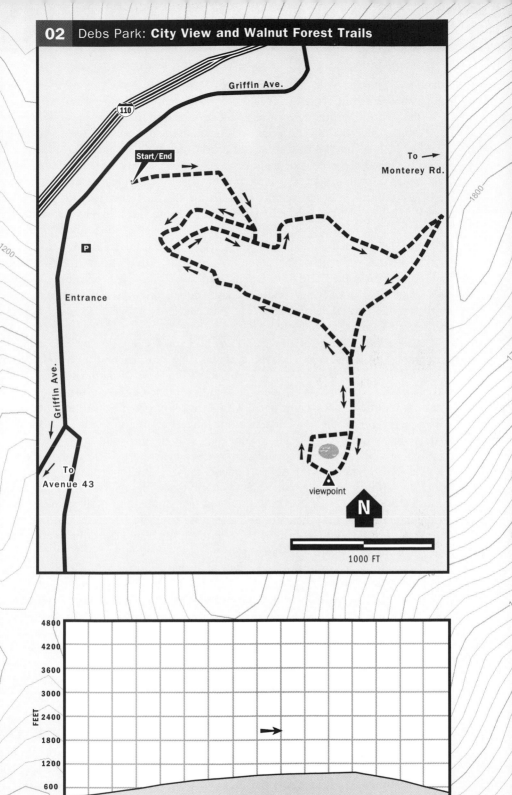

Griffin Ave.

110

Start/End

To →
Monterey Rd.

P

Entrance

Griffin Ave.

To
Avenue 43

viewpoint

N

1000 FT

4800
4200
3600
3000
2400
1800
1200
600
0

FEET

0.65   1.3   1.95   2.6
MILES

City View Trail to the pond at the park's peak. There is also a short, easy Butterfly Loop just behind the nature center that's popular with parents with infants and strollers.

To reach the Walnut Forest Trail, walk back toward the entrance from the parking lot to the fire-road gate. Turn right and head up the dirt path as it winds north on a gradual incline. You'll pass a couple of narrow dirt trails on the left, but continue to stay to the right on the wide path. After a brief dip downward, the Walnut Forest Trail begins to climb gradually past coastal sage scrub, toyon (Christmas berry) bushes, and eucalyptus and walnut trees. In the spring, you can also expect to see arroyo lupine, goldenbush, laurel sumac, and morning glories along this route. On the left you'll see (and hear) the Pasadena Freeway, as well as the rooftops of hillside homes in the distance. At about 0.4 miles, you'll pass stone steps on your left that lead nowhere as the path curves around to the right. You'll also pass an unmarked trail on the right at 0.6 miles. This is the City View Trail. It's a steeper, more exposed climb than the Walnut Forest Trail. I recommend sticking to the Walnut Forest Trail on the way up and taking the City View Trail, which can also be accessed from the north near the pond, on the way back.

After about 1 mile, the dirt path ends and you'll come to a paved road. Turn right and follow it past a gazebo with a picnic table and benches on the left. As the path climbs, pass a few more benches on the left and more toyon bushes and walnut and palm trees. On a clear day, you'll be able to see views of downtown L.A. straight ahead. At about 1.4 miles, come to a **Y** with a cluster of pine trees in the center. Continue to the right on the unmarked Summit Ridge Trail and follow it a few hundred yards to the entrance to the pond on your right. The pond sneaks up on you. It's not far off the trail, but it's well camouflaged by trees and shrubs. With its hillside location and views of downtown L.A. and Dodger Stadium, it reminds me of nature's version of the infinity pool, a popular L.A. swimming pool design that makes the water seem like it meets the sky. You might want to allot some time to linger here before turning around; there are benches and the pond is stocked with largemouth bass, bluegill, and black bullhead (fishing is permitted). It's truly a beautiful setting in an area of Los Angeles where you least expect it.

From the pond, you can retrace your steps back to the Walnut Forest trail, or return along the City View Trail (the City View trailhead is 0.4 miles on the left as you walk back along the Summit Ridge Trail). The City View trail is narrower and less shady, but it has better views of downtown L.A. and the Arroyo Seco, the dry riverbed that runs parallel to the Pasadena Freeway, than the other trails. You can also see the Metro Gold Line's Highland Park station and the nineteenth-century adobe architecture of the Southwest Museum from here.

I hiked this trail on a Saturday afternoon and only encountered a handful of people. Most of the hikers were parents with young kids in tow.

▶ NEARBY ACTIVITIES

The Audubon Center at Debs Park is worth a stop, not only for its trail maps and reasonably priced energy bars but also for its environmentally friendly architecture. The walls are reinforced by melted-down handguns and scrap metal; the carpeting is woven with leaves from the Mexican agave plant, and the cabinets are made with pressed sunflower seeds. An education room fills you in on the details of the construction. For more information, go online to www.audubon-ca.org/debs_park.htm.

Another possible activity while you're in Highland Park is a house tour. The Sycamore Grove area of Highland Park is one of L.A.'s oldest neighborhoods, known for its Victorian and Craftsman homes and the Southwest Museum, a national historic site that features a replica of a circa-1800 hacienda. The Los Angeles Conservancy leads tours of the area four times a year; for more information, go online to www.laconservancy.org. Nearby, North Figueroa Street is an urban strip of art galleries, restaurants, and Mr. T's Bowl, a neighborhood institution that is a diner and bowling alley by day and a cool live-music venue by night.

A view of Highland Park from the City View Trail

ELYSIAN PARK: ANGELS POINT TO BISHOPS CANYON

UTM Trailhead Coordinates for Elysian Park: Angels Point to Bishops Canyon

UTM Zone (WGS84)   11S

Easting   385332

Northing   3772387

▶ IN BRIEF

A mix of paved road and rugged dirt path, this hike through L.A.'s oldest park leads to a bluff-top recreation area with sweeping views of Dodger Stadium and the San Gabriel Mountains.

▶ DESCRIPTION

The 600-acre Elysian Park, which includes Dodger Stadium and the Los Angeles Police Academy, is the city's oldest park and second only in size to Griffith Park. No stranger to controversy, this park saw three of its communities uprooted to make room for the stadium in 1950, and later it was divided in half by the Pasadena Freeway.

Still, it's a great place for a solitary run or hike, though its lack of good trail maps can be confusing for those unfamiliar with the area. Birders also frequent the park; recent sightings include red-tailed hawks, Western bluebirds, a black-headed grosbeak, and Lucy's warbler. On weekends, the park is full of picnicking families, exercise hounds, and nature lovers. If there happens to be a home baseball game, the area is even livelier; just try to plan your visit so it doesn't coincide with the beginning or end of a game, or you will likely find yourself caught in a massive traffic jam.

The first time I hiked Elysian Park, I showed up without a plan, figuring the trail system was small enough to make that unnecessary. In reality, the park has many and varied trails spread over its 600 acres. A couple of trail maps are posted within the park, but it's hard to get a sense of

▶ DIRECTIONS

From the I-5 freeway, exit at Stadium Way and follow signs to Dodger Stadium. Turn right at Grace E. Simons Lodge and park along the curb or further down the road in the parking lot adjacent to the lodge. The trailhead is just behind you to the right.

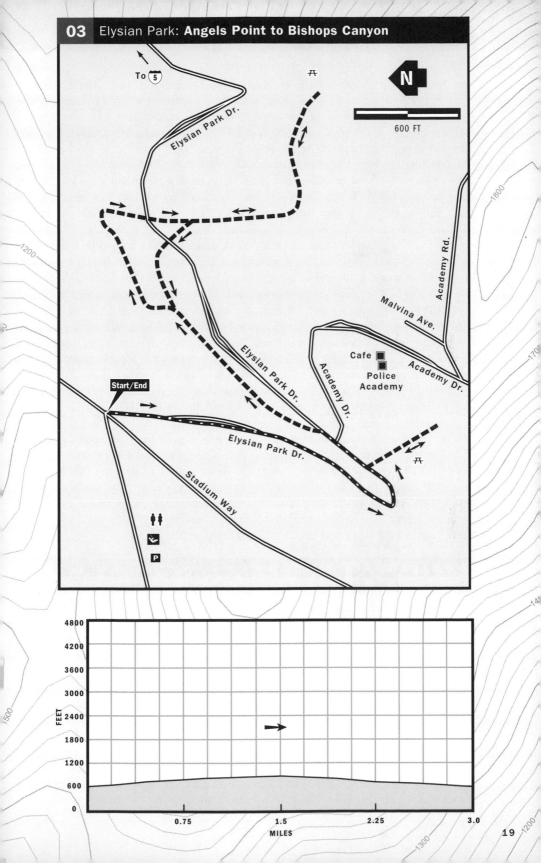

To ⑤

Elysian Park Dr.

N

600 FT

Academy Rd.

Malvina Ave.

Elysian Park Dr.

Academy Dr.

Cafe
Police
Academy

Academy Dr.

Start/End

Elysian Park Dr.

Elysian Park Dr.

Stadium Way

4800
4200
3600
3000
2400
1800
1200
600
0

FEET

0.75   1.5   2.25   3.0
MILES

how long or difficult they are. So my husband, a baseball fan, and I just decided to wander uphill in the direction of Dodger Stadium, where we figured (correctly) that we would find nice views of the venerable sports venue. The hike we cobbled together begins in the parking lot of Grace E. Simons Lodge. We crossed Stadium Way and headed uphill along Angels Point Drive, a paved road that is blocked to car traffic during the week. At about half a mile, you'll come to Angels Point, a clearing with a playground, picnic tables, and good views of downtown Los Angeles. Walk a little farther and you'll come to a dirt path bordered by a chain-link fence on the right. Follow the path a short way downhill for views of the stadium. Return to the road and continue walking north. On weekends this road gets a good deal of car traffic, but there is plenty of room for pedestrians, and it's nicely framed by palm trees. To your right, you'll get a bird's-eye view of the Los Angeles Police Academy's shooting range. At about 2 miles, you'll come to a gate and a dirt trail on the left. Follow that as it winds away from the paved road and past views of the northwestern side of Elysian Park. You'll pass a water tower on the right and views of Glendale and the Verdugo Mountains on the left. Continue on the trail as it loops back to Elysian Park Drive and passes a baseball/softball field. Just past this, you'll see a sign for Elysian Fields; turn left on Park Road and walk by picnic pavilions, a parking area, and a large playground. All this used to be the Bishops Canyon landfill, a collection point for tons of household and construction refuse that was sealed in 1969 and turned into a recreational area by sanitation and park officials in the 1990s.

The area differs from the rest of Elysian Park in that there are few trees or shrubs here, but its bluff-top views make it worth a visit. The road ends at another cluster of picnic tables and a rocky promontory with views of the stadium and downtown L.A. This provides an even better view of the stadium (from the "Think Blue" side) than Angels Point. On weekends, this area gets very busy with ball players and families and groups celebrating birthday parties and other events under the picnic pavilions, which are often reserved in advance. From here you can retrace your steps along Elysian Park Drive and back to the parking lot.

▶ NEARBY ACTIVITIES

Take some time before or after your hike to walk through the open-air Chavez Ravine Arboretum near the parking lot for Grace E. Simons Lodge. Founded in 1893 by the Los Angeles Horticultural Society, the arboretum has more than 1,000 varieties of trees from around the world, including redwoods from northern California, pines from the Rocky Mountains, and eucalyptus from Australia. For more information, call (213) 485-5054 or visit www.laparks.org/dos/horticulture/chavez.htm.

For a bite to eat in an unusual setting, try the Academy Café, the commissary of the Los Angeles Police Academy, located within the park. After sampling a Hot Squad club sandwich, you can stroll through a circa-1950 rock garden that is adjacent to the academy's shooting range. The café is located at 1880 North Academy Road and is open daily for breakfast and lunch.

Finally, baseball fans will want to catch a game at Dodger Stadium. You can plan your hike to coincide with game time and soak up the spirit from a distance, but watch out for traffic jams. For ticket and schedule information, go to www.dodgers.com.

ELYSIAN PARK: WILDFLOWER TRAIL

▶ IN BRIEF

Yellow wildflowers and birds dominate this easy loop trail in the spring. It's a popular jogging path year-round, but it never seems overcrowded. A small secluded garden with a bench can be found at the midway point.

▶ DESCRIPTION

The 600-acre Elysian Park is the city's oldest park and second only in size to Griffith Park. No stranger to controversy, the park saw three of its communities uprooted to make room for Dodger Stadium in 1950, and later it was divided in half by the Pasadena Freeway.

Still, it's a great place for a solitary run or hike, though its lack of good trail maps can be confusing for those unfamiliar with the area. Birders also frequent the park; recent sightings include red-tailed hawks, western bluebirds, a black-headed grosbeak, and Lucy's warbler. On weekends, the park is full of picnicking families, exercise hounds, and nature lovers. If there happens to be a home baseball game, the area is even livelier; try to plan your visit so it doesn't coincide with the beginning or end of a game, or you will likely find yourself caught in a massive traffic jam.

The Wildflower Trail begins just beyond a lush, grassy picnic area landscaped with palm trees and picnic tables. Look for the white fire-road gate near the sign for Grace E. Simons Lodge, a rental facility for birthday parties, weddings, and corporate gatherings. Begin walking on

ⓘ KEY AT-A-GLANCE INFORMATION

LENGTH: 2.8 miles

CONFIGURATION: Loop

DIFFICULTY: Easy

SCENERY: Wildflowers, birds, groves of ficus, oak, and sycamore trees

EXPOSURE: Sun and shade

TRAFFIC: Moderate

TRAIL SURFACE: Packed dirt

HIKING TIME: 1.25 hours

ACCESS: Free; open daily

MAPS: At kiosk near Grace E. Simons Lodge; USGS Los Angeles

FACILITIES: Restrooms, picnic tables, water fountains, playground

SPECIAL COMMENTS: No bikes are allowed on this trail, and dogs must be leashed.

▶ DIRECTIONS

From the I-5 freeway, exit at Stadium Way and follow signs to Dodger Stadium. Turn right at Grace E. Simons Lodge and park along the curb or further down the road in the parking lot adjacent to the lodge. The trailhead is just behind you to the right.

UTM Trailhead Coordinates for Elysian Park: Wildflower Trail

UTM Zone (WGS84) 11S

Easting 385301

Northing 3772481

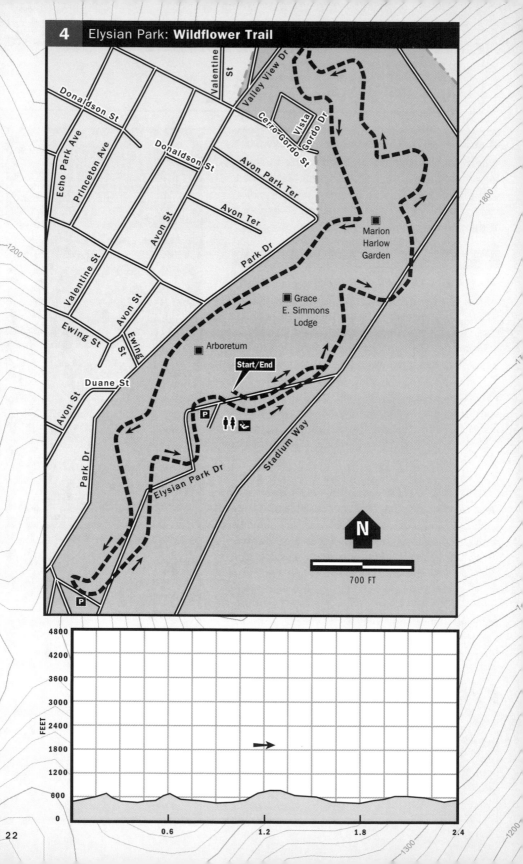

Thick patches of yellow wildflowers give this trail its name.

the dirt trail past rows of tall pine and sycamore trees. To your right is a shady ravine that serves as a buffer to Stadium Way, which runs parallel with the first leg of the trail. In the spring, you'll soon reach the thick patches of yellow wildflowers that give the trail its name. At about 0.5 miles, the path dips downward and gives way to prominent views of both sides of I-5 freeway, one of L.A.'s busiest roads. Hiking this trail during rush hour makes it all the sweeter as you look down on the gridlock below. Beyond the freeway and industrial areas that surround it, there are also nice views of the Verdugo and San Gabriel Mountains from here. It's not long, however, before the path curves around to the left and heads uphill away from the freeway. Just shy of 1 mile, you'll pass a green water tower on the left and glimpse private homes on the right, though they are well shrouded by trees and brush. As the uphill path levels, you'll reach a shady resting place with a bench, trash cans, and landscaping. This is the Marion Harlow Garden, according to the trail map, although there is no sign or plaque at the actual site. Whatever its back story, it's a peaceful place to stop and rest for a moment.

For a shorter hike, take the path to the left of the garden back to the trailhead. To extend this hike, you can continue to the right for another mile or so. The trail widens a bit here and on clear days has views of the downtown L.A. skyline—first filtered through the trees, then wide-open views. You will probably see more foot traffic along this leg of the trail, as it can also be easily accessed from a small parking lot on Academy Road. At 1.2 miles, you'll pass another trail that leads back to the parking lot. I had intended to take this trail back to my car, but the cloudless day made me want to prolong the hike, so I continued on the main trail as it loomed over Grace E. Simons Lodge and the Chavez Ravine Arboretum on my left. After about a half mile, I reached the Academy Road parking lot and reversed course on a paved path that led back to the parking lot.

▶ NEARBY ACTIVITIES

Take some time before or after your hike to walk through the open-air Chavez Ravine Arboretum near the parking lot for Grace E. Simons Lodge. Founded in 1893 by the Los Angeles Horticultural Society, the arboretum has more than 1,000 varieties of trees from around the world, including redwoods from northern California, pines from the Rocky Mountains, and eucalyptus from Australia. For more information call (213) 485-5054 or visit www.laparks.org/dos/horticulture/chavez.htm.

For a bite to eat in an unusual setting, try the Academy Café, the commissary of the Los Angeles Police Academy, located within the park. After sampling a Hot Squad club sandwich, you can stroll through a circa-1950 rock garden that is adjacent to the academy's shooting range. The café is located at 1880 N. Academy Road and open daily for breakfast and lunch.

Finally, baseball fans will want to catch a game at Dodger Stadium. You can plan your hike to coincide with game time and soak up the spirit from a distance, but watch out for traffic jams. For ticket and schedule information, go to www.dodgers.com.

FRANKLIN CANYON: CROSS MOUNTAIN AND HASTAIN TRAILS

▶ IN BRIEF

Beginning at a bucolic 3-acre reservoir and duck pond, this well-graded path winds through patches of oak forest before a gradual ascent leads to scenic views of Santa Monica and the Pacific Ocean. You will see pockets of development along the way, but heavy woodland and chaparral-covered slopes make this hike seem deeper in the wilderness than it actually is.

▶ DESCRIPTION

Looking for a way to distribute water brought from the Owens Valley to southern California, William Mulholland and the Department of Water and Power created a reservoir and power system in Franklin Canyon in the early 1900s. Luckily for today's hikers, this move helped prevent further development of the canyon, which today is

▶ DIRECTIONS

From downtown L.A., take the 101 Freeway north to the exit for Coldwater Canyon Drive and follow it south for 2 miles to Mulholland Drive or take Sunset Boulevard to Beverly Drive to Coldwater Canyon until you reach the stoplight at Mulholland. Turn right (west) onto Franklin Canyon Drive and head straight on a narrow twisting road past a sign that reads ROAD CLOSED 800 FEET (a small sign on the right reads FRANKLIN CANYON PARK). Soon you'll come to the entrance gate. Continue about a half mile to a stop sign. You can either park in the large lot on the left or continue to a smaller gravel parking lot on the left in front of Franklin Canyon Lake. Gates are open from 7 a.m. to sunset.

Alternate Directions: From Sunset Boulevard, follow Beverly Drive north to Coldwater Canyon. Veer left and follow to the intersection of Mulholland Drive. Turn left and head straight on Franklin Canyon Drive, then continue as above.

❶ KEY AT-A-GLANCE INFORMATION

LENGTH: 4.2 miles

CONFIGURATION: Out-and-back

DIFFICULTY: Moderate

SCENERY: Views of the water; wild chaparral, birds

EXPOSURE: Filtered shade and full sun

TRAFFIC: Moderate

TRAIL SURFACE: Paved road and packed dirt

HIKING TIME: 2 hours

ACCESS: Free; daily, 7 a.m.–sunset

MAPS: Available at Sooky Goldman Nature Center near the Coldwater Canyon entrance and at kiosks along the trails; USGS Beverly Hills

FACILITIES: Public restrooms at nature center and Franklin Canyon Ranch

SPECIAL COMMENTS: For additional information, go to www.nps.gov/samo/maps/franklin.htm.

UTM Trailhead Coordinates for Franklin Canyon: Cross Mountain and Hastain Trails

UTM Zone (WGS84)   11S

Easting   369930

Northing   3776445

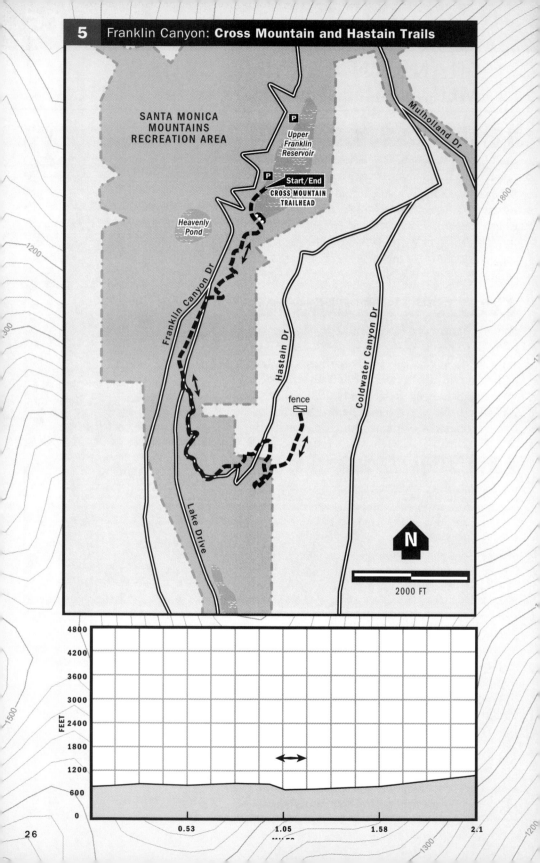

SANTA MONICA
MOUNTAINS
RECREATION AREA

Mulholland Dr

P

Upper
Franklin
Reservoir

P

Start/End
**CROSS MOUNTAIN
TRAILHEAD**

Heavenly
Pond

Franklin Canyon Dr

Hastain Dr

Coldwater Canyon Dr

fence

Lake Drive

N

2000 FT

surrounded by the densely populated neighborhoods of Coldwater Canyon and Beverly Hills. The family of oil baron Edward L. Doheny used the south end of the canyon for a retreat in the 1930s. After several attempts were made to turn the property into private housing developments, the Santa Monica Mountains Conservancy purchased it and turned over ownership to the National Park Service in 1981. Its 605 acres include an upper and lower reservoir, a nature center, an outdoor amphitheater, and the original Spanish-style home built by Doheny in 1935. The William O. Douglas Outdoor Classroom is a popular site for school groups.

From the parking lot of the Sooky Goldman Nature Center, walk south on Franklin Canyon Drive. The Upper Franklin Reservoir is on your left, though it is shrouded by thick forest. To your right is Heavenly Pond, a hidden pond with a few benches and an abundance of big-bellied frogs and ring-necked ducks. Follow the paved road to the left across the dam. Here's where you can get a good look at the reservoir, which resembles a tranquil lake and has been the site of many film and TV shoots, including *Combat!* and the opening fishing sequence of *The Andy Griffith Show*. More recently, TV shows like *Matlock* and *Quantum Leap* and such films as *Dr. Doolittle 2* and *Nightmare on Elm Street* have been shot here. (A complete list is available at the park's nature center.)

At the end of the dam, you can either continue on Franklin Canyon Drive or head up a narrow dirt path called Cross Mountain Trail. The latter path is more serene, passing through patches of thick brush, poison oak, and sycamore trees (in contrast, you'll probably encounter some cars and bicycles along Franklin Canyon Drive). After about half a mile, the dirt path starts to descend back down to the paved road.

At this point, you'll reach a fork in the road where Franklin Canyon meets Lake Drive. The white stone structure in front of you is known as the apple press building, though the Doheny family allegedly used it as a horse stable. Follow Lake Drive to the left for about a half-mile until you reach a trail kiosk and a small gravel parking lot. Turn left and follow the sign for Hastain Trail. The wide dirt path rises steadily up a chaparral-covered slope, with huge clusters of cactus and a scattering of expensive homes lining the hills to your right. Don't expect to see many people along here, even on weekends; I've never passed more than half a dozen on my visits. Here's where you'll want to make sure you have plenty of water and sunscreen, because there is little shade. As the trail continues to curve upward, you'll see dozens of white structures that resemble file cabinets tucked into a lush glade on your left 100 yards away. These are actually long-standing beehives that sit on private land that abuts the park. If you listen hard, you might hear a cacophony of buzzing—a sign that the bees are content.

Despite the proximity to busy Coldwater Canyon Drive, wildlife is common throughout the park. Recent sightings by Park Service rangers include red-tailed hawks, bobcats, coyotes, and plenty of gray squirrels. From the beehive site, continue up the dirt path 0.25 miles to a level area where you can take in the cityscape views of west Los Angeles. On a clear day, you should be able to see the Pacific Ocean from Santa Monica down to San Pedro. From here, the path continues to climb another quarter mile until it reaches a fenced-off area that is under construction; it will become a private housing development and is expected to be finished in 2006.

Before you head back, turn your back on the bulldozers and take in the spectacular views of water and sky to the south. After retracing your steps back to the upper reservoir, stop at Sooky Goldman Nature Center for water refills and bathroom facilities. The center also has trail maps, a few generic nature displays about the Santa Monica Mountains, and information on recent wildlife sightings within the park. Those interested in exploring Franklin Canyon further might want to look into the free docent-led hikes offered regularly by the conservancy. Themes include "Nature Rambles," "Franklin Canyon and the Movies," and "Morning Birds." An updated schedule is available at the nature center.

▶ NEARBY ACTIVITIES

Tree People, a conservation group whose headquarters are located directly across Coldwater Canyon Boulevard from the eastern end of Franklin Canyon Drive, regularly holds tree-care workshops and full moon– or holiday-themed hikes. During the summer, the group hosts concerts, plays, children's shows, and staged readings at its outdoor amphitheater. For more information, go to their Web page at www.treepeople.org.

GRIFFITH PARK: AMIR'S GARDEN

▶ IN BRIEF

A steep but manageable path leads past green hills and a large water tower to a 2-acre oasis of palm trees, ferns, succulents, and other native plants and flowers.

▶ DESCRIPTION

Griffith Park, tucked into the eastern end of the Santa Monica Mountains, is the largest municipal park in the United States. Its 4,100 acres include the Los Angeles Zoo, a 1926 merry-go-round, four municipal golf courses, a world-renowned observatory, and miles of hiking trails that make you forget you're in the middle of the nation's second-largest city. A comprehensive list of trails in the park is available at the Griffith Park Visitor Center at 4730 Crystal Springs Drive. I have picked three, Bronson Caves, Hollyridge, and Amir's Garden, that I think offer a good representation of the park's trails, but there are many other options.

Amir Dialameh was an Iranian immigrant who created a lush garden on a hillside in Griffith Park after a brush fire swept through the area in 1971. Dialameh cared for the garden until his death in 2003 at the age of 71. He could be found tending the terraced hillside on most days, and he once told a local newspaper that the secrets to a

ⓘ KEY AT-A-GLANCE INFORMATION

LENGTH: 1 mile

CONFIGURATION: Out-and-back

DIFFICULTY: Moderate

SCENERY: Chaparral-covered hills, city views

EXPOSURE: Sunny

TRAFFIC: Light

TRAIL SURFACE: Packed dirt

HIKING TIME: 45 minutes

ACCESS: Free; park is open to the public 6 a.m.–10 p.m. daily

MAPS: Available at Griffith Park Ranger Headquarters, 4730 Crystal Springs Drive; USGS Burbank

FACILITIES: None

SPECIAL COMMENTS: Bring a book or journal and spend the morning relaxing on a bench in Amir's peaceful garden.

▶ DIRECTIONS

From the Golden State Freeway (I-5), exit at Los Feliz Boulevard and turn right on Crystal Springs Drive. Just past the park ranger headquarters on the right, turn left at the stop sign onto Griffith Park Drive and continue past Harding Municipal Golf Course to the Mineral Springs Picnic Area. Park at the picnic area.

Alternate Directions: From the 134 Freeway in Burbank, exit at Forest Lawn Drive. Make a left on Zoo Drive and a right onto Griffith Park Drive and follow to the Mineral Springs Picnic Area.

UTM Trailhead Coordinates for Griffith Park: Amir's Garden

UTM Zone (WGS84) 11S

Easting 380747

Northing 3778995

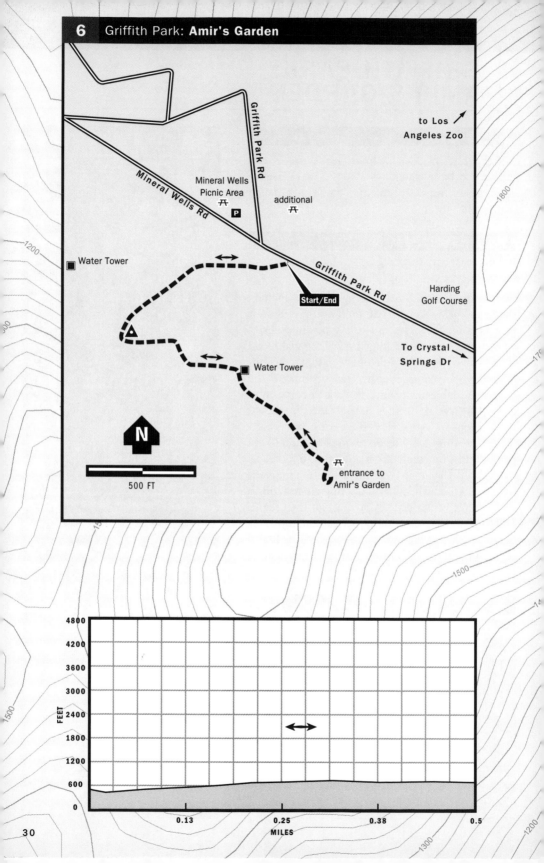

Griffith Park Rd

to Los Angeles Zoo

Mineral Wells Rd

Mineral Wells Picnic Area

additional

Water Tower

Griffith Park Rd

Start/End

Harding Golf Course

To Crystal Springs Dr

Water Tower

N

500 FT

entrance to Amir's Garden

4800
4200
3600
3000
2400
1800
1200
600
0

FEET

0.13   0.25   0.38   0.5
MILES

healthy, happy life were staying away from doctors and lawyers and "hiking, lots of hiking." A couple of hikers who developed a friendship with Amir help keep up the garden. To get to the trailhead, walk to the lower end of the Mineral Springs parking lot. You will want to take the middle dirt trail up a fairly steep grade. You'll see green hills to your left and city views of Glendale and the Verdugo Mountains behind you. At about 0.3 miles, the path curves sharply around and heads toward a large green water tower. It will appear as if the path ends at the water tower, but it actually just curves around it to the left and continues upward. The ascent starts to become more gradual here. You'll be able to see the Harding Golf Course below and city sprawl giving way to the Verdugo Mountains on your left. Soon you will see the wobbly painted benches that mark the entrance to Amir's Garden. There are also trash cans and a hitching post with a sign cautioning horses to keep out of the garden. Inside the makeshift entrance are a few picnic tables; groves of Christmas berry, pepper, and pine trees; and gardens of asparagus ferns, oleander, jade, geraniums, and ice plants. Take a deep breath and revel in the garden's restorative scent. A small shrine near the tables honors the man who created the garden with a photo and brief history. There is also a large rock honoring various local Boy Scout troops that have helped care for the garden over the years. Beyond this, you can follow a flight of stone steps down a terraced hillside to explore the garden further. The circular path leads back to the picnic tables where you started.

The one small disadvantage of this trail is you're likely to hear traffic noise from nearby I-5 and the 134 Freeway all the way to the garden. It doesn't fully disappear until you reach the garden entrance. On the flip side, this trail is rarely crowded. When I hiked it on a weekday morning, I only ran into two people as I made my way back down. It was a couple who seemed to be in their 60s; they were holding hands and humming a tune, slowly making their way up the path.

▶ NEARBY ACTIVITIES

The Griffith Observatory, the park's best-known attraction, has been closed for renovations since 2001 and is slated to reopen in the second half of 2006. In the meantime, a satellite facility is open with planetarium shows and limited exhibits. For more information, go to www.griffithobs.org. Another place within the park worth checking out is the Museum of the American West, a spacious complex of cowboy and Indian art and artifacts funded by the late Gene Autry. To get there from Bronson Caves trail (p. 32), follow Franklin Avenue east to Western Avenue. Turn left, and then make an immediate right onto Los Feliz Boulevard and continue to Crystal Springs Drive. Turn left; the museum is about 5 miles ahead on the right. For more information, go to www.museumoftheamericanwest.org.

GRIFFITH PARK: BRONSON CAVES

KEY AT-A-GLANCE INFORMATION

LENGTH: 1.8 miles

CONFIGURATION: Out-and-back

DIFFICULTY: Strenuous

SCENERY: Caves; city and observatory views

EXPOSURE: Sunny

TRAFFIC: Light

TRAIL SURFACE: Dirt path

HIKING TIME: 1.5 hours

ACCESS: Park is open to the public 6 a.m.–10 p.m. daily; gate to the parking lot closes at sunset

MAPS: Available at Griffith Park visitor center, 4730 Crystal Springs Drive, or call (323) 913-7390; USGS Hollywood

FACILITIES: None

SPECIAL COMMENTS: Expect puddles and muddy conditions if you visit this trail after a big rainstorm. Be sure to wear boots or sturdy shoes.

UTM Trailhead Coordinates for
Griffith Park: Bronson Caves

UTM Zone (WGS84)   11S

Easting   378823

Northing   3776752

▶ IN BRIEF

On this little-used Griffith Park trail, check out the caves that were featured in the 1960s *Batman* TV series and countless B-movies, then get a brief uphill workout that ends with a flat walk along cliffs offering good views of the Los Angeles basin and the Hollywood Hills.

▶ DESCRIPTION

Griffith Park, tucked into the eastern end of the Santa Monica Mountains, is the largest municipal park in the United States. Its 4,100 acres include the Los Angeles Zoo, a 1926 merry-go-round, four municipal golf courses, a world-renowned observatory, and miles of hiking trails that make you forget you're in the middle of the nation's second largest city. A comprehensive list of trails in the park is available at the Griffith Park visitor center at 4730 Crystal Springs Drive. I have picked three, Bronson Caves, Hollyridge, and Amir's Garden, that I think offer a good representation of the park's trails, but keep in mind that there are many other options.

When you arrive at the Hollywoodland Camp parking lot, you will likely see scads of hikers streaming past the north gate. This leads to a moderate path to Mount Hollywood and is one of the most popular hikes in the park. To get to the less-traveled Bronson Caves trail, walk south from

▶ DIRECTIONS

Take the Hollywood Freeway (101) to the Gower Road exit. Head north on Gower to Franklin Avenue and turn right. Make a left on Bronson and continue until it intersects with Canyon Drive. Follow Canyon about a mile north until the road dead-ends at a small parking lot just before a gate marked Hollywoodland Camp. There is also parking along the road near the picnic area to the south.

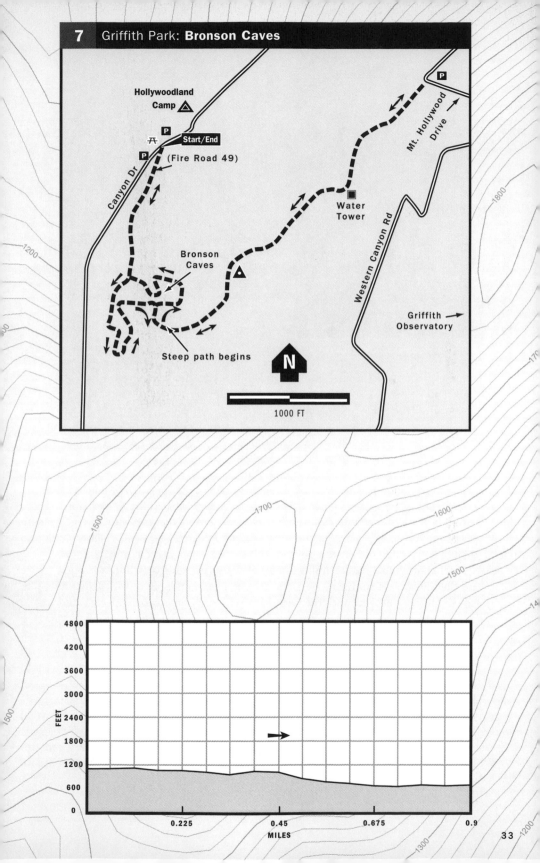

Hollywoodland Camp

P

Start/End

(Fire Road 49)

Canyon Dr

Bronson Caves

Steep path begins

N

1000 FT

Water Tower

Mt. Hollywood Drive

P

Western Canyon Rd

Griffith Observatory →

—1200—

—1800—

—1700—

—1600—

—1500—

—1700—

—1400—

—1500—

—1300—

—1200—

FEET

4800
4200
3600
3000
2400
1800
1200
600
0

0.225   0.45   0.675   0.9

MILES

The famous "Hollywood" sign

the end parking lot to Fire Road 49 and follow the dirt path upward for about 0.25 miles. To your right are hilltop homes, and below is the overflow parking lot and a grassy area with a few picnic tables. As the path winds east, you'll see the caves and big granite cliffs that were part of a rock quarry in the early part of the twentieth century. *Batman* fans will likely recognize the larger of the two caves as the opening out of which the Batmobile roared during the title scene of the 1960s TV series. Episodes of *Little House on the Prairie, Gunsmoke,* and *Star Trek Voyager* were also shot here. Some movies that featured the cave include the original *Invasion of the Body Snatchers,* Frank Capra's *Lost Horizon,* and *The Searchers* with John Wayne and Natalie Wood. On a dry day, you can walk through the caves, but they quickly fill up with water after it rains. Many people turn back to the parking lot from here, happy to snap a few pictures or let their dogs or kids romp around the boulders.

To continue the hike, follow the narrow dirt trail to the right of the biggest cave up the hill. It gets confusing here because there are a couple of wider dirt trails that go off to the right. You want the narrowest trail that is closest to the cave and immediately starts to ascend. The trail, which is surrounded by wild fennel, toyon (red berry), and other native plants, is very steep for about 0.75 miles. Parts of the trail are covered in scratchy branches and shrubs, so it's a good idea to wear long pants to avoid getting scratched up. Soon after passing some graffiti-covered rocks, you'll be at the top of the cliffs heading northeast on another semi-shrouded dirt trail. From here, you'll be able to look down and get a bird's-eye view of the Bronson caves. The trail also offers good views of the Griffith Observatory to the east and the Hollywood Hills and downtown Los Angeles to the southwest. The trail continues hugging the cliff, so it's important to be extra-careful with your footing at this point. You can also carve your own path parallel to the one closer to the cliff's edge a little further inland if walking along the edge becomes too teeth-rattling.

The trail flattens out for about 0.25 miles until it meets up with the Mount Hollywood trail near a large green water tower (with more graffiti) on the right. From here, the dirt path widens and continues northeast up a slight incline to the paved Mount Hollywood Drive, reaching an elevation of 1,200 feet. You'll probably encounter other hikers and drive-by tourists here, as the road is also accessible via car (there is a small parking lot to the east).

From here, you can retrace your steps back to the Bronson caves and the parking lot.

▶ NEARBY ACTIVITIES

The one-block stretch of Franklin Avenue between Cheremoya Avenue and Bronson Avenue is home to a newsstand, coffeehouse, several casual restaurants, and a used book and record store. It's a nice place to while away a couple of hours, especially in the early evening.

The Griffith Observatory, the park's best-known tourist attraction, has been closed for renovations since 2001 and is slated to reopen in the second half of 2006. In the meantime, a satellite facility is open with planetarium shows and limited exhibits. For more information, go to www.griffithobs.org. Another place within the park worth checking out is the Museum of the American West, a spacious complex of cowboy and Indian art and artifacts funded by the late Gene Autry. To get there from Bronson Caves Trail, follow Franklin Avenue east to Western Avenue. Turn left, and then make an immediate right onto Los Feliz Boulevard and continue to Crystal Springs Drive. Turn left; the museum is about 5 miles ahead on the right. For more information, go to www.museumoftheamericanwest.org.

GRIFFITH PARK: HOLLYRIDGE TRAIL

KEY AT-A-GLANCE INFORMATION

LENGTH: 2.6 miles

CONFIGURATION: Out-and-back

DIFFICULTY: Easy

SCENERY: Hills, Griffith Observatory, Hollywood sign

EXPOSURE: Sunny

TRAFFIC: Heavy

TRAIL SURFACE: Paved road and dirt path

HIKING TIME: 1.75 hours

ACCESS: Free; parking gate open from sunrise to sunset

MAPS: Available at Griffith Park visitor Center, 4730 Crystal Springs Drive; USGS Burbank

FACILITIES: None

SPECIAL COMMENTS: It's tempting, but resist any urges to scale the fences that keep you from getting a perfect snapshot of yourself standing next to the Hollywood sign—it's illegal.

UTM Trailhead Coordinates for Griffith Park: Hollyridge Trail

UTM Zone (WGS84)   11S

Easting   378718

Northing   3777203

▶ IN BRIEF

Great views of the Hollywood sign and chaparral-covered hills dominate this busy Griffith Park trail.

▶ DESCRIPTION

Griffith Park, tucked into the eastern end of the Santa Monica Mountains, is the largest municipal park in the United States. Its 4,100 acres include the Los Angeles Zoo, a 1926 merry-go-round, four municipal golf courses, a world-renowned observatory, and miles of hiking trails that make you forget you're in the middle of the nation's second largest city. A comprehensive list of trails in the park is available at the Griffith Park visitor center at 4730 Crystal Springs Drive. This trail, along with Bronson Caves and Amir's Garden offer a good representation of what the park has to offer, but keep in mind that there are many other options.

You'll drive through one of L.A.'s hippest neighborhoods before reaching the base of the Hollyridge Trail. Beachwood Canyon has been home to Madonna, Humphrey Bogart, Aldous Huxley, and countless aspiring actors who fill the many apartment buildings on lower Beachwood Drive. In the 1920s, the area was part of an upscale real estate development known as Hollywoodland (look for the stone gates and guard tower as you drive toward the trail base). As an advertising gimmick, the developers erected a huge sign with the development's name atop Mount Lee, which looms above the canyon. The

▶ DIRECTIONS

From the 101 Freeway, exit at Gower Street and head east on Franklin Avenue. Make a right on Beachwood Drive and follow it about 2 miles until it dead-ends. Park on North Beachwood Drive or in a dirt lot just past the entrance gate.

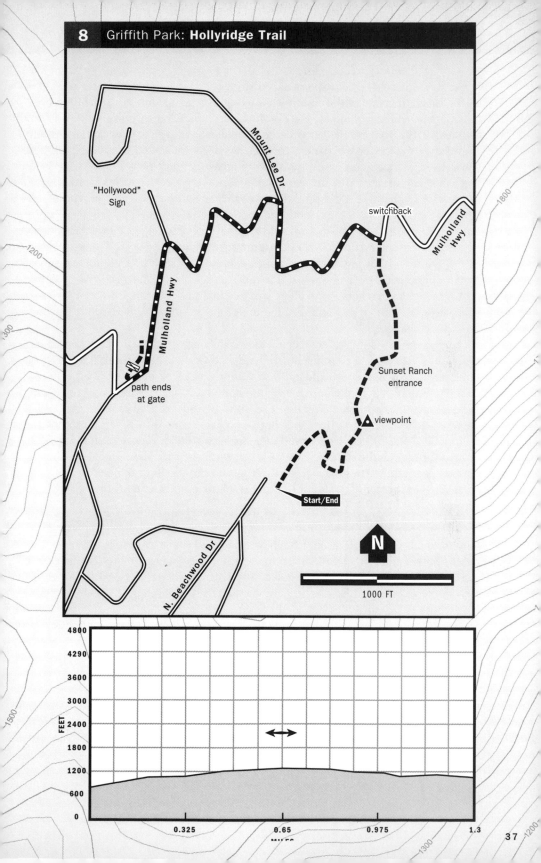

Mount Lee Dr

"Hollywood" Sign

switchback

Mulholland Hwy

Mulholland Hwy

path ends at gate

Sunset Ranch entrance

viewpoint

Start/End

N. Beachwood Dr

N

1000 FT

4800
4290
3600
3000
2400
1800
1200
600
0

FEET

0.325   0.65   0.975   1.3

MILES

letters were refurbished and shortened to Hollywood (thanks to gale-force winds) in 1949. This trail is one of the easiest ways to get a close-up view of the famous sign.

From the dirt parking lot just south of the Sunset Ranch horse stables, follow the sign for Hollyridge Trail. The wide dirt trail climbs moderately for 0.25 miles past a leveled area with views of the Los Angeles basin. As you round the corner, the Hollywood sign will suddenly come into view. You may see some people snapping photos here; this path attracts as many starstruck tourists as it does residents because of its proximity to Hollywood. I did this hike on a rainy day during the first weekend of January, and it still had a decent amount of traffic. The crowds were largely made up of out-of-town sports fans who had come to L.A. for the annual Rose Bowl game and festivities and were determined to check out the sign before they left, bad weather or no.

Continue following the path north, and you'll pass an entrance to Sunset Ranch on the left. Don't be surprised if you also see a few horseback riders on this trail. The ranch rents horses and offers weekly dinner rides through Griffith Park that begin here. To your right, you'll be able to see green hills and the Griffith Observatory in the distance.

After about 0.5 miles, you'll come to a switchback on the left that follows a dirt trail uphill. Take that to continue on Hollyridge. If you go straight, you'll wind up on Mulholland Trail, and eventually in Brush Canyon, near the Bronson Caves.

From here, the trail climbs gently to about 1,200 feet, giving way to sweeping views of the L.A. basin on a clear day. Continue another 0.25 miles until you reach a paved road, Mount Lee Drive. From here, you can either turn right and follow the steep trail to Mount Lee, which overlooks the sign from an elevation of about 1,500 feet, or turn left and walk past a water tower until the road dead-ends at a housing development and a gate that warns you to go no farther. Both options will net you great views of the sign; the Mount Lee trail is a little more strenuous than Hollyridge.

▶ NEARBY ACTIVITIES

Sunset Ranch, just north of the Hollyridge trailhead, is a sprawling horse ranch that boards horses and rents by the hour. It's worth a peek before or after hiking even if you're not interested in renting a horse. The ranch has been in operation since the 1920s; the original red barn is still the facility's main building. Its popular Friday Night Dinner Ride includes a guided sunset ride through Griffith Park, dinner at a Mexican restaurant, and a moonlit ride back to the ranch. For more information, go online to www.sunsetranchhollywood.com.

MOUNT WASHINGTON: JACK SMITH TRAIL

▶ IN BRIEF

Named for a beloved *Los Angeles Times* metro columnist, this trail begins with a rigorous climb up five flights of steps, then tapers to a gradual incline through the pretty hillside neighborhood of Mount Washington, tracing the route of a former railway that carried residents to and from their homes in the early 1900s.

▶ DESCRIPTION

I found this hike by default. I had intended to hike a trail in Elyria Park, an urban oasis bordered by the neighborhoods of Mount Washington, Glassell Park, and Cypress Park. But when I arrived at the entrance at the end of a residential street, the gate was locked and the paths were overgrown, unwieldy, and unwelcoming. As I tried to find out if there was another way to access the park, I came across information on another trail in the hillside neighborhood of Mount Washington and decided to check it out. This one turned out to have less of a wilderness feel than the first, but it was no less interesting and contemplative, and it's a good introduction to a little-known gem of a Los Angeles neighborhood.

The trail is named for Jack Smith, the late *Los Angeles Times* columnist and Mount Washington resident who often wrote about the quirks and beauty of his longtime neighborhood. After Smith died in 1996, his wife, Denise (a.k.a. Denny) and other members of the community worked to name an urban trail in his honor.

▶ KEY AT-A-GLANCE INFORMATION

LENGTH: 3.2 miles

CONFIGURATION: Out-and-back

DIFFICULTY: Moderate to strenuous

SCENERY: City views, residential development, black walnut woodland

EXPOSURE: Sun and shade

TRAFFIC: Light

TRAIL SURFACE: Paved sidewalk, steps

HIKING TIME: 1.5 hours

ACCESS: Free

MAPS: USGS Los Angeles

FACILITIES: None

SPECIAL COMMENTS: A rapid elevation gain of 500 feet puts this urban hike on the strenuous side. It's best if combined with a visit to the Southwest Museum and a meditation garden that is open to the public Tuesday–Sunday.

▶ DIRECTIONS

From the Pasadena Freeway (110), take the Avenue 43 exit, head west to Figueroa Boulevard and turn right. Turn left onto West Avenue 45, then make another left onto Marmion Way and park along Marmion near the intersection with West Avenue 43. Walk up West Avenue 43 to the flight of stairs that ascends west.

UTM Trailhead Coordinates for
Mount Washington: Jack Smith Trail

UTM Zone (WGS84)   11S

Easting   388377

Northing   3773464

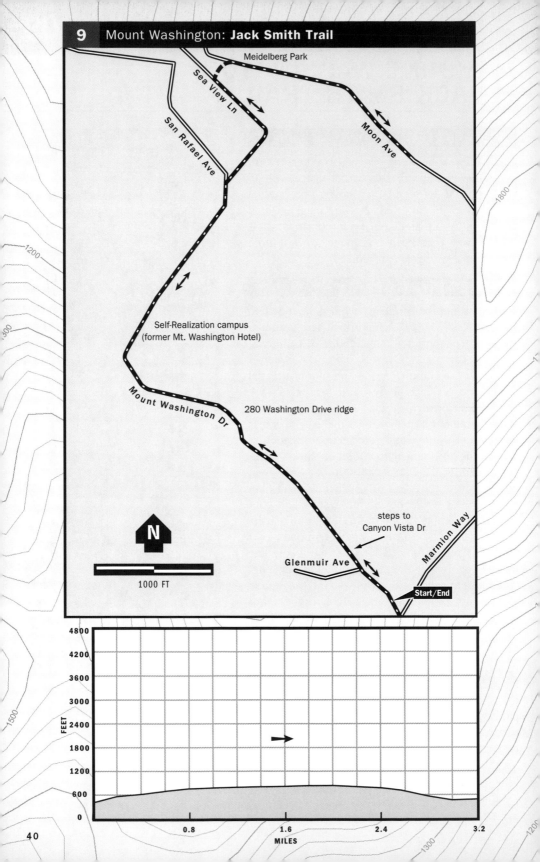

Meidelberg Park

Sea View Ln

San Rafael Ave

Moon Ave

Self-Realization campus
(former Mt. Washington Hotel)

Mount Washington Dr

280 Washington Drive ridge

N

1000 FT

steps to
Canyon Vista Dr

Marmion Way

Glenmuir Ave

Start/End

1200

1300

1800

1300

1500

4800
4200
3600
3000
2400
1800
1200
600
0

FEET

0.8   1.6   2.4   3.2
MILES

Located just north of downtown Los Angeles, Mount Washington is a close-knit enclave of historic houses, wide streets, and nature parks. It was used for sheep and cattle-raising in the nineteenth century before a couple of developers targeted it for residential homes. A two-car railway carried residents up and down the hillside between their homes and the flatlands in the early 1900s. The Mount Washington Hotel, now the headquarters for the Self-Realization Fellowship, a religious organization founded by Paramahansa Yogananda, once attracted celebrities like Charlie Chaplin for its city-to-ocean views and get-away-from-it-all environment. The mayor of Los Angeles, Antonio Villaraigosa, owns a home here.

Begin the hike by walking up Avenue 43 from Marmion Way. The paved road ends at Glenmuir Avenue, and you will see a flight of stairs in front of you. Climb the steps (there are about 70 of them), which are flanked by cactus plants, lilacs, and oak trees, until you reach Canyon Vista Road. Follow Canyon Vista via the sidewalk as it continues to climb past an interesting variety of houses, from Spanish-style to modernist, some shrouded from view by fences or shrubs, others brightly colored with open landscapes. On the left, weather permitting, you will be able to see views of downtown Los Angeles. Behind you is the hillside neighborhood of Montecito Heights.

At about 0.4 miles, Canyon Vista Road merges with Mount Washington Drive. You'll want to bear right and continue climbing uphill along a white-fenced ridge on the left side of the road. On a clear day, this portion of the hike offers uninhibited views of the downtown Los Angeles skyline. Continue following Mount Washington Drive until it dead-ends at San Rafael Avenue. Turn right on San Rafael, and you will find yourself on one of Mount Washington's finest streets, marked by architecturally stunning homes and big landscaped yards. On the right side of the road, fronted by big iron gates, sits the former Mount Washington Hotel, now the international headquarters for the Self-Realization Fellowship. An interesting architectural note: It was built by the same firm that built the famous Graumann's Chinese Theatre in Hollywood. At 0.75 miles, you will pass Mount Washington Elementary School on the left. If you time your hike for the early afternoon, as I did, don't be surprised at the noise and traffic levels here as school lets out. This is also the site of the Jack and Denny Smith Library and Community Center, another effort to honor the L.A. columnist and his wife.

The housing gets a little denser here as San Rafael Avenue crosses Sea View Lane and curves around to the right. For a short detour, hang a left on Sea View and follow it about 0.25 miles until the road turns to dirt; on a clear day, you can see as far as Catalina Island and the Palos Verdes Peninsula. Walk down the hill to the stop sign at Moon Avenue. Turn right on Moon, and you will see a sign for Heidelberg Park on the right. This is Mount Washington's newest designated open space area. The Santa Monica Mountains Conservancy purchased the land in 2002, thanks to an effort by residents to protect the area from development. Formerly known as Rainbow Canyon, the park is home to one of the best remaining examples of black walnut woodland in all of southern California. Birds that make their home here include the great horned owl, hooded oriole, American crow, the red-breasted nuthatch, and Cooper's hawk.

Follow Moon Avenue as it skirts the park on the left. Private homes line the right side of the road. At Crane Boulevard, you can either turn left and follow it down the hill to the Southwest Museum at 234 Museum Drive, or turn around and retrace your steps back to San Rafael Avenue and stop by the Self-Realization Fellowship gardens before heading back to the car. Note that the Southwest Museum and its lauded collection of Native American art and artifacts was purchased by the Autry Museum of Western Heritage in 2003. At press time, the Autry Museum, which is located in Griffith Park, was researching long-term uses for the century-old historic landmark. Go to www.southwestmuseum.org for updates.

▶ NEARBY ACTIVITIES

The Mount Washington Hotel, at 3880 San Rafael Avenue, opened in 1909 as a mountaintop retreat for movie stars like Charlie Chaplin. It is now the international headquarters for the Self-Realization Fellowship, a religious organization founded by Paramahansa Yogananda. The first floor of the building and the surrounding gardens are designated spots of quiet contemplation open to the public from 10 a.m. to 5 p.m. Tuesday through Saturday and 1 to 5 p.m. Sunday. One a clear day, you can see the San Gabriel Mountains to the east and Catalina Island and the Pacific Ocean to the southwest.

RUNYON CANYON

▶ IN BRIEF

This 130-acre park two blocks north of Hollywood Boulevard offers a peaceful respite right in the middle of the city. The trail is popular with dog owners and local residents looking for an energetic outdoor workout that comes with spectacular views of the Los Angeles basin.

▶ DESCRIPTION

Runyon Canyon has three entrances: two are at the bottom, or south end, of the park, and one begins at the north end, off Mulholland Drive. For the best workout and views, most hikers begin at the Fuller Avenue gate on the park's southeast corner and follow it counterclockwise. Once known as No Man's Canyon, the property takes its current name from Carman Runyon, a coal magnate from the East who used the property in the 1930s as a hunting and riding retreat. The city and the Santa Monica Mountains Conservancy bought the property in 1984 and turned it into a public park. Its former life as a playground for Hollywood stars is evidenced by the dilapidated tennis courts and the remains of terraces and building foundations along the main trail loop.

From the gate, take the lower fire road as it starts to climb upward past a grassy children's play area on the left and several exposed picnic tables. Expect to see a good number of dogs romping around a water pump here. The park also attracts its share of impossibly beautiful people, thanks to

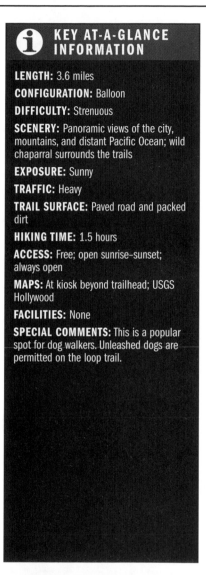

ℹ KEY AT-A-GLANCE INFORMATION

LENGTH: 3.6 miles

CONFIGURATION: Balloon

DIFFICULTY: Strenuous

SCENERY: Panoramic views of the city, mountains, and distant Pacific Ocean; wild chaparral surrounds the trails

EXPOSURE: Sunny

TRAFFIC: Heavy

TRAIL SURFACE: Paved road and packed dirt

HIKING TIME: 1.5 hours

ACCESS: Free; open sunrise–sunset; always open

MAPS: At kiosk beyond trailhead; USGS Hollywood

FACILITIES: None

SPECIAL COMMENTS: This is a popular spot for dog walkers. Unleashed dogs are permitted on the loop trail.

▶ DIRECTIONS

Take the 101 Freeway to the Cahuenga Boulevard exit and follow Cahuenga south to Franklin Avenue. Turn right on Franklin and follow it for a mile, past the La Brea Boulevard intersection. Turn right on Fuller Avenue and park on the street (there's a two-hour limit in most areas). The road dead-ends at the Runyon Canyon gate.

UTM Trailhead Coordinates for Runyon Canyon

UTM Zone (WGS84) **11S**

Easting **375577**

Northing **3774652**

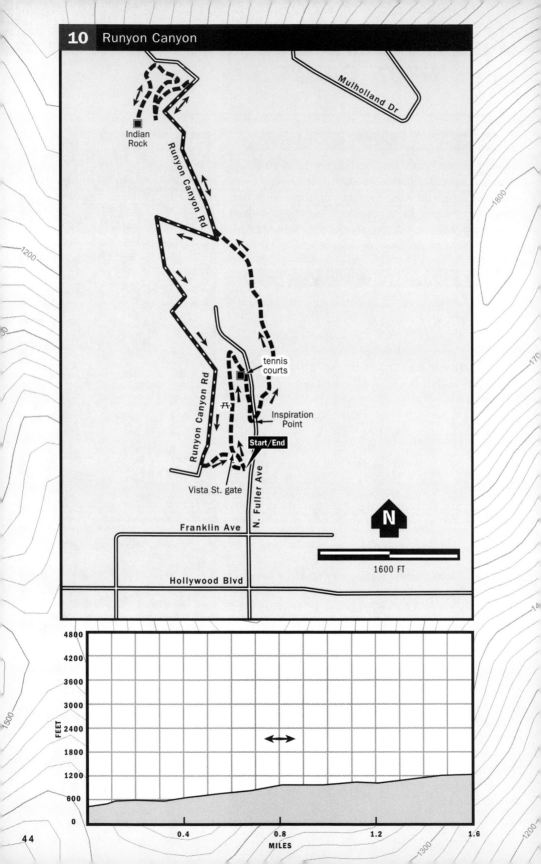

its proximity to Hollywood and the surrounding hills of million-dollar mansions. I spotted actor Robert Forster here once; other celebrities seen on the trail include Brad Pitt and William H. Macy. Bobcats, deer, raccoons, and rattlesnakes also inhabit the canyon, but daylight sightings are rare.

From the picnic tables, continue north on the fire road. After about 0.5 miles, the road curves sharply around and winds past the old tennis courts, now used as a setting for yoga classes. Soon you'll approach Inspiration Point, a level area with a long bench and views of the city stretching below and to the east and west. Here, the paved road ends and you'll begin a steep climb up steps and a sloped dirt path surrounded by brush and cactus. Watch for the occasional dog or runners making their way swiftly down the narrow path. On a clear day, you'll be able see the Hollywood sign and the Griffith Observatory in the distance to your right. Be sure to bring lots of water and sunscreen, as there are few shady areas and the afternoon sun can be brutal.

The steep climb ends at Cloud's Nest, another stopping point with a couple of benches (usually occupied) and even better views of the city. From here the dirt path levels and continues about 0.5 miles to a fork, where you can turn left and head downhill along a paved pathway known as Runyon Canyon Road (no cars are allowed, but you might pass a few baby strollers), which winds back to the Fuller gate.

Instead of heading back down the hill, you may opt to veer right on Runyon Canyon Road and continue north for another (slightly easier) climb to Indian Rock. To get to Indian Rock, go through the iron gate. Dogs must be leashed at this point. You'll pass several private gated homes and a small horse ranch on the right. Just past the ranch, turn left and follow the dirt path uphill past a few unsightly antenna towers. You'll soon come to a T in the path; turn right (the left path dead-ends to a private home) and walk another 0.25 miles or so. You'll reach a narrow path almost covered in shrubs that continues climbing upward. As you approach the top, you may start to hear echoes of "wow" and "awesome" from the hikers who made it to the top before you. At nearly 1,300 feet, this observation point offers a truly stunning view of Los Angeles, especially on clear days after it rains. The entire city stretches below you, framed by the Pacific Ocean to the right and, in the winter, the snowcapped San Gabriel Mountains to the left. One of the best times to take it all in is in the early evening just before sunset. This point can also be accessed easily from Mulholland Drive. There's a small parking lot, but be aware that it closes punctually at sunset.

From here, you'll retrace your steps down the hill and back to the main loop. When you reach the bottom, turn left away from the Vista Street gate and walk along a shady path, lined with palm trees and drought-resistant evergreens, until you reach the children's play area and the Fuller Avenue gate.

▶ NEARBY ACTIVITIES

The bustling corner and neon lights of Hollywood Boulevard at Highland Avenue, about half a mile from Runyon Canyon's southeast entrance, provide a stark contrast to the nature park you've just left. The Hollywood and Highland complex has several restaurants, including a Wolfgang Puck brasserie and a California Pizza Kitchen, upscale shops, and a parking garage. It is also home to the Kodak Theatre, host of the Academy Awards ceremonies. For more information, go to www.hollywoodandhighland.com.

SILVER LAKE RESERVOIR

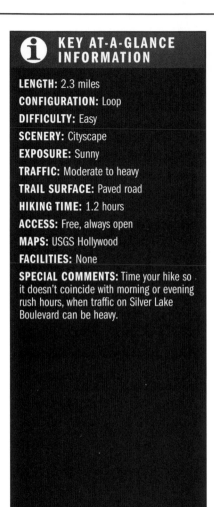

KEY AT-A-GLANCE INFORMATION

LENGTH: 2.3 miles

CONFIGURATION: Loop

DIFFICULTY: Easy

SCENERY: Cityscape

EXPOSURE: Sunny

TRAFFIC: Moderate to heavy

TRAIL SURFACE: Paved road

HIKING TIME: 1.2 hours

ACCESS: Free, always open

MAPS: USGS Hollywood

FACILITIES: None

SPECIAL COMMENTS: Time your hike so it doesn't coincide with morning or evening rush hours, when traffic on Silver Lake Boulevard can be heavy.

UTM Trailhead Coordinates for Silver Lake Reservoir

UTM Zone (WGS84)   11S

Easting   383343

Northing   3773073

IN BRIEF

This flat, suburban loop around a reservoir and an architecturally rich neighborhood is popular with local joggers and power walkers. A busy dog park on one end means you'll also see a fair number of dog walkers along the route.

DESCRIPTION

This isn't the most picturesque of hikes, and a large part of it requires walking along fairly busy roads, but it's an easy way to get some exercise if you live or work nearby. It's also a good place to take out-of-town friends who want to see a business-as-usual side of Los Angeles that goes beyond the glitz of Hollywood and Malibu. Silver Lake is a diverse and architecturally rich neighborhood about 5 miles from downtown Los Angeles. It was the center of the burgeoning entertainment industry in the 1930s, housing the Mack Sennett, Walt Disney, and ABC studios and attracting celebrity residents such as Gloria Swanson, Stan Laurel, and Oliver Hardy. Today, it's more of a hip, bohemian neighborhood full of nightclubs, cafés, and somewhat claustrophobic residences. The Department of Water and Power established the reservoir in the early 1900s as part of a citywide

DIRECTIONS

From the Golden State Freeway (I-5), exit at Fletcher Drive. Turn right on Fletcher, then make an immediate left on Glendale Boulevard. Go 0.2 miles and turn right on Silver Lake Boulevard. Follow the reservoir (on your right) around to Van Pelt Place, turn right and park on the street.

Alternate Directions: Head east on Sunset Boulevard toward Echo Park. Turn left on Silver Lake Boulevard and follow about 0.7 miles to Van Pelt Place and the southern rim of the reservoir. Park on the street.

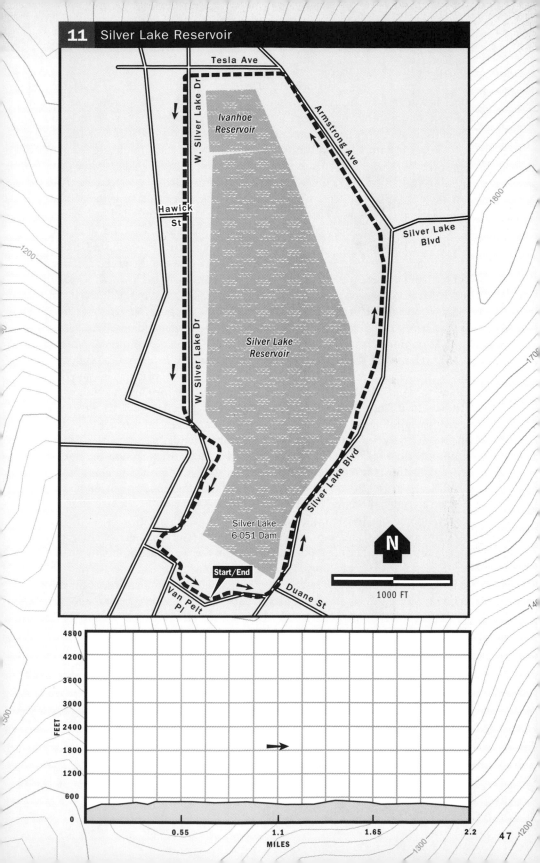

Tesla Ave

W. Silver Lake Dr

Ivanhoe
Reservoir

Armstrong Ave

Hawick
St

Silver Lake
Blvd

W. Silver Lake Dr

Silver Lake
Reservoir

Silver Lake Blvd

N

Silver Lake
6-051 Dam

Start/End

1000 FT

Van Pelt
Pl

Duane St

4800								
4200								
3600								
3000								
2400								
1800								
1200								
600								
0								

FEET

0.55   1.1   1.65   2.2
MILES

system of water storage and delivery. There has been much debate over the years about how to find alternative sources of water for the city and improve the area around the reservoir for public use; a plan is in the works to add a landscaped median and a paved pathway for pedestrians and joggers.

To begin, turn left onto Van Pelt Place from Silver Lake Boulevard, then make a right onto West Silver Lake Drive as it curves uphill around a small grassy park. (You can also make the loop counterclockwise and head north up Silver Lake Boulevard past the dog park; I prefer the clockwise route because it offers better views of the mountains on clear days.) The reservoir is to your right surrounded by a barbed-wire fence. When I walked this trail in late December, there was a good deal of road construction on the east side of Silver Lake Drive, so most people were using the sidewalk across from the reservoir. My walk still yielded good views of the water, and because it had just rained, there were also great views of the snowcapped San Gabriel Mountains in the distance. As soon as you turn onto Silver Lake Drive, the path levels into easy walking. To your right, the reservoir is lined with mature pine trees and grassy patches. To your left is an interesting cross-section of well-tended residences. Architects such as R. M. Schindler and Frank Lloyd Wright were hired to build homes here in the 1930s, and many of them have retained a heavy Spanish Mediterranean influence with stucco, arches, and red roof tiles. At the intersection of Hawick Street and Silverlake Boulevard, to the right you'll see the dam that separates the smaller Ivanhoe reservoir from the Silver Lake reservoir. Continue another 0.25 miles to Tesla Street and turn right to keep following the fence surrounding the water. You'll come to a stop sign, where you'll want to make a right on Armstrong Avenue, passing a preschool at the southwest corner of the reservoir. The pine trees and shrubs around the reservoir are dense along this part of the path, but you can still glimpse the water as you walk. To your left, the road is lined with more homes that maximize their views of the reservoir; they are considered prime Silver Lake property.

Continue on Armstrong for about 0.5 miles until you reach a stop sign. Turn right on Silver Lake Boulevard to keep hugging the reservoir. You can either cross the street and walk on the sidewalk here, or stay on the west side of the bike path. It's a busy street, but the traffic noise is made less annoying by the bucolic views of trees and water to your right. The reservoir ends at about the 2-mile marker, and you'll see a dog park ahead of you to the right at Duane Street. It's open from 5 a.m. to 10:30 p.m. and is quite popular with L.A. dog owners. (There's even a separate area for small or timid dogs.) Continue following Silver Lake Boulevard as it curves around the dog park, and you'll be back at your starting point, Van Pelt Place. If you want to rest or people-watch, there's a small fenced-in park on the corner that has a basketball court and several picnic tables set up under shade trees. (No dogs are allowed.)

▶ NEARBY ACTIVITIES

The Back Door Bakery, 1710 Silver Lake Boulevard, is a casual dog-friendly café with outdoor seating that serves tasty breakfasts, sandwiches, and desserts. There's also the Red Lion Tavern, a well-regarded German pub at 2355 Glendale Boulevard, with a beer garden that's always packed. Besides a wide selection of beer, its pub menu features beef roulade, schnitzel, bratwurst, and other hearty fare.

WEST

(including San Fernando Valley, Verdugo Mountains, Santa Monica Mountains)

ARROYO SEQUIT TRAIL

LENGTH: 2.2 miles

CONFIGURATION: Balloon

DIFFICULTY: Moderate

SCENERY: Wildflowers, chaparral, open meadow

EXPOSURE: Sunny

TRAFFIC: Light

TRAIL SURFACE: Dirt

HIKING TIME: 1 hour

ACCESS: Daily, sunrise to sunset;

MAPS: Posted at kiosk near trailhead; USGS Triunfo Pass

FACILITIES: None

SPECIAL COMMENTS: The 2005 rains washed out two of the trail's stream crossings, leaving 8-foot banks that are navigable, but small kids and out-of-shape adults may find it a bit challenging.

UTM Trailhead Coordinates for Arroyo Sequit Trail

UTM Zone (WGS84)   11S

Easting   325574

Northing   3773608

IN BRIEF

This low-profile trail off Mulholland Highway in the western Santa Monica Mountains crosses an open meadow, then weaves in and out of a gorge bursting with an impressive variety of wildflowers each spring.

DESCRIPTION

Arroyo Sequit, which means "dry riverbed," is a former ranch that was taken over by the Santa Monica Conservancy in the mid-1980s. Besides its role as a hiking destination, it is also used by Santa Monica College as an astronomical observation area. Naturalists estimate that the 155-acre park is home to more than 50 species of wildflowers, including Indian warrior, scarlet pitcher sage, monkey flower, deer weed, owl's clover, bush sunflowers, and morning glory. It is best visited in the spring, when the wildflowers and views of chaparral-covered mountains dominate the trail. During other times of the year, the scenery can be a bit brown and uninspiring. Even in the spring, this path is uncrowded. My husband, son, and I hiked this on a Saturday afternoon during the peak spring wildflower season, and we had the entire place to ourselves.

To get to the trailhead, follow the paved road about 0.2 miles to a small house. Follow the signs for the nature trail, which winds around to the left past another small house, an outhouse, and a cluster of benches used by astronomy

DIRECTIONS

From the 101 Freeway, take the exit for Westlake Boulevard south and follow it about 2 miles until it runs into Mulholland Highway. Turn right on Mulholland and follow it several winding miles to the park entrance on the left. The small sign and gate are easy to miss. The address is 34138 Mulholland Highway.

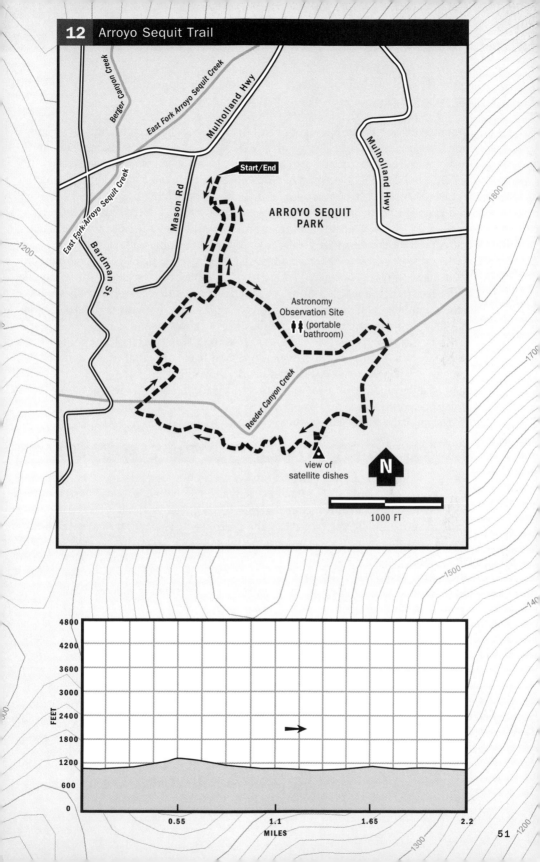

students at Santa Monica College. We spotted what appeared to be corn and wild artichoke plants growing along this part of the trail.

The paved road ends just past the observation benches, and the trail turns to dirt and grass and passes a few large coast live oak trees and picnic tables before crossing an open meadow and giving way to nice views of Boney Mountain to the northwest. Exposure is high on this part of the trail, so be liberal with the sunscreen. After peaking at about 1,300 feet, the trail descends into the canyon via long switchbacks and has a few patches of shade. After about nearly a mile, you will come to the first (and easiest) stream crossing. Look for a seasonal waterfall on the left as you cross.

At 0.7 miles, look to your right and you will see three large white satellite dishes jutting from otherwise green hills. Continue downhill and, at about the 1-mile marker, you will reach another stream crossing, this one much steeper and more difficult than the first. Winter 2005's heavy rains apparently washed out large chunks of the stream banks and left them steep and high. It's passable, but it does require some scrambling and stone-hopping. Wear appropriate footwear and keep in mind that the hike might not be as kid-friendly as it once was.

The situation is similar at the next stream crossing, just a few hundred yards away. After the fourth stream crossing, the path begins to climb again and you will come to a T. Take the right path uphill and follow the wall of the gorge back to the open meadow and picnic area. This is a good place to stop and rest or have a snack under one of the oak trees. From here, you can retrace your steps past the private homes and back to the parking area.

▶ NEARBY ACTIVITIES

Visit the Santa Monica Mountains Recreation Area's headquarters and visitor center at 401 West Hillcrest Drive in Thousand Oaks to stock up on maps, get updated trail conditions, and check out rotating art and wildlife exhibits. Also featured is *Mountains, Movies & Magic*, a film coproduced by the Discovery Channel that highlights the history and resources of the Santa Monica Mountains. To get there from western Mulholland Highway, take Westlake Boulevard north to the Ventura Freeway (101) North and exit at Moorpark Road. Turn right, then make an immediate left onto Hillcrest Drive and follow 0.7 miles to the visitor center. For more information, call (805) 370-2301.

CABALLERO CANYON TRAIL

▶ IN BRIEF

There's not much in terms of scenery along this trail near one of L.A.'s busiest freeways, but its steady 700-foot elevation gain via switchbacks provides a good workout. It is also a popular link to Dirt Mulholland, a wide, no-cars path that leads to several major hiking destinations in the Santa Monica Mountains

▶ DESCRIPTION

The Caballero Canyon Trail was around long before the nearby gated residential developments and landscaped Mulholland Gateway Park showed up. It's a favorite Sierra Club hike in part because it leads to Dirt Mulholland, the 7-mile unpaved stretch of Mulholland Drive between Encino and Woodland Hills. From here, hikers can access the Santa Monica Mountains Backbone Trail, Temescal Canyon, and other trails leading all the way to the Pacific Ocean. Today, more hikers seem to use the shiny new gateway park (it opened in 2000) to connect with other mountain trails, but Caballero Canyon still attracts its share of hikers, mountain bikers, and others who don't want to pay the $3 parking fee at Mulholland Gateway Park.

Look for the trailhead on the east side of Reseda Boulevard just north of the entrance to Braemar Country Club. The dirt-and-gravel trail begins a gradual descent past a dusty trail kiosk that hasn't been updated in ages. I encountered more mountain bikers than hikers on this trail on a Saturday afternoon. Most of them were headed north on the trail toward Reseda Boulevard.

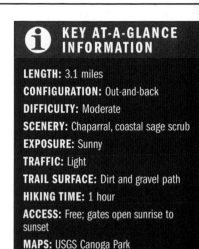

ⓘ KEY AT-A-GLANCE INFORMATION

LENGTH: 3.1 miles

CONFIGURATION: Out-and-back

DIFFICULTY: Moderate

SCENERY: Chaparral, coastal sage scrub

EXPOSURE: Sunny

TRAFFIC: Light

TRAIL SURFACE: Dirt and gravel path

HIKING TIME: 1 hour

ACCESS: Free; gates open sunrise to sunset

MAPS: USGS Canoga Park

FACILITIES: None at trailhead; public restrooms available a mile up Reseda Boulevard at Mulholland Gateway Park

SPECIAL COMMENTS: Don't be put off by the gated communities that line Reseda Boulevard near the trailhead. This path quickly disappears into chaparral and sage scrub and makes you feel like you're a world away from urban sprawl

▶ DIRECTIONS

From the Ventura Freeway (101), take the Reseda Boulevard exit and head south about 2 miles. Park on Reseda across from Braemar Country Club and look for the trailhead on the left side of the road.

UTM Trailhead Coordinates for Caballero Canyon Trail

UTM Zone (WGS84) 11S

Easting 357936

Northing 3779050

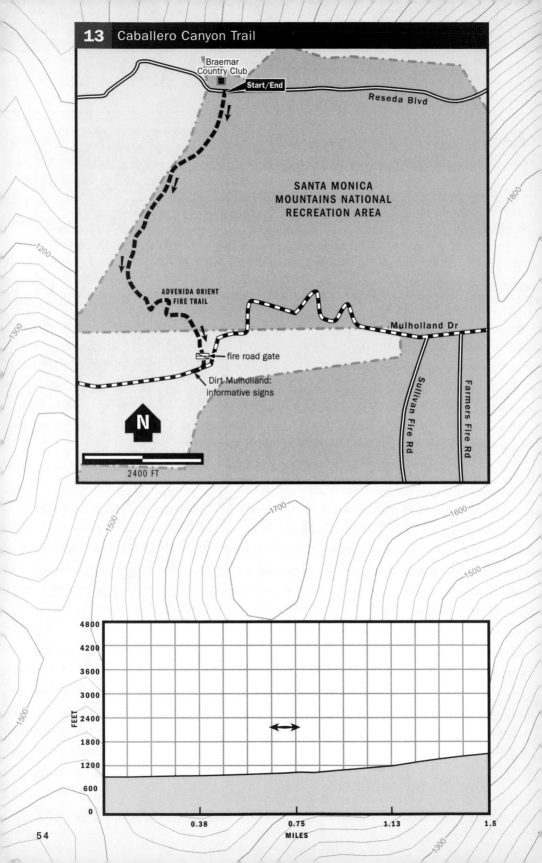

Braemar
Country Club

Start/End

Reseda Blvd

SANTA MONICA
MOUNTAINS NATIONAL
RECREATION AREA

ADVENIDA ORIENT
FIRE TRAIL

fire road gate

Mulholland Dr

Dirt Mulholland:
informative signs

Sullivan Fire Rd

Farmers Fire Rd

N

2400 FT

4800
4200
3600
3000
2400
1800
1200
600
0

FEET

0.38   0.75   1.13   1.5
MILES

At about 0.75 miles, you will come to a turnoff for an unmarked narrow trail on the left. This leads to a seasonal streambed, though you won't be able to see it or hear it well from the canyon trail. You want to continue straight in tandem with Reseda Boulevard. Most of the path is flanked by tall grass, a scattering of sycamore trees, and coastal sage shrub, with the crest of the Santa Monica Mountains in full view most of the time. In the spring and summer, you can also spot clumps of California dodder, a leafless parasitic weed with orange buds that resembles spun sugar.

The path makes a sharp left at the 1-mile marker, heading east toward the hills before climbing south again. There is little shade along most of the path, so bring plenty of sunscreen and insect repellent. The path continues to climb past a bench and water fountain, then reaches a fire-road gate. If you look behind you at this point, you will get nice views of the San Fernando Valley on a clear day. Walk 50 more yards uphill and you will reach Dirt Mulholland and signs for other Santa Monica Mountains paths, including Topanga State Park, Temescal Ridge, and Westward Ridge, which leads to a former missile observation post that was folded into the Santa Monica Mountains Recreation Area in 1996 and turned into a park. From here, you can retrace your steps back to the parking lot or turn right and follow Dirt Mulholland west toward Mulholland Gateway Park, which empties you back on Reseda Boulevard. The downside to this loop route is that the last mile requires you to walk past the aforementioned residential developments. It's a bit jarring after the wilderness feel of Caballero Canyon, which is why I prefer to take the out-and-back option and return via the canyon.

▶ NEARBY ACTIVITIES

Ventura Boulevard is teeming with restaurants and shops. One standout place to get a bite is Empanada's Place, a pretty little diner specializing in empanadas, the meat- or cheese-stuffed pies from Argentina that make a great picnic offering. Choose from 16 varieties or opt for the tamales or Milanesa sandwiches with chimichurri sauce. It's located a few blocks west of Reseda Boulevard at 18912 Ventura Boulevard. For hours, call (818) 708-8640.

CALABASAS PEAK TRAIL

KEY AT-A-GLANCE INFORMATION

LENGTH: 3.8 miles

CONFIGURATION: Out-and-back

DIFFICULTY: Difficult

SCENERY: Chapparral- and boulder-covered hills, suburban landscape

EXPOSURE: Sunny

TRAFFIC: Moderate

TRAIL SURFACE: Dirt fire road

HIKING TIME: 1.5 hours

ACCESS: Free; always open

MAPS: USGS Malibu Beach

FACILITIES: Water fountains, picnic area, pit toilet at Red Rock Canyon Park on trail

SPECIAL COMMENTS: During the hot summer months, hike this trail in the early evening and enjoy the sunset and cooler air.

UTM Trailhead Coordinates for
Calabasas Peak Trail

UTM Zone (WGS84)   11S

Easting   347810

Northing   3773989

▶ IN BRIEF

Serene hills and dramatic sandstone rock formations dominate the scenery of this uphill Santa Monica Mountains trail, which has an elevation gain of nearly 1,000 feet.

▶ DESCRIPTION

From the parking lot, cross Stunt Road to the white gate and begin walking uphill along the fire road. There is very little shade on this trail, so bring plenty of sunscreen and water. The path continues on a gradual ascent, giving way to splendid vistas of hillsides covered by rocky outcrops and toyon, laurel sumac, sagebrush, buckwheat, and *ceanothus* shrubs. In no time at all, you'll feel worlds away from the city bustle. This is also a good place to spot Santa Susana tarweed, a native, hard-to-find plant with yellow, bell-shaped flowers that blooms between June and August and tends to grow amid the area's sandstone rock formations. Other wildflowers found here are cliff aster, sunflowers, *clarkia,* and golden bush.

This trail is fairly well known among L.A. hikers, but I've never seen more than a handful of people here. Mountain bikers and horseback riders also use the trail on a regular basis. At about 0.8 miles, you'll come to a right turnoff for Red Rock Canyon Park, a former Boy Scout camp that was purchased by the Santa Monica Mountains Conservancy in 1986. The park has water fountains, a picnic area, and a pit toilet; it can also be accessed by car from Topanga Canyon Boulevard.

▶ DIRECTIONS

From the 101 Freeway, exit Topanga Canyon Boulevard and head south to Mulholland Highway. Turn right and follow Mulholland for 4 miles to Stunt Road. Make a left on Stunt and drive about 1 mile to a pullout parking area on the right.

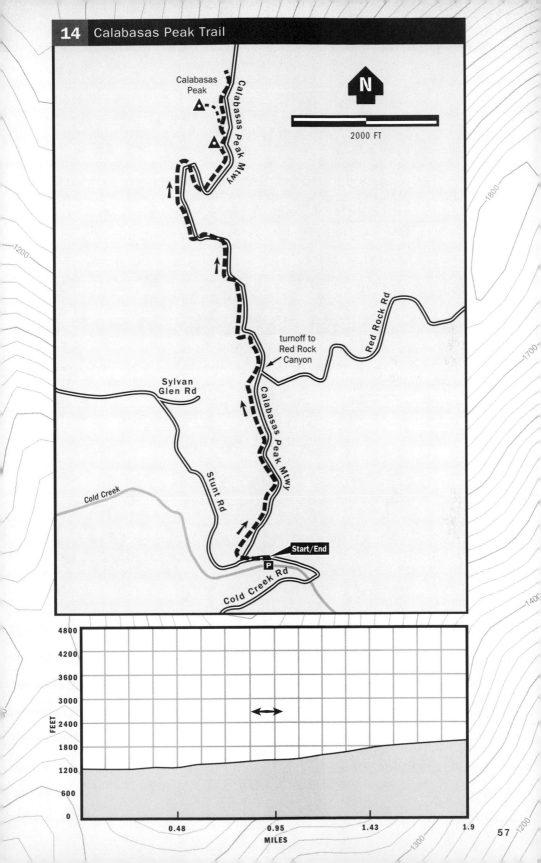

Calabasas Peak

Calabasas Peak Mtwy

N

2000 FT

Red Rock Rd

turnoff to
Red Rock
Canyon

Calabasas Peak Mtwy

Sylvan
Glen Rd

Stunt Rd

Cold Creek

Start/End

P

Cold Creek Rd

1200

1800

1700

1400

1300

1200

FEET

4800
4200
3600
3000
2400
1800
1200
600
0

0.48   0.95   1.43   1.9
MILES

To reach Calabasas Peak, take the left fork on the fire road and continue on the uphill climb. The dramatic rock formations you see on the right are the result of centuries of wind and water erosion. They lend an otherworldly element to the hike, making the trail seem much farther from the suburban sprawl and traffic-choked highways than it actually is. The trail continues to steepen as it makes a switchback to the right and approaches the peak.

The trail gives way somewhat abruptly to sweeping views of the San Fernando Valley, Santa Monica Mountains, and Pacific Ocean. You can rest here and call it a day, or get extra credit by following a left narrow trail uphill to an elevation of 2,100 feet and even better vistas. The fire road continues northeast toward Old Topanga Canyon Road from here, but most hikers turn back at this point. You can retrace your steps back to the Stunt Road lot, or if you'd like to extend the hike, consider turning off at the Red Rock Canyon path on the way back down. This tacks on about 3 miles to the hike.

▶ NEARBY ACTIVITIES

If you want a cool drink and festive atmosphere after your hike, La Paz, at 4505 Las Virgenes Road in Calabasas, stocks 50 different kinds of tequila and specializes in Yucatán cuisine.

FRYMAN CANYON LOOP

▶ IN BRIEF

There's nothing awe-inspiring about this hike, but it is a reliable, well-maintained exercise route that's easily accessible from Hollywood and the San Fernando Valley. It's also dog-friendly, with plenty of trashcans, plastic-bag dispensers, and water troughs. Most people take the moderately strenuous loop that begins with an uphill climb under sycamore trees, gives way to valley views, and empties into a street of private homes and back to the parking lot.

▶ DESCRIPTION

Look for the Betty B. Dearing Mountain Trail sign to the right of the parking lot entrance. The trailhead begins here, and you'll probably see a jogger or two warming up by the gate and a few dogs getting their leashes strapped on by their owners. Fryman Canyon is part of the 128-acre Wilacre Park, which also includes Franklin and Coldwater Canyon Parks and is run by the Santa Monica Mountains Conservancy.

Follow the paved fire road as it curves upward past toyon (Christmas berry) bushes and sycamore trees. You'll see quite a mix of hikers—from serious runners to dog walkers and moms with kids—yet the path is wide enough that it never seems overly crowded. The traffic noise from Laurel Canyon Boulevard below you to the right can be heavy, but it will soon fade as you get

ⓘ KEY AT-A-GLANCE INFORMATION

LENGTH: 2.6 miles

CONFIGURATION: Loop

DIFFICULTY: Moderate

SCENERY: Native plants, trees; hill and valley views

EXPOSURE: Mostly sun, some shade

TRAFFIC: Heavy

TRAIL SURFACE: Paved road and packed dirt

HIKING TIME: 1 hour, 20 minutes

ACCESS: $3 lot fee; open 8 a.m.–sunset daily; free street parking, but be aware of the no parking zones

MAPS: USGS Van Nuys

FACILITIES: Public restrooms at parking lot

SPECIAL COMMENTS: This path can get crowded on weekends.

▶ DIRECTIONS

From the 101 Freeway, take Laurel Canyon Boulevard south about 2.4 miles to Fryman Road. Turn right on Fryman and make an immediate right into a gravel parking lot. There is also free street parking along Fryman Road. From Hollywood, head north on Laurel Canyon Boulevard until you reach Fryman Road. Turn left at the light and right into the parking lot.

UTM Trailhead Coordinates for Fryman Canyon Loop

UTM Zone (WGS84) 11S

Easting 371666

Northing 3777808

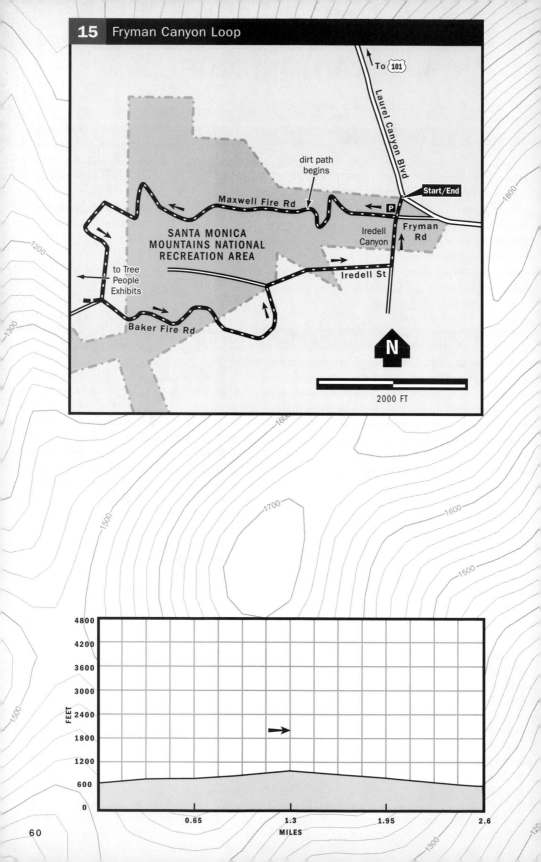

To ⬡101

Laurel Canyon Blvd

dirt path begins

Maxwell Fire Rd

Start/End

P

SANTA MONICA MOUNTAINS NATIONAL RECREATION AREA

Iredell Canyon

Fryman Rd

to Tree People Exhibits

Iredell St

Baker Fire Rd

N

2000 FT

A hiker enjoying the walk along
Fryman Canyon

farther into the canyon. Don't get too comfortable with the shade—the trail soon
gives way to sky and the often-brutal valley sun. It continues to ascend somewhat
sharply for about a mile, until it reaches a rusty barbed-wire fence on the left and the
remains of a driveway that leads nowhere. At 0.3 miles, the path turns to packed dirt,
and the ascent becomes more gradual and open. This path gets slick and muddy after
it rains, but it usually dries up quickly.

Through the trees to the right, you'll see a scattering of hillside homes (some
look more like villas) in the distance and the entire sprawling San Fernando Valley
beyond that. At 0.6 miles, an inviting wooden bench appears on the right (courtesy
of a Santa Monica Mountains Conservancy donor)—it's a good place to rest, guzzle
some water, and take in the valley views. From here, the dirt path curves sharply to
the south and winds upward again. Rattlesnake warning signs dot this area, but I've
never spotted one; occasional coyote sightings are also possible. At about 1.3 miles,
you'll come to a wide clearing covered with loose wood chips. The path to the right
leads to Coldwater Canyon Boulevard and the entrance to the headquarters of Tree
People, a nonprofit group that promotes energy and water conservation and holds
summer concerts and other events in its outdoor amphitheater. The group is in the
middle of building an eco-friendly center of community forestry that will include a
nursery, conference hall, and outdoor labyrinth, slated to open in 2006.

To the left are a couple of benches, water fountains for dogs and people, and
more views of shrouded hills and the valley. Continue straight (south) on the path
until you reach a dirt path on the right with a wooden guardrail. Follow it upward for
a quick detour to check out a small display (courtesy of Tree People) on native rock
formations and the trees of Fryman Canyon, including valley oaks, the only decidu-
ous oak in the Santa Monica Mountains, and black walnut trees.

Back on the dirt path, continue south about 0.25 miles until you reach a yellow gate that marks the perimeter of the state-owned park. You can either turn back

here and retrace your steps to the parking lot or continue straight down Iredell Lane, a low-traffic street that will instantly let you know that you're back in Los Angeles proper, with its imposing security gates, buzz of weed whackers, and Mercedes-filled driveways. The road empties into Fryman Road and takes you back to the trailhead.

▶ NEARBY ACTIVITIES

DuPar's, a classic Los Angeles diner at 12036 Ventura Boulevard, is a great place to scarf down some nearly perfect flapjacks after your hike. If you'd rather take some snacks with you on the trail, just behind DuPar's is Trader Joe's market, which sells trail mix, energy bars, ready-made sandwiches, and other supplies. There is also a decent farmer's market on Sunday mornings on Ventura Place, just north of the boulevard at Laurel Canyon. It's very much geared toward kids, with face-painting, pony rides, and a petting zoo, but you can also pick up fresh fruit, vegetables, and flowers. For more information, go to www.studiocitychamber.com/farmers_market.htm.

GROTTO TRAIL

▶ IN BRIEF

Located on the grounds of a former Boy Scout camp about 5 miles north of the Pacific Coast Highway, this trail offers a nice sampling of the scenery that characterizes Santa Monica Mountains hiking: open fields, shady streambed, live oak forest, and volcanic-rock walls. It ends at a cool and somewhat gloomy grotto where you can splash around before making the arduous uphill trek back to the car. A difficult scramble over boulders for the last 200 yards puts this hike in the strenuous category.

▶ DESCRIPTION

The Circle X Ranch was a working ranch until 1948, when a service organization called Circle X bought the property and donated it to the Boy Scouts for a wilderness retreat. Tucked away in one of the more remote areas of the western Santa Monica Mountains, it is home to Sandstone Peak, the highest point in the mountain range at 3,100 feet and a rare Mediterranean ecosystem that includes coastal sage scrub and red shank chaparral, a tree-like shrub with reddish-brown bark, thread-like leaves, and small bunches of seasonal white flowers. From the 101, it's a teeth-clenching drive along a mountain ridge off Mulholland Drive to the ranch, but that's part of

▶ DIRECTIONS

From the 101 Freeway, take the Westlake Boulevard exit and head south for several miles until it merges with Mulholland Highway. Turn right on Little Sycamore Canyon Road (it will become Yerba Buena Road at the Ventura County Line) and follow it about 4.5 miles to Circle X Ranch. The entrance is on the left side of the road.

Alternate Directions: Take Pacific Coast Highway to Yerba Buena Road. Turn right and follow the road about 5.5 miles to Circle X Ranch.

ⓘ KEY AT-A-GLANCE INFORMATION

LENGTH: 3.2 miles

CONFIGURATION: Out-and-back

DIFFICULTY: Moderate

SCENERY: Grassland, Boney Mountain, oak forest

EXPOSURE: Sun and shade

TRAFFIC: Moderate

TRAIL SURFACE: Dirt fire road

HIKING TIME: 1.5 hours

ACCESS: Free; open 8 a.m.–sunset, daily

MAPS: Available at ranger station; USGS Triunfo Pass

FACILITIES: Restrooms, water, picnic tables

SPECIAL COMMENTS: The drive to Circle X Ranch from the 101 Freeway is a bit of a roller-coaster ride: full of sharp curves and hairpin turns. Allow for extra drive time and watch out for mountain bikers. No bikes are allowed past the picnic area, and dogs must be leashed.

UTM Trailhead Coordinates for Grotto Trail

UTM Zone (WGS84)   11S

Easting   321349

Northing   3775894

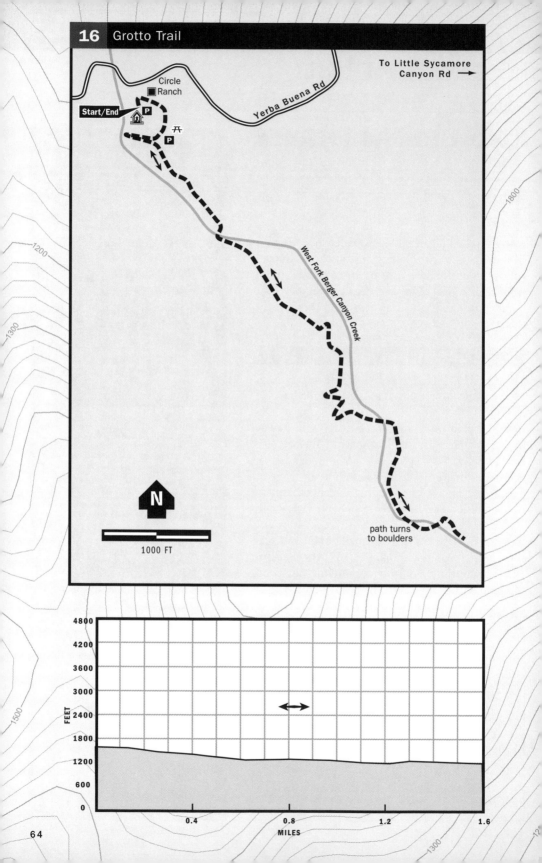

To Little Sycamore
Canyon Rd →

Circle
Ranch

Start/End

Yerba Buena Rd

West Fork Berger Canyon Creek

N

1000 FT

path turns
to boulders

4800

4200

3600

3000

2400

1800

1200

600

0

FEET

0.4

0.8

1.2

1.6

MILES

the adventure and prepares you for the interesting hike to come. It's tough not to be impressed by the views of the Conejo and San Fernando valleys, especially if you're a passenger in the car and do not have to concentrate on the hairpin turns. Other trails that can be accessed from Circle X are Sandstone Peak, which leads to the highest peak in the Santa Monica Mountains, and Canyon View, an easy 2-mile hike that spurs off the Grotto trail. Also nearby but not accessible from the main parking lot is the Mishe Mokwa trail, a challenging 6-mile loop known for its dramatic cliffs, rock formations, and valley and ocean views. The trailhead for that is next to a dirt pull-out about a mile north of the main entrance.

The original Circle X Ranch is now a ranger office. It is located at the upper parking lot and is a good place to stop for maps and information on the history of the property. Old photos from the ranch's heyday decorate the walls. A shaded bench, water fountain, and unisex bathroom are just outside the office.

From the parking lot, take the paved road south toward the picnic area and Grotto trailhead. The road winds downhill past another office complex and a basketball court to the shady picnic area. The Grotto trailhead is at the far end of the picnic area. You can also leave your car here, but keep in mind that the small lot fills up quickly with picnickers on weekends. If there are no spaces, you will have to turn around and drive back to the upper lot.

After leaving the picnic area, the trail turns into a single-track dirt path and reaches the turnoff for Canyon View Trail after 0.4 miles. Continue straight and cross a dry streambed, then follow the trail uphill briefly before it levels and winds through a wide open field. Behind you are distant views of the rugged cliffs and pinnacles of Boney Mountain. Soon after crossing the meadow, the trail begins a steep descent toward the bottom of the gorge and shady oak forest. Turn left at the stream and head downstream to a pond. At this point, it seems as if the trail ends, but the best is yet to come.

Keep in mind that dogs are not allowed from this point on. To get to the upper grotto, you will have to scale a narrow rock ledge and a few large boulders for about 0.2 miles, then climb down to the pool of water surrounded by a small cavern. You will likely find other hikers here cooling off, aware that they face a steady uphill climb back to the park entrance. Be sure to conserve some water for the trek back.

▶ NEARBY ACTIVITIES

Visit the National Park visitor center at 401 West Hillcrest Drive in Thousand Oaks to stock up on maps, get updated trail conditions, and check out rotating art and wildlife exhibits. Also featured is *Mountains, Movies & Magic,* a film coproduced by the Discovery Channel that highlights the history and resources of the Santa Monica Mountains. To get there from western Mulholland Highway, take Westlake Boulevard north to the Ventura Freeway (101) and exit at Moorpark Road. Turn right, then make an immediate left onto Hillcrest Drive and follow it 0.7 miles to the visitor center. It's open daily from 9 a.m. to 5 p.m. For more information, call (805) 370-2301.

M*A*S*H TRAIL, MALIBU CREEK STATE PARK

 KEY AT-A-GLANCE INFORMATION

LENGTH: 6 miles

CONFIGURATION: Out-and-back

DIFFICULTY: Moderate

SCENERY: Oak forest, creek, abandoned TV show sets

EXPOSURE: Sun and shade

TRAFFIC: Moderate

TRAIL SURFACE: Dirt path, dry creek bed

HIKING TIME: 2.5 hours

ACCESS: Park is open 7 a.m.–sunset; $8 per car day-use fee

MAPS: USGS Malibu Beach

FACILITIES: Restrooms, water, picnic areas, campsites, visitor center open weekends only

SPECIAL COMMENTS: Weekends draw lots of families with small children to this area.

UTM Trailhead Coordinates for *M*A*S*H* Trail, Malibu Creek State Park

UTM Zone (WGS84) 11S

Easting 341588

Northing 3774184

▶ IN BRIEF

This no-dogs-allowed trail starts off flat and easy as it passes through shady valleys of live oaks and wildflowers, then turns rugged with boulders and brush before arriving at the now-desolate site of the old *M*A*S*H* TV series. Worthwhile detours include a rock pool and climbing wall and a manmade lake that fans of the 4077th might also recognize.

▶ DESCRIPTION

The 20th Century Fox studio purchased this 4,000-acre property from a group of homeowners in the late 1940s. Besides *M*A*S*H*, movies and TV shows filmed here include *Butch Cassidy and the Sundance Kid*, *Dr. Dolittle*, and *Fantasy Island*, though few remnants of the sets remain. Fox sold the property to the state of California in 1974 and it opened to the public in 1976.

The *M*A*S*H* trail begins at the bottom of a flight of steps in front of the restrooms at the southwestern corner of the parking lot. Follow it down across a small bridge, past signs marked BACKCOUNTRY TRAILS and NO DOGS ALLOWED. After about 0.3 miles, you'll see another bridge in front of you (during rainy season, it's usually flooded and impassable). This leads to the Rock Pool, a swimmable stretch of water framed by volcanic cliffs that has served as a backdrop for *The Swiss Family Robinson,* the Tarzan movies, *Planet of the Apes* and many other films.

To get to the *M*A*S*H* site, you want to continue straight on the fire road past an open

▶ DIRECTIONS

From the Ventura Freeway (101), exit at Las Virgenes Canyon Road and head south 4 miles to Malibu Creek State Park. The entrance is on your right. Follow the entrance road to the far western corner of the lot, near the restrooms.

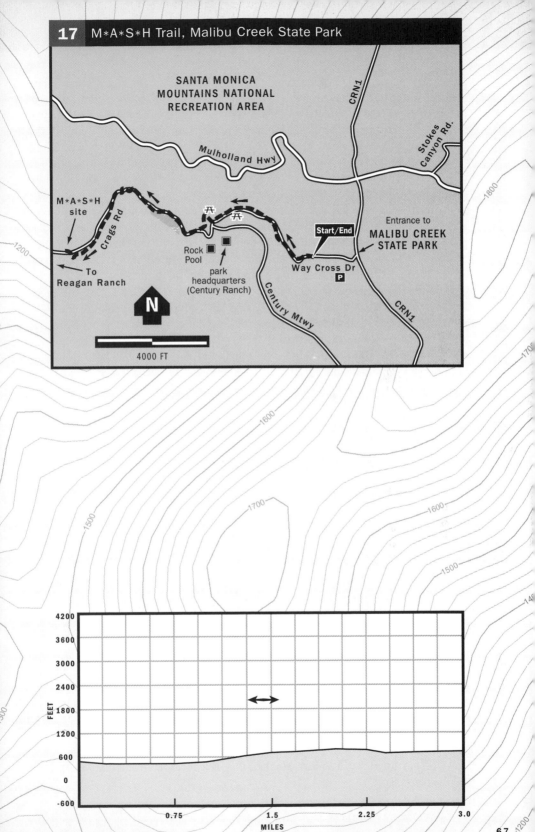

SANTA MONICA
MOUNTAINS NATIONAL
RECREATION AREA

Mulholland Hwy

CRN1

Stokes
Canyon Rd.

1800

M∗A∗S∗H
site

Crags Rd

← To
Reagan Ranch

Rock
Pool

park
headquarters
(Century Ranch)

Start/End

Entrance to
**MALIBU CREEK
STATE PARK**

Way Cross Dr
P

Century Mtwy

CRN1

1700

N

4000 FT

1200

1600

1700

1500

1600

1500

140

FEET

MILES

4200
3600
3000
2400
1800
1200
600
0
-600

0.75   1.5   2.25   3.0

grassy area dotted with newly planted trees. On weekends, this area is usually swarming with families who have come to the park to picnic, ride bikes, and splash around the creek. This trail is often billed as an easy walk because it's mostly flat, but it's not for kids. The latter half of the hike isn't well marked and requires quite a bit of scrambling around boulders and heavy brush, especially in the winter when the creek floods parts of the trail. I recommend bringing lots of water and a walking stick. Also, despite the proximity to the Pacific Ocean, this area gets very hot in the summer; bring plenty of sunscreen and insect repellent.

After you pass a left turnoff for the visitor center and campground at 0.9 miles, it gets a little more tranquil. The road is shaded by live oaks, and there are also a few picnic tables tucked discreetly out of the way. The path will begin to narrow and climb gradually upward past pleasant views of hills covered with boulders and chaparral. As you continue to climb, you'll pass a turnoff on the left that leads to a building foundation, perhaps one of the original adobe homes that sat on the property before it was sold to Fox. Soon you'll also pass turnoffs for Lookout Trail (to the right), which leads uphill to a ridge overlooking the valley, and Century Lake (to the left). The lake—a bucolic marshland setting that is home to ducks, coots, herons, and redwing blackbirds—is worth a detour if you have time, but keep in mind that it's another 2 miles to the M*A*S*H site. Stay on Crags Road as it follows Malibu Creek on your left. At about 2.5 miles, you'll come to a bridge, and you'll want to bear right after crossing it and follow a dry streambed. Again, in winter, this area can flood, so you may have to turn right before you cross the bridge and hike through brush and debris to get back on the trail. You might start to feel like you're lost and in the middle of nowhere, but it probably won't last long. Just keep following Crags Road and the dry creek bed for another 0.5 miles until you reach the M*A*S*H site. Chances are, you'll run into other hikers at the site, because it can also be accessed from Kanan Road on the western end of the park. You'll also know you've made it when you come to two rusted-out vehicles—a jeep and an ambulance once used as props on the show—and a lone picnic table. Nearby a small hill leads to a clearing that served as a helicopter landing pad. This is all that's left of the outdoor set of one of TV's most popular shows.

From here, you can continue following the Crags Road trail to Reagan Ranch and Malibu Lake, or retrace your steps back to the main parking lot.

▶ NEARBY ACTIVITIES

Take time to stop by the park visitor center, about a mile's walk from the main parking lot via the lower or higher roads and open only on weekends. Besides maps and restrooms, it has black-and-white photos of Hot Lips, Hawkeye, Radar, and the rest of the M*A*S*H cast, plus native plant and wildlife exhibits. Movie buffs might also recognize the rustic building as Cary Grant's rural Connecticut dream home in the 1948 film *Mr. Blandings Builds His Dream House.*

If you want a cool drink and festive atmosphere after your hike, La Paz, at 4505 Las Virgenes Road in Calabasas, stocks 50 different kinds of tequila and specializes in Yucatán cuisine.

MULHOLLAND GATEWAY PARK: HUB JUNCTION TRAIL

▶ IN BRIEF

This popular trail offers an excellent introduction to the Santa Monica Mountains trail system. After a steep ascent, it eases to a gradual incline on a well-maintained dirt path flanked by chaparral and seasonal wildflowers. It also connects with several other trails with varying degrees of difficulty.

▶ DESCRIPTION

Named after a Los Angeles city councilman who championed the preservation of the Santa Monica Mountains, Marvin Braude Mulholland Gateway Park opened in 2000 and encompasses 17 acres of once-rugged land above the unpaved portion of Mulholland Drive known as Dirt Mulholland. Environmental groups protested that the landscaped park and its irrigation system would have a negative effect on the hillsides of nearby Caballero Canyon. Despite the opposition, the park opened as a slightly scaled-down version of the original plan. Local families and exercise hounds pack the place on weekends. Don't be put off by the upscale gated communities you see on the way up Reseda Boulevard to the park. Once you pass through the fire-road gate, you will feel as if you're a world away from urban sprawl. The farther south you walk, the more serene and natural it gets.

To get to the main trailhead, walk up the fire road at the park's southernmost end. To the left are two pathways that lead to a short landscaped loop with rock benches and mountain and valley

ⓘ KEY AT-A-GLANCE INFORMATION

LENGTH: 5.5 miles

CONFIGURATION: Out-and-back

DIFFICULTY: Moderate

SCENERY: Chaparral-covered hills, San Fernando Valley views

EXPOSURE: Sunny

TRAFFIC: Moderate to heavy

TRAIL SURFACE: Packed dirt

HIKING TIME: 2 hours, 15 minutes

ACCESS: $3 fee at self-pay station or street parking; park closed sunset–sunrise

MAPS: USGS Canoga Park

FACILITIES: Restrooms, water, picnic area

SPECIAL COMMENTS: For additional information, go to www.lamountains.com/parks.asp?parkid=34

▶ DIRECTIONS

From the Ventura Freeway (101), take the Reseda Boulevard exit and head south about 3.2 miles past residential developments until the road ends at the park. Parking is along the street. Don't forget to check in at the self-pay parking station, or park on the street outside the gate before you reach the signs marked FEE PARKING.

UTM Trailhead Coordinates for Mulholland Gateway Park: Hub Junction Trail

UTM Zone (WGS84)   11S

Easting   356782

Northing   3777859

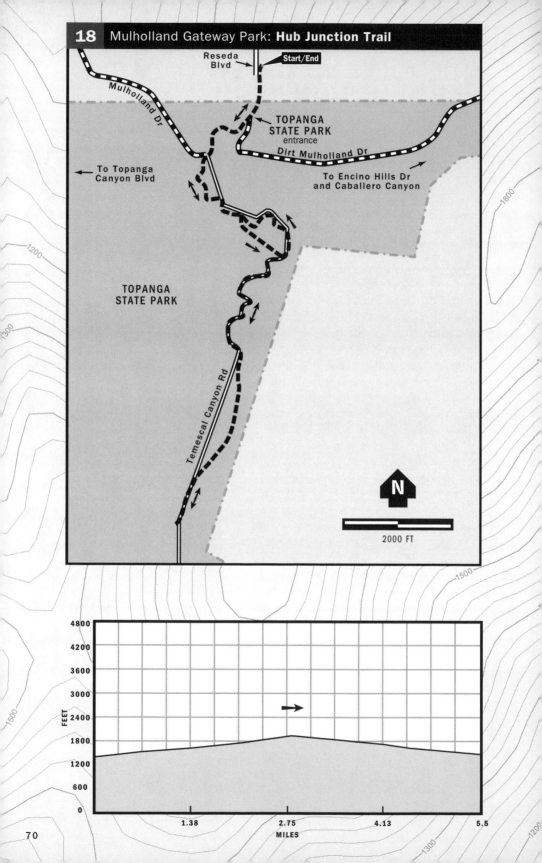

Reseda Blvd

Start/End

Mulholland Dr

TOPANGA
STATE PARK
entrance

Dirt Mulholland Dr

← To Topanga
Canyon Blvd

To Encino Hills Dr
and Caballero Canyon →

TOPANGA
STATE PARK

Temescal Canyon Rd

N

2000 FT

1800

1200

1300

1500

1500

1300

1200

FEET

4800
4200
3600
3000
2400
1800
1200
600
0

1.38   2.75   4.13   5.5
MILES

views. This is a nice spot to have a picnic or rest after your hike. There is also a grassy hillside just before the trailhead on the left with a bench and plenty of room for sprawling.

Walk up the wide, dirt fire road about 0.2 miles until you reach a Y and a sign marking the entrance to Topanga State Park, an 11,000-acre park known for its 36 miles of hiking trails, views of the Pacific Ocean, and variety of geologic formations.

To the left is Dirt Mulholland and turnoffs for Caballero Canyon and Encino Hills Drive. You want to turn left and follow Dirt Mulholland west toward Temescal Canyon Fire Road 30 and Topanga Canyon Boulevard. After 0.3 miles, you will come to another Y. Take the left-hand path south, following the brown sign for Temescal Ridge Road and Hub Junction. From here, it's a gentle uphill 2-mile hike past open grassland, chaparral slopes, and coast live oaks to Hub Junction, a four-way junction that links up with the Backbone Trail, Will Rogers State Park, and Eagle Spring, a loop trail known for its series of boulder outcroppings. Hub Junction also has good views of a cluster of red sandstone rocks known as the Sespe Formation, a non-marine layer of rock that accumulated as the sea filled with sediment about 50 million years ago.

From here, you can retrace your steps back to the parking lot or extend the hike a few more miles and head deeper into the mountains on any of the aforementioned trails.

▶ NEARBY ACTIVITIES

Ventura Boulevard is teeming with restaurants and shops. One standout place to get a bite is Empanada's Place, a pretty little diner specializing in empanadas, the meat- or cheese-stuffed pies from Argentina that make a great picnic offering. Choose from 16 varieties, or opt for the tamales or Milanesa sandwiches with chimichurri sauce. It's located a few blocks west of Reseda Boulevard at 18912 Ventura Boulevard. For hours, call (818) 708-8640.

PARAMOUNT RANCH: HACIENDA TRAIL TO BACKDROP TRAIL

 KEY AT-A-GLANCE INFORMATION

LENGTH: 3.6 miles

CONFIGURATION: Out-and-back

DIFFICULTY: Easy to moderate

SCENERY: Rolling hills, meadows, woodland

EXPOSURE: Sunny

TRAFFIC: Moderate

TRAIL SURFACE: Dirt and gravel

HIKING TIME: 2 hours

ACCESS: Free; open sunrise–sunset, daily

MAPS: Available at kiosk at entrance to Western Town; USGS Point Dume

FACILITIES: Restrooms in parking lot, water fountains, picnic tables

SPECIAL COMMENTS: Towering over the area from the south is Sugarloaf Peak, at 1,515 feet the highest point in the Santa Monica Mountains.

UTM Trailhead Coordinates for Paramount Ranch: Hacienda Trail to Backdrop Trail

UTM Zone (WGS84) 11S

Easting 336430

Northing 3776550

▶ IN BRIEF

Ideal for families and fans of Hollywood westerns, this sun-scorched trail meanders through grassy meadows to the former site of TV's *Dr. Quinn, Medicine Woman* and other movies and TV shows with western themes. Its links to other unmarked trails within the ranch property encourages wandering, but the relatively small size of the property (400 acres) and the visibility of major roads from the paths make it tough to get lost.

▶ DESCRIPTION

In 1927, Paramount Pictures bought rural property in the Santa Monica Mountains and for 20 years used it as a setting for shooting dozens of westerns, including *The Virginian*, *Wells Fargo*, and *Gunsmoke*. The ranch has also been the setting for western-themed TV shows like *The Cisco Kid* and *Bat Masterson*. It was used as a racetrack in the 1950s before the National Park Service bought part of the property in 1980 and revitalized the old movie ranch and added hiking trails. The area is still used as a working movie ranch. From 1992 to 1997, it served as the early Colorado setting of *Dr. Quinn, Medicine Woman*. It's quite popular with tourists and families, but the trails never seem crowded because most visitors show up to gawk at the cluster of faux western buildings at the ranch entrance without venturing to the trails beyond them.

Paramount Ranch's handful of trails are named for the ranch's celluloid past, though few props remain beyond the facades of Western Town. Medicine Woman Trail leads past the site

▶ DIRECTIONS

From the 101 Freeway, exit at Kanan Road and follow south to Cornell Road. Bear left onto Cornell. Paramount Ranch is on your right, just before the intersection with Mulholland Highway. Park in the lot.

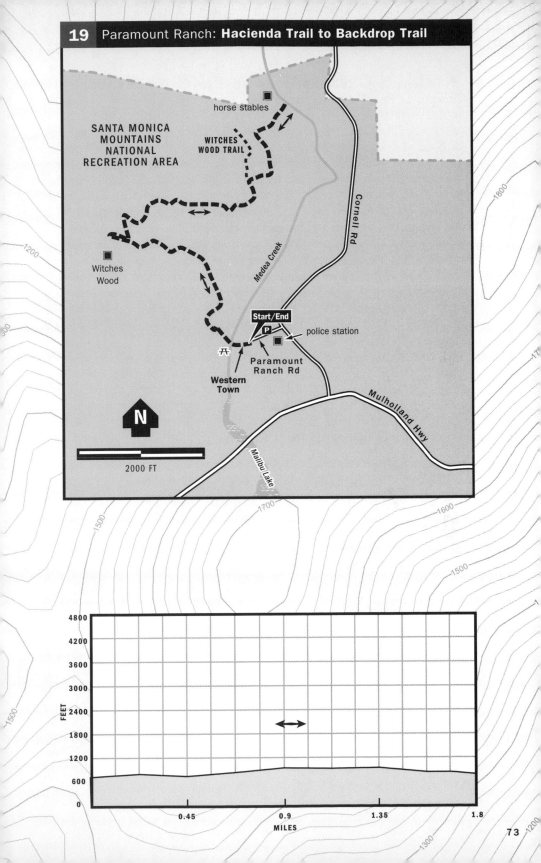

SANTA MONICA
MOUNTAINS
NATIONAL
RECREATION AREA

horse stables

WITCHES
WOOD TRAIL

Witches
Wood

Medea Creek

Cornell Rd

Start/End
P
police station

Paramount
Ranch Rd

Western
Town

Mulholland Hwy

Malibu Lake

N

2000 FT

1800

1700

1600

1500

1700

1600

1500

1300

1200

FEET

4800
4200
3600
3000
2400
1800
1200
600
0

0.45   0.9   1.35   1.8
MILES

where *Dr. Quinn* was shot. The Bwana Trail takes you through the grasslands of Africa as featured in the 1952 movie *Bwana Devil*. And the Backdrop Trail is a nod to the area of the ranch that can be used for any type of shot because it has no telephone poles or other distinctive features, according to a brochure available at the entrance.

None of the trails are marked with signposts, but they are all well maintained and easy to navigate. To get to the Hacienda Trail, walk past the dusty streets and storefront facades of Western Town and turn right on the wide gravel path located behind the barber shop. You will pass a large picnic pavilion on the right; to the left is the train depot that was used in *Dr. Quinn*. At 0.3 miles, the gravel trail narrows and comes to a T. Turn left and follow the trail up a gradual incline past brush and seasonal golden currant flowers. You'll see chaparral-covered hills in the distance. The bulk of this hike is shadeless, so bring plenty of sunscreen and water.

Just after crossing a small seasonal stream, you'll come to a Y in the trail. The left path leads past Witches Wood, a narrow dirt trail on a gradual incline shaded partially by oak trees. This area got its name from the fortune tellers who set up booths here for the Renaissance Pleasure Faire during the 1970s and 1980s, according to a park brochure.

I made a quick detour up this path, then reversed course back to the Y and headed right. After crossing another small drainage area, the trail turns narrow and flat with heavy sun exposure. It is flanked by tall grassy meadow on both sides.

I wasn't a regular watcher of *Dr. Quinn*, but it was easy to picture Jane Seymour (a.k.a. Dr. Mike) ministering to rattlesnake bites and other nineteenth-century maladies amid this pristine landscape. I was also reminded of the opening scene in *Little House on the Prairie,* when Laura, Mary, and Carrie Ingalls run tumbling down a grassy meadow.

At about 1.3 miles, the path descends gradually, then climbs again and brings you back to the twenty-first century as the Spanish-tile rooftops of Calabasas and Cornell Road come into view. It turns a little more secluded before reaching another Y. The right-hand path leads to the nonmaintained Paramount Ridge Trail (and eventually private homes), whereas a left turn will take you downhill past a horse stable before the trail hits Medea Creek and, beyond that, private property. From here, you may retrace your steps back along the backdrop trail or hook up with the Bwana Trail, which runs parallel to the Backdrop Trail and Medea Creek and leads back to Western Town and the parking lot.

▶ NEARBY ACTIVITIES

Western Town is worth a stop on your way to or from your hike. It is still used regularly as a site for filming movies and TV shows (the main street recently served as a 1930s California town for the HBO series *Carnivale*) and remains open to the public during shooting.

Every May, the ranch hosts the annual Topanga Banjo Fiddle Contest, a one-day festival of live music, dancing, food, and cowboy storytelling. For more information, go online to www.topangabanjofiddle.org.

PETER STRAUSS TRAIL

▶ IN BRIEF

This low-traffic trail switchbacks up a hillside and through an oak- and sycamore-shaded glen on a property once owned by actor Peter Strauss. The vast lawn in front of the ranch house is perfect for a picnic—if you don't mind being serenaded by the squawks of the resident peacock.

▶ DESCRIPTION

This 40-acre property in the Santa Monica Mountains operated as a resort known as Lake Enchanto from the mid-1930s to the 1960s. The swimming pool, now closed to the public, was once the largest pool on the West Coast, holding 650,000 gallons of water and accommodating 3,000 people at a time. Actor Peter Strauss bought it in 1976 after falling in love with the area while shooting the *Rich Man, Poor Man* TV series at nearby Malibu Lake. He restored the house and grounds, then six years later sold it to the Santa Monica Mountains Conservancy for $1.2 million, a reported $1 million more than he had paid for it. One of the alleged conditions of the sale was that the ranch and trail be named after him, according to a local newspaper report.

This is easily the least-traveled path that I have experienced in the Santa Monica Mountains. I did this hike on a perfect-for-hiking sunny Saturday afternoon and didn't encounter a soul,

ⓘ KEY AT-A-GLANCE INFORMATION

LENGTH: 1.5 miles

CONFIGURATION: Balloon

DIFFICULTY: Easy

SCENERY: Chaparral, oak, eucalyptus, and sycamore trees

EXPOSURE: Mostly shady

TRAFFIC: Light

TRAIL SURFACE: Dirt path

HIKING TIME: 45 minutes

ACCESS: Free; daily 8 a.m.–sunset

MAPS: Available online at www.nps.gov/samo/maps/peter.htm; USGS Point Dume

FACILITIES: Restrooms

SPECIAL COMMENTS: The parking lot for the ranch is often closed in the weeks following heavy rains, but the property itself usually opens to hikers after a couple of days. Street parking is available across Mulholland Highway along Waring Street.

▶ DIRECTIONS

From downtown L.A. and the San Fernando Valley, take the 101 Freeway to the Kanan Road exit and follow it south 3 miles to Troutdale Drive. Turn left on Troutdale and follow to Mulholland. The pedestrian entrance to the ranch will be right in front of you. Turn left on Mulholland and follow signs to parking lot on the right. If parking lot is closed, there is street parking across Mulholland along Waring Drive.

UTM Trailhead Coordinates for Peter Strauss Trail

UTM Zone (WGS84)   11S

Easting   335860

Northing   3776257

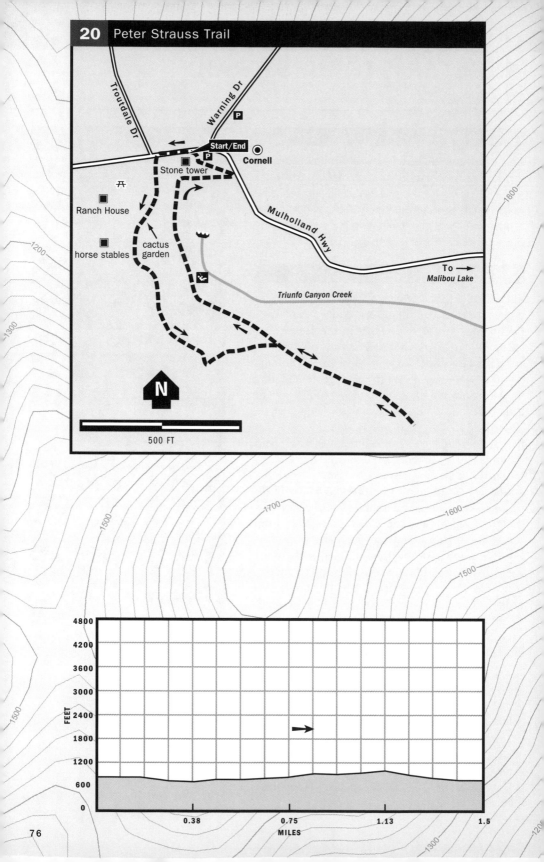

Troutdale Dr

Warning Dr

P

Start/End

P

Cornell

Stone tower

Ranch House

horse stables

cactus garden

Mulholland Hwy

To →
Malibou Lake

Triunfo Canyon Creek

N

500 FT

1800

1700

1600

1500

1300

1200

FEET

4800
4200
3600
3000
2400
1800
1200
600
0

0.38   0.75   1.13   1.5
MILES

unless you count the peacock that lives on the property. It's also an excellent hike when summer temperatures reach the triple digits in the San Fernando Valley because the hot sun rarely penetrates the thick groves of oak and sycamore trees that shade most of the trail.

The biggest challenge is figuring out where to park, because the ranch parking lot tends to be closed more often than it's open. I parked on Waring Street, a residential street on the north side of Mulholland after checking to make sure there were no restricted parking signs, then walked across the street to the ranch gate.

Look for the stone tower and a sign that reads PETER STRAUSS RANCH, LAKE ENCHANTO and pass through the gate between them. The original ranch house is on the right just beyond a lush green lawn with a couple of picnic tables. To the left is Triunfo Canyon Creek and the remains of a dam built in the 1940s by the owners of Lake Enchanto.

Follow the driveway past the circular cactus garden and look for a sign that says AMPHITHEATRE to the left of the house. Don't be surprised if you are greeted by the honking of the ranch's peacock. Other birds spotted here include the canyon wren, great blue heron, and a black-headed grosbeak.

Follow the dirt path past the amphitheater and a grove of eucalyptus trees as it switchbacks up a hillside. The path is a little rugged here with drainage ruts, but it soon gets smooth and well maintained. When you reach the horse stables, follow the path uphill and to the left. It will start to get shady with a few patches of sun. The trail levels for a quarter mile or so and gets sunny, and you will be able to see million-dollar homes peeking out amid the trees on the left. It then descends down wooden steps into an oak- and sycamore-shaded glen. You can hear some car and motorcycle noise from nearby Mulholland Highway, but the cool tunnel of shade that surrounds you helps muffle it and make it seem like you're a million miles away from civilization. In the spring, wildflowers blooming here include milkmaids, wild sweetpea, crimson pitcher sage, Angel's gilia, and purple nightshade. I also spotted chickweed, mountain mahogany, spring vetch, and wild cucumber plants during my trek.

At about 0.75 miles, the trail descends to a T. The path to the right extends the hike by about 0.25 miles and dead-ends at a chain-link fence that separates the ranch from private property. Retrace your steps back to the T and follow the path straight. Soon you'll reach a playground and the driveway that leads back to the trailhead.

▶ NEARBY ACTIVITIES

On Sunday afternoons in the summer, the ranch opens its doors to bands who perform free outdoor concerts under the oak trees at the amphitheater. For a schedule, go online to www.topangabanjofiddle.org.

Alternatively, if you're looking for a daytime family-oriented activity, the aptly named Troutdale Rainbow Trout at the corner of Kanan and Troutdale Roads is a manmade pond stocked with, yep, trout. On weekends, it fills up with families who picnic under the oak trees with their freshly caught fish (barbecue pits and cleaning facilities are available). Admission is $5 per person and includes equipment and fishing license, plus there's a fee charged for each fish caught. The place is open daily. For more information, call (818) 889-9993.

SAN VICENTE MOUNTAIN: OLD NIKE MISSILE SITE

 KEY AT-A-GLANCE INFORMATION

LENGTH: 3 miles

CONFIGURATION: Out-and-back

DIFFICULTY: Easy

SCENERY: Wildflowers, valley, and canyon views

EXPOSURE: Sunny

TRAFFIC: Light

TRAIL SURFACE: Packed dirt

HIKING TIME: 1 hour

ACCESS: Free; park gate is open sunrise to sunset

MAPS: USGS Canoga Park

FACILITIES: Picnic tables, benches, restrooms

SPECIAL COMMENTS: For additional information, go to www.lamountains.com/parks.asp?parkid=54

UTM Trailhead Coordinates for San Vicente Mountain: Old Nike Missile Site

UTM Zone (WGS84)   11S

Easting   361432

Northing   3777389

▶ IN BRIEF

This easy Santa Monica Mountains hike begins at the east end of the dirt road extension of Mulholland Drive and maintains a steady ascent past sweeping views of the San Fernando Valley to a former Nike missile control site that has been turned into a mountaintop park.

▶ DESCRIPTION

This trail certainly isn't the most picturesque or serene of all the hikes in the Santa Monica Mountains trails, but it offers a unique peek at Cold War–era Los Angeles amid the multimillion-dollar mansions and mountain-bike culture that now mark the area, and it reminds the young that Nike wasn't always another word for sneaker. Between 1954 and 1968, this park was one of 16 missile control sites established to guard the skies of Los Angeles from a nuclear attack by Soviet planes. Situated on a mountaintop 1,950 feet above sea level with sweeping views of downtown L.A., the Pacific Ocean, and the San Fernando Valley, the area was considered an ideal site for detecting planes from up to 100 miles away. It closed in 1968, but the radar tower, guard shack, and barbed-wire fence remain. The Santa Monica Mountains Conservancy acquired the site in 1995, which planted oak trees, added picnic

▶ DIRECTIONS

From the 405 Freeway, exit at Mulholland Drive and follow it 2.7 miles until it intersects with Encino Hills Drive. At the intersection of Encino Hills Drive, turn left onto Dirt Mulholland, an unpaved section of the road, and continue about a mile to a nondescript cluster of small buildings. Park by the chain-link fence and look for the fire-road gate. Keep in mind that the gate to Dirt Mulholland closes at sunset, and the road is often closed following heavy rains.

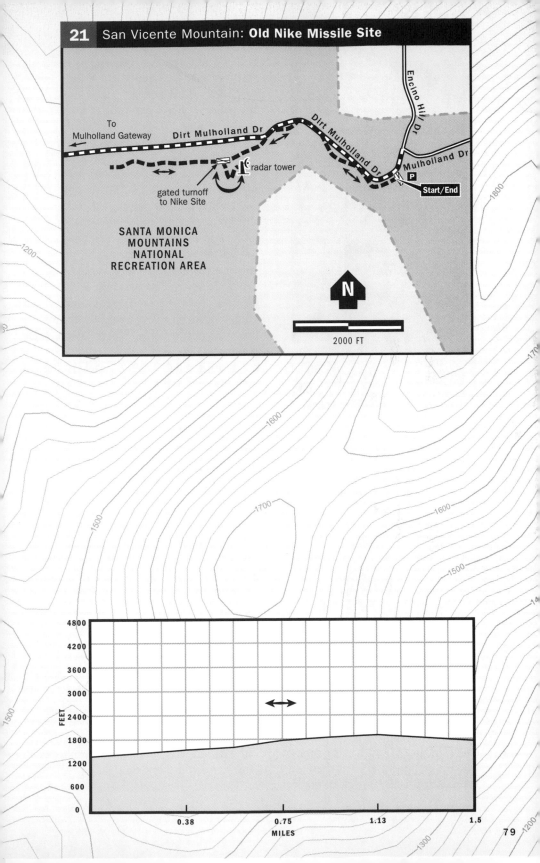

To
Mulholland Gateway

Dirt Mulholland Dr

Dirt Mulholland Dr

Encino Hill Dr

Mulholland Dr

radar tower

gated turnoff
to Nike Site

P

Start/End

SANTA MONICA
MOUNTAINS
NATIONAL
RECREATION AREA

N

2000 FT

4800

4200

3600

3000

2400

1800

1200

600

0

FEET

0.38   0.75   1.13   1.5
MILES

HIGH SECURITY

Remnants of the Cold War

tables, and turned the officers' barracks into restrooms. It's a strange place for a picnic, with the disassembled radar tower and barbed-wire fence looming above, and it seems to attract more mountain bikers looking for a pit stop than hikers. But it's quieter than most other Santa Monica Mountains trails, and the panoramic views are tough to match.

From the dirt parking lot, walk around the fire-road gate and follow the wide dirt path up a gradual incline. The path is flanked by yellow wildflowers in the spring. To the right are wide-open views of the San Fernando Valley. The next mile is completely exposed, so come prepared with a hat and plenty of sunscreen, especially during the hot summer months. There aren't many landmarks or items of interest until you reach a dilapidated guard shack and chain-link fence after about a mile or so. Look for the sign LA96C—the name bestowed by the U.S. Army on the military site—and head left up the dirt path. Soon you will come to a T. A small parking lot (for authorized vehicles only) and public restrooms are on the right; on the left are picnic tables, the radar tower, and a couple of interpretive signs that explain the site's former role.

One sign explains the reason for the site's closure. In the 1960s, the United States and the Soviets had developed intercontinental ballistic missiles that traveled so fast and so high that they rendered the Nike missiles obsolete. Another sign details the site's use of a bulky computer system that "recorded, plotted and coordinated every event to locate, intercept and destroy an enemy target." The work these computers, which occupied an entire building, did in 1961 can be done by handheld computer today. Also, according to a *Los Angeles Times* story about the park's grand opening, soldiers kept a garden with cactus and other plants to pass the time and "as a sign of hope." Another interesting tidbit: For security purposes, the soldiers weren't allowed to know how the entire missile defense system worked, so their knowledge was limited to their specific jobs.

From the T, turn left and walk up to the former helicopter platform (now the site of picnic tables and clusters of young oak trees), then climb the steps to the slate-gray tower platform. From here, it is 15 miles to downtown Los Angeles and 10 miles to Venice Beach. If it's a clear day, you can check out the city-to-ocean views, though with decidedly less intensity than the Army officers who staffed the site once did. The place still has an ominous Cold War–era feel to it and doesn't exactly encourage lingering. I was here on a stifling hot day in May, though, and that may have added to the unwelcoming feel.

On returning to the guard station, you can either head back to the parking lot or turn left on Dirt Mulholland to extend the hike by another mile or more. The path is flat and the scenery is similar to the first mile of the hike: wildflowers, coastal sage scrub, and views of the valley to the north and chaparral-draped mountains to the south. The dirt road continues another 8 miles or so past Mulholland Gateway Park and links to other Santa Monica Mountains trails, including Caballero Canyon, Temescal Ridge, and Hub Junction.

▶ NEARBY ACTIVITIES

Encino Town Center has a five-screen movie theater and many shops and restaurants. From the entrance to Dirt Mulholland, drive straight on Encino Hills Drive about 2 miles to Hayvenhurst Drive. Turn left on Hayvenhurst and follow it to Ventura Boulevard. Turn left, and drive about 1 mile until you see Encino Town Center on the right. The address is 17200 Ventura Boulevard, between Amestoy and Louise avenues.

EAST
(including Glendale, Pasadena, San Gabriel Mountains)

ARROYO SECO/ GABRIELINO TRAIL

KEY AT-A-GLANCE INFORMATION

LENGTH: 5 miles

CONFIGURATION: Out-and-back

DIFFICULTY: Easy to moderate

SCENERY: Arroyo rocks, oak forest

EXPOSURE: Shady

TRAFFIC: Heavy

TRAIL SURFACE: Packed and loose dirt, boulders

HIKING TIME: 2.5 hours

ACCESS: Free; gate open dawn–dusk

MAPS: USGS Pasadena

FACILITIES: Picnic areas at several points along trail

SPECIAL COMMENTS: Besides hikers, this path attracts a wide range of outdoors types: birders, mountain bikers, horseback riders, picnickers, and joggers. Everyone seems to coexist peacefully, but this path is not for you if you prefer solitude on the trails.

UTM Trailhead Coordinates for Arroyo Seco/Gabrielino Trail

UTM Zone (WGS84)   11S

Easting   392393

Northing   3784308

▶ IN BRIEF

This mostly flat hike begins along a paved service road with industrial views of the NASA Jet Propulsion Laboratory, then becomes increasingly bucolic as it follows a wide gurgling stream past several picnic area, thick groves of oak and sycamore, and big-leaf maple trees.

▶ DESCRIPTION

The Gabrielino Trail is one of several in the Angeles National Forest designated as a multiuse national recreation trail. It follows the route of an original 1920s road that ran from Pasadena north up the canyon past wilderness resorts and old rustic cabins. The road lost its appeal after the Angeles Crest Highway was built, but today it has reinvented itself as a multiuse trail for hikers, horseback riders, mountain bikers, and birders.

This hike, known as the Arroyo Seco stretch, covers the well-maintained lower end of the Gabrielino Trail and features the part of the Arroyo Seco that doesn't live up to its Spanish name of "dry riverbed." Much of the hike follows a sparkling, gurgling stream past thick groves of live oak, sycamore, Douglas fir, and big-leaf maple trees. Except for the first half mile, the path is almost entirely in the shade, making it a great year-round hike. Some hikers prefer to begin at the northern end of the Gabrielino Trail, heading south into the forest from Switzer Falls Picnic Area and ending at the Arroyo Seco trailhead.

▶ DIRECTIONS

From the Foothill Freeway (I-210) in Pasadena, take the Arroyo Boulevard/Windsor Avenue exit. Drive 0.75 miles north on Windsor and turn left into the small parking lot just before the stop sign at Ventura Avenue. Look for the fire road across the street from the parking lot.

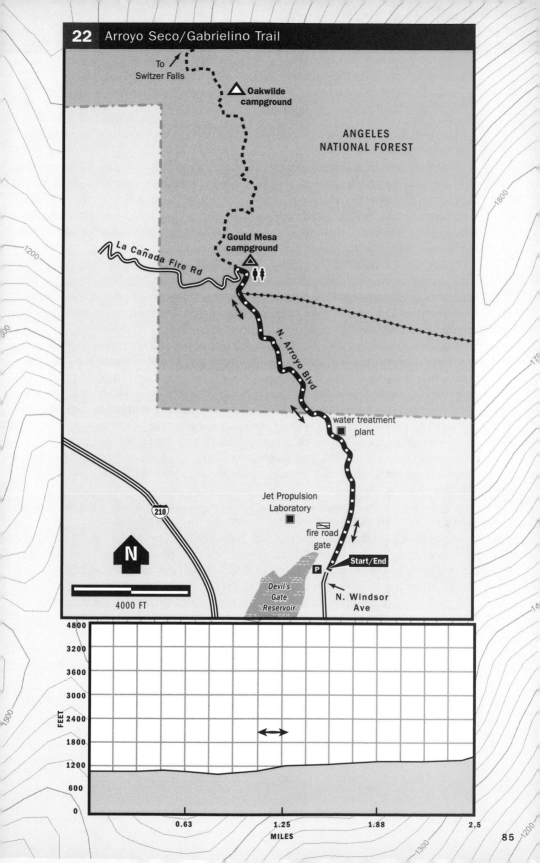

To
Switzer Falls

△ Oakwilde
campground

ANGELES
NATIONAL FOREST

La Cañada Fire Rd

**Gould Mesa
campground**
△ 🏃🏃

N. Arroyo Blvd

water treatment
plant

Jet Propulsion
Laboratory

210

fire road
gate

N

Start/End

P

N. Windsor
Ave

Devil's
Gate
Reservoir

4000 FT

1800

1200

1700

1400

1300

1200

1500

FEET

4800
3200
3600
3000
2400
1800
1200
600
0

0.63   1.25   1.88   2.5
MILES

To get to the trailhead from the parking lot, walk across Ventura Avenue to the yellow fire-road gate and a sign for the Gabrielino National Recreation Trail and follow the paved road as it heads north into the canyon. (The paved road to the left of the trailhead leads to a back entrance of the Jet Propulsion Laboratory, NASA's high-security spacecraft research hub.)

The left side of the road is lined with shrubs and large arroyo boulders; on the right you will pass the backyards of private homes. Soon you will pass a clearing on the left and the sprawling JPL complex will come into view, as well as the Devil's Gate Reservoir, one of Los Angeles County's oldest reservoirs. Its dam was deemed seismically unsafe in the 1970s, and heavy rains have left it looking more like a no-man's-land full of silt and debris than a water basin.

The first 0.5 miles of the hike has little shade and isn't very attractive. You will pass a water treatment plant on the right and may even hear generator-type roars coming from JPL. Just past the water treatment plant, you will come to a fork in the trail. The left-hand path leads to the back side of JPL. You want to continue straight on the paved road.

Things start to get a little more natural here—hillsides sprouting chaparral, sage scrub, and seasonal wildflowers come into better view on either side of the trail. Soon you'll come to a concrete-and-stone bridge, the first of several you'll encounter on your walk. Now the stream is on the right and the path turns shady and pleasant.

After about a mile, you will pass another water treatment plant on the right and cross an old wooden bridge. Just after the bridge, a sign tells you that you have officially entered the Angeles National Forest. Continue walking alongside the stream past groves of sycamore, oak, and maple trees. Expect to see some people splashing around in the stream here. Big boulders along the edge and shallow waters make it a popular spot.

Soon you'll pass a signed turnoff for Brown Mountain Trail on the right, and a primitive NO SHOOTING sign. Continue straight on the Gabrielino Trail.

At about 1.2 miles, a couple of small private homes pop up on the right, as well as a water trough made of arroyo rocks. The trail then passes through the gate of a chain-link fence and curves around to the right (north). You are now walking on loose dirt and have a good view of the stream on the left.

At 1.5 miles, the trail crosses over another wooden bridge. On the left just after the bridge is a picnic area known as Teddy's Outpost. This is a fine spot for a picnic, but if you can hold out for another mile or so, the picnic areas to the north of Gould Mesa Campground such as Paul Little or El Niño are much nicer, . The trail continues north and passes more bridges and an occasional backless bench where you can rest and watch the creek gurgle.

Your first of several wide stream crossings comes at 2 miles. The crossings aren't difficult, but this is often a turnaround point for parents with infants or small children. From here the creek is on the right and the path turns into gravel for awhile. At 2.1 miles, you will come to a Y. You want to take the lower trail to the right and keep hugging the stream. It is briefly exposed here, but quickly descends back into the shady forest. This is one of the coolest and loveliest sections of the trail. Groves of oaks and alders line the stream, and green ivy covers either side of the trail in abundance. After some more boulder-hopping, the dirt path widens and you will pass a bench under an old oak tree. Soon Gould Mesa Campground will come into view. There are public restrooms, water, and a sign-in kiosk here. This is another popular spot to relax and enjoy the stream. Birders also testify to this area's tendency to attract all kinds of warblers, such as the Western tanager, owls, even an occasional American dipper. According to the Pasadena Audubon Society, more than 180 species of birds have been spotted along the Arroyo Seco.

You can turn around here, or extend the hike by another 2.5 miles and follow the trail as it narrows into a single-track path to Oakwilde Campground, the site of a rustic inn in the 1930s and a great spot for a leisurely picnic.

▶ NEARBY ACTIVITIES

The Jet Propulsion Laboratory offers free walking tours of its facility for individuals or groups. You must call ahead and make a reservation, and tours often fill up months in advance. Highlights of the 2.5-hour tour include a multimedia presentation called "Welcome to Outer Space" and a visit to JPL's space flight operations and spacecraft assembly areas. For more information, go online to www.jpl.nasa.gov/pso/pt.cfm. From the trailhead parking lot, turn right on Ventura Boulevard. Make another right at the first traffic light at Woodbury and follow it until it turns into Oak Grove and dead-ends at the entrance to the JPL.

BIG DALTON DAM TRAIL

KEY AT-A-GLANCE INFORMATION

LENGTH: 4.6 miles

CONFIGURATION: Out-and-back

DIFFICULTY: Easy

SCENERY: Oak forest, chaparral slopes, rocky stream

EXPOSURE: Sunny

TRAFFIC: Light

TRAIL SURFACE: Paved

HIKING TIME: 2 hours

ACCESS: No Adventure Pass required because parking is outside of the Angeles National Forest; open daily sunrise–sunset

MAPS: USGS Glendora

FACILITIES: Restrooms and picnic area at Big Dalton Campground, a mile into the hike

SPECIAL COMMENTS: For historical information on the San Dimas Experimental Forest, go to www.fs.fed.us/psw/ef/san_dimas.

UTM Trailhead Coordinates for
Big Dalton Dam Trail

UTM Zone (WGS84) 11S

Easting   423064

Northing   3779887

IN BRIEF

This tranquil hike follows a wide, paved fire road and boulder-strewn creek deep into the Angeles National Forest, ending at a concrete dam and small reservoir that is home to a variety of birds. Chances are good that you will only encounter a handful of people during your visit.

DESCRIPTION

Don't expect heavy traffic on this trail. Despite its proximity to the towns of Glendora, San Dimas, and Claremont, it doesn't draw the crowds that other San Gabriel trails do. From either side of the paved road, adventurous hikers can access several more trails that wander deep into the forest, though these can get overgrown and tough to navigate following heavy rains. This path traverses Glendora Wilderness Park and then skirts the San Dimas Experimental Forest, 27 square miles of land located within the Angeles National Forest. Since the 1930s, the forest has been used as an outdoor laboratory for the U.S. Forest Service. Budget cuts have scaled back its use dramatically, but scientists still use it as an experimental watershed to test land-management measures to increase water yield, reduce fire hazards, and control erosion. It is one of about 80 experimental forests in the United States. According to the *Los Angeles Times,* it represents "a perfect specimen of

DIRECTIONS

From the Foothill Freeway (210) in Pasadena, head east to Grand Avenue in Glendora. Take Grand north to Sierra Madre Boulevard and turn right. Just before the road ends, turn left on Glendora Mountain Road. Continue uphill for about 0.7 miles to Big Dalton Canyon Road and turn right. Parking is on the side of the road just outside the fire-road gate. The road in closes at sunset.

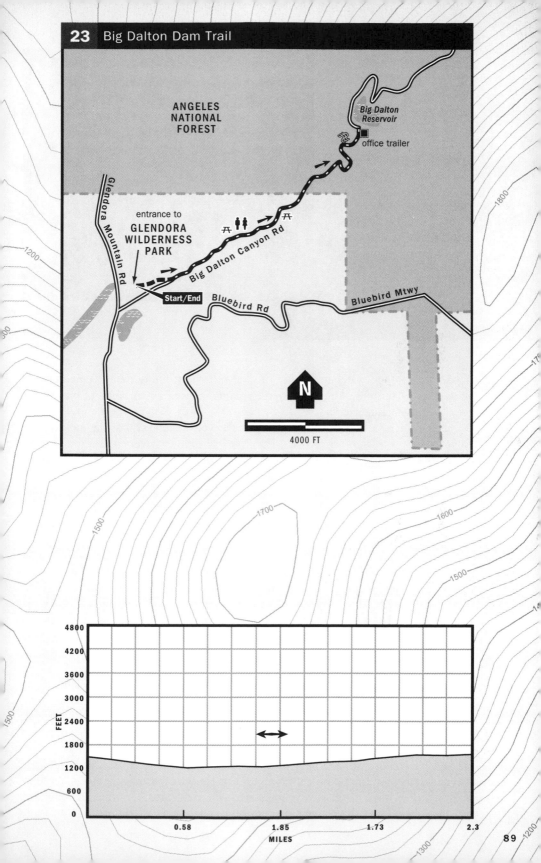

ANGELES
NATIONAL
FOREST

*Big Dalton
Reservoir*

office trailer

Glendora Mountain Rd

entrance to
**GLENDORA
WILDERNESS
PARK**

Big Dalton Canyon Rd

Start/End

Bluebird Rd

Bluebird Mtwy

N

4000 FT

4800
4200
3600
3000
2400
1800
1200
600
0

FEET

0.58   1.85   1.73   2.3
MILES

Big Dalton Reservoir is a haven for wild birds such as herons and ducks.

chaparral forest and watershed land." It is also home to more than 80 members of the *asteraceae* family—a kind of flowering plant—as well as 14 kinds of bats and 3 types of lungless salamanders.

Begin the hike by following Big Dalton Canyon Road east past the locked gate. On your right is a large debris dam. The first half mile isn't very scenic—a barbed-wire fence runs along the right side of the road—but things improve once you pass a couple of private homes on the left and cross a stream. Hills covered in chaparral, oak trees, and California dopper flank both sides of the road, and the gurgling stream provides pleasant background noise. Other plants that thrive in the hills here include rosemary, toyon (Christmas berry), wild sweet pea, cliff aster, white-stem filaree, and Mediterranean mustard.

After about a mile, you will see a sign for the San Dimas Experimental Forest on your right. A trail called Wilderness Cabin just beyond the sign leads uphill to a small building and a couple of picnic tables, then keeps going farther into the forest. To continue to Big Dalton Dam, stay on the paved road and continue to follow the stream. The road gets a little narrower here. When I was here in spring 2005, debris and fallen trees and branches littered the stream—the leftover effects of the 2004–2005 rains that pelted southern California. Nothing was impeding hiking conditions on the main path, however.

At about 1.5 miles on the left, there is a small seasonal waterfall on the left and the road narrows and climbs gradually uphill. A sign warns that you are in mudslide territory, and if you look around you, you will see concrete drainage walls covering some of the hillsides. Another 0.2 miles brings you to a gate and a small bridge. The path curves around to the left and you may spot some small seasonal waterfalls on the right.

At 1.7 miles, you will pass through another gate and cross over a concrete drainage tunnel, and the path curves around to the left. You may be able spot some small waterfalls in your right. As you approach the 2-mile marker, you will come to a road that leads to a private home on the right and a small sign directing you to go straight to Big Dalton Dam. The path gets steep here as it switchbacks up the mountain ridge; continue climbing and soon you will pass a waterfall on the left and be able to look down and see the private home you passed on the way up. Straight ahead is a good view of the south side of Big Dalton Dam, which was built in the early 1900s as a flood-control mechanism. Continue walking up the hill toward the dam.

Just past an office trailer on the right, the road levels and reaches a small reservoir, attractively framed by forest-covered hills. There are no benches or viewpoints, but it's a good place to stop and look out over the water. Bring binoculars, and see if you can spot some of the many species of birds that dwell here. Among those spotted recently are blue herons, mallard ducks, and yellow finches. From here, you can retrace your steps back to the parking area. Keep in mind that a permit is required of anyone who goes beyond this point.

▶ NEARBY ACTIVITIES

On your way up Grand Avenue after exiting the freeway, you will pass both Ralph's and Vons—two major grocery chains where you can stock up on picnic supplies to bring on your hike.

BRAND FIRE ROAD TRAIL: VERDUGO MOUNTAINS

 KEY AT-A-GLANCE INFORMATION

LENGTH: 4 miles

CONFIGURATION: Out-and-back

DIFFICULTY: Moderate to difficult

SCENERY: Chaparral-covered hills, seasonal waterfall, panoramic valley and city views

EXPOSURE: Sunny

TRAFFIC: Heavy on weekends, moderate weekdays

TRAIL SURFACE: Paved; loose dirt and gravel

HIKING TIME: 2 hours

ACCESS: Gate open sunrise–sunset

MAPS: USGS Burbank

FACILITIES: Restrooms, water

SPECIAL COMMENTS: The best time of year to do this nearly shadeless hike is late winter or early spring, when the stream is gushing at full force and the wildflowers are in bloom. If you do hike this during the summer, bring plenty of water and sunscreen and plan your visit for the morning or late afternoon.

UTM Trailhead Coordinates for Brand Fire Road Trail: Verdugo Mountains

UTM Zone (WGS84)   11S

Easting   382332

Northing   3783414

IN BRIEF

This hike follows a wide fire road that climbs 800 feet from the base of Brand Park in Glendale to the ridge of the Verdugo Mountains. Your reward is a lookout with sweeping views of the Los Angeles Basin and the San Fernando Valley. In the winter and spring, a detour along a stream to the base of a waterfall adds another easy half-mile to the hike.

DESCRIPTION

Brand Park, at the base of the Verdugo Mountains in Glendale, is on the grounds of an estate known as El Mirador. Today, it's a meticulously kept neighborhood park, with a baseball field, basketball courts, picnic areas, library, and Japanese tea garden. It gets crowded on weekends with families, Little League teams, and exercise hounds, but I have never had a problem finding a parking space in the lot.

To get to the Brand Fire Road Trail, leave your car near the Doctors' House at the park's northwest corner and follow the paved path to the right. The path winds uphill behind the house to a white gate. You'll see a large, unsightly debris basin on the right. This part of the trail is completely exposed,

DIRECTIONS

From the I-5 Freeway, take the Western Avenue exit, head east, and turn right on Mountain Street. At the intersection of Mountain and Grandview, turn right into the Brand Park parking lot (on Brand Park Drive).

Alternate Directions: Take the Pacific Avenue exit off the 134 Freeway in Glendale, head north, turn left on Kenneth Road, then right on Grandview. The park entrance is at the corner of Grandview and Kenneth. Look for the ornate archway that says EL MIRADOR.

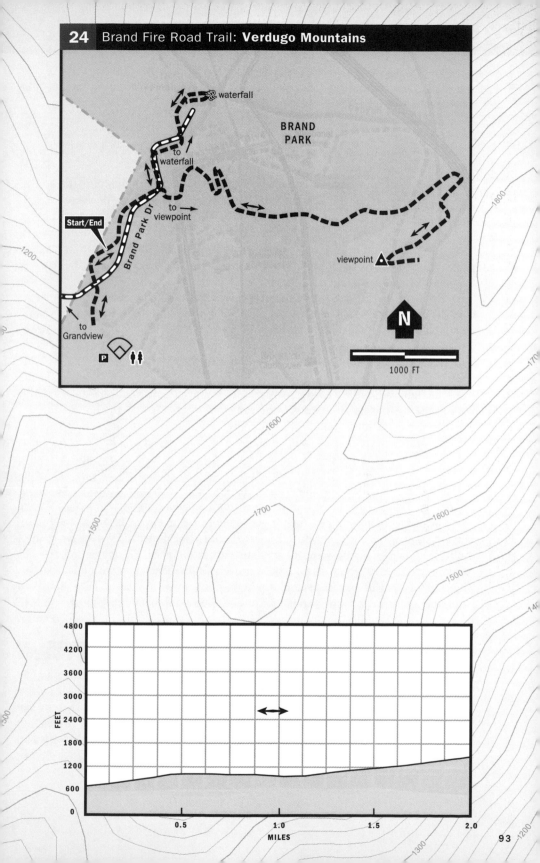

waterfall

BRAND
PARK

to
waterfall

to →
viewpoint

Brand Park Dr

Start/End

viewpoint △

to
Grandview

N

1000 FT

P ♀♂

FEET

4800

4200

3600

3000

2400

1800

1200

600

0

0.5   1.0   1.5   2.0
MILES

and there is little vegetation. Don't be discouraged by the lack of scenery, though—the longer you walk, the better it gets.

At about 0.4 miles, you'll come to a fork in the path and see a set of stone steps that lead nowhere (the remains of the El Mirador estate, most likely). The Brand Fire Road curves uphill to the right of the steps. You may also take a brief detour from the fire-road trail by following the rocky dirt path to the left. This borders a seasonal stream and leads to a pretty waterfall. It is the shadiest part of the hike. It's a good idea to have hiking boots if you take this path. It requires fording the stream at several points, stomping through dense vegetation and climbing over a few fallen trees that partially block the path. Just before the waterfall, you'll see a couple of primitive chairs that someone has formed out of large stones next to the stream. Excellent photo opportunity! When I did this hike midday on a Saturday in March, the sun was beating down hard, so I didn't linger.

Back on the fire road, the trail continues to steadily ascend past chaparral-covered hills, coastal sage scrub, palm trees, and seasonal yellow wildflowers. You'll begin to see views of Glendale and the San Fernando Valley as you walk. Expect to see lots of hikers and mountain bikers here on weekends; the trail also attracts many hiking groups. (I passed four on my Saturday afternoon hike.) The fire road is wide enough, however, that it's easy to overtake them if you're motivated. At about 1 mile from the trailhead, the fire road curves around to the left and you'll see a narrow dirt path to the right. (The dirt path is a shortcut that meets up with the fire road.)

At about 1.2 miles, you'll pass a chained-off construction site, which explains the bulldozers and trucks that you'll likely pass on your way up the trail. The road narrows into a packed dirt-and-gravel path here and winds around to the right, then levels briefly at an elevation of 1,150 feet before it starts to climb again. If you look down and to the left, you'll also be able to spot the seasonal waterfall that sits at the end of the detour. This stretch of the trail requires more boulder-hopping, as well as scaling a couple of big drainage pipes, then it gets smooth again as you approach the mountain ridge. At about 2 miles, you'll come to a dirt clearing with an elevation gain of 1,600 feet. The sweeping views of the San Fernando Valley, Glendale, and the Los Angeles Basin are tough to match; you can even see the Pacific Ocean on a clear day. There are no benches or picnic tables up here, but it's worth a pause. From here, you can retrace your steps to the parking lot or continue climbing another quarter mile to the ridge of the Verdugo Mountains for access to other trails within the Verdugo range.

▶ NEARBY ACTIVITIES

The Doctors' House is a restored Queen Anne–Eastlake-style home built in the late nineteenth century. It was once the residence and office space for three successive Glendale physicians. It was relocated to Brand Park in 1979. It was restored to its late nineteenth-century appearance by the local historical society. Tours are given every Sunday between 2 and 4 p.m. Highlights include displays of medical implements and supplies of the era and a room set aside for the sale of books and materials on local history. For more information, go online to www.glendalehistorical.org/doctors.html.

DESCANSO GARDENS: CHAPARRAL NATURE TRAIL

▶ IN BRIEF

This hike covers several unmarked dirt trails within the pristine landscaped Descanso Gardens. It's an easy way to introduce small children or visitors to L.A.'s natural side without worrying about getting lost or having the right hiking gear.

▶ DESCRIPTION

Descanso Gardens, a secluded 160 acres of woodlands, gardens, and chaparral in the San Rafael Hills north of Glendale, was once the home of E. Manchester Boddy, publisher and owner of the *Los Angeles Daily News*. Boddy lived here with his family from 1937 until the 1950s. He deeded the land to Los Angeles County in 1957. Today, a private guild runs the gardens, which include a live oak forest, more than 500 varieties of lilacs, an international rosarium, and southern California's largest public collection of irises.

This isn't your typical southern California hiking trail. It includes a manmade koi pond, Zen garden, and enough benches to fill the Hollywood Bowl, and most "hikers" do little more than shuffle from one landscaped exhibit to another. But it's worth pointing out that there are several rugged trails within the garden grounds that aren't labeled on the visitor map, and it's easy to miss them without a little guidance. The unmarked trails are a nice way to introduce small children and visitors to suburban nature. Just when you feel as if you are in the middle of the wilderness, the paved road pops up to lead you back to civilization (and restrooms).

To access the Chaparral Nature Trail, follow the paved road to the right after exiting the entrance

❶ KEY AT-A-GLANCE INFORMATION

LENGTH: 1.8 miles

CONFIGURATION: Loop

DIFFICULTY: Easy

SCENERY: Woodlands, fern garden, mountain views

EXPOSURE: Partly sunny

TRAFFIC: Moderate

TRAIL SURFACE: Paved and dirt

HIKING TIME: 1.25 hours

ACCESS: Daily 10 a.m.–5 p.m.; entrance fees: $7 adults; $5 students and senior; $2 kids aged 5–12

MAPS: Available at entrance station; USGS Pasadena

FACILITIES: Restrooms, water, picnic tables; gardens are open daily 10 a.m.–5 p.m.

SPECIAL COMMENTS: The facility offers regular fitness walks, yoga, outdoor tai chi classes, and other seasonal "wellness" programs. Check the web site for information: www.descanso.org/site/wellnessprograms.cfm.

UTM Trailhead Coordinates for Descanso Gardens: Chaparral Nature Trail

UTM Zone (WGS84) 11S

Easting 388493

Northing 3785116

▶ DIRECTIONS

From the Foothill Freeway (210), exit at Verdugo Avenue in Glendale and turn right (east). Make another right on Descanso Drive and look for the garden entrance on right. Park in the large lot.

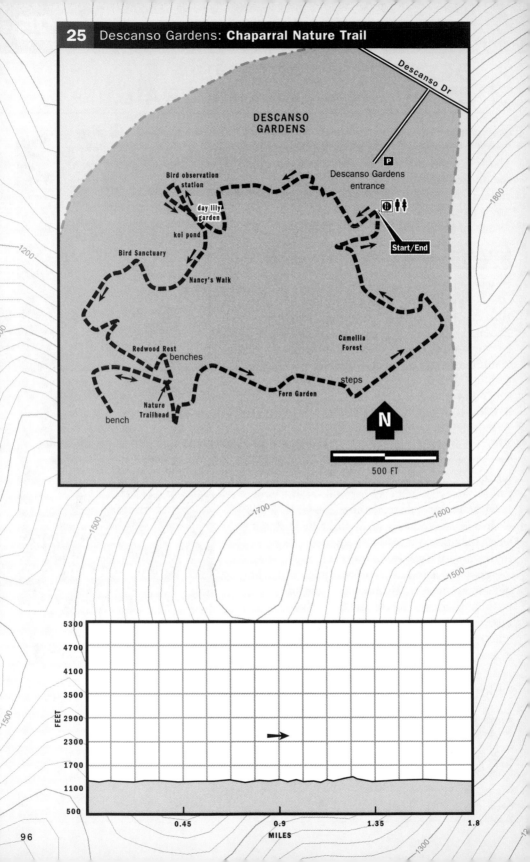

DESCANSO
GARDENS

Descanso Dr

P

Descanso Gardens
entrance

Bird observation
station

day lily
garden

Start/End

koi pond

Bird Sanctuary

Nancy's Walk

Camellia
Forest

Redwood Rest
benches

steps

Nature
Trailhead

Fern Garden

bench

N

500 FT

FEET

5300
4700
4100
3500
2900
2300
1700
1100
500

0.45   0.9   1.35   1.8
MILES

area. Across from the tram stop is the entrance to the international rosarium, worth a detour, especially if you are here during the peak blooming season of May to October. Exit the Rose Garden at the northeastern end, and you will find yourself back on the main paved path. To the right of you is a pretty koi pond stocked with super-size Japanese carp. Look for the unmarked narrow dirt path between the pond and the day lily garden and follow it straight past a pretty stream and waterfall, then up a hill through a dense forest of pine trees. This path winds past a bench, then ends next to a bird observation station that overlooks an algae-ridden lake (confession: I didn't see any birds during my visit).

Exit the bird-watching station and take the main path to the right and up the hill toward the California (native plant) garden. Look for a sign marked NANCY'S WALK on the right, and follow the dirt trail over a footbridge. This trail takes you past California palms, cactus, orange ocotillo plants, California poppies, and red monkey flowers, then winds under a grove of scrub oak and black oak trees before emptying back to the main path. Just past some laurel sumac shrubs, you will see another dirt path on the left. It meanders a short way past coast redwood trees, scrub oak, and Monterey and Jeffrey pine trees. Be sure to breathe deeply—you will forget that you are five minutes from a busy L.A. freeway and feel as if you've been suddenly transported to northern California.

Soon after rejoining the main path, you will pass a lookout area called Redwood Rest on the right. Continue on the main path as it dips down, then back up again past a gnarled old oak tree to a sign marked NATURE TRAIL. Don't embark on this path just yet. Instead, take the path to the right of the nature trail and follow it past Torrey and pinyon pines and California juniper trees as it winds uphill behind the Redwood Rest. Soon it will give way to some nice views of the San Gabriel Mountains to the north. Continue west on the narrow trail as it hugs a chain-link fence and eventually ends at a wooden bench that overlooks the city of La Cañada-Flintridge. This is a wonderful spot to sit for a while and savor the serenity (when I was here in the spring, the bench was picturesquely draped in orange monkey flowers). Even on weekends when the gardens are filled with tram-riding tourists, this area of the property is nearly deserted. This is one of the trails that isn't on the visitor map, but it's well worth the detour.

From here, retrace your steps back to the Chaparral Nature Trailhead. This trail *is* marked on the visitor map. Take the packed-dirt trail into dense woodland, and soon you will see a bench to the left that overlooks a dry creekbed. Follow the trail past the bench and a plaque marking the spot where disaster occurred after 10 days of record rains on January 25, 1969. The large boulders in front of the bench were pushed there from the hills above by mudslides caused by the rainstorms.

Just past the bench you will come to a Y in the trail. The lower path leads back to the main road briefly, then rejoins the nature trail again. The upper trail is shadier and more natural and winds above the main road, then down to a cool and lush fern garden. Scenes from the 1970s TV series *Land of the Lost* were filmed here. The trail passes a bench (another good place to stop and breathe deeply—you will feel as if you're in a rain forest) and clusters of birds of paradise on the right, then empties back to the main road. Continue walking until you come to a set of benches overlooking the East Camellia Forest, home to an oak forest that features thousands of camellias. (The best time to view the flowers is late winter.) Look for the set of concrete steps just past the benches and follow them into the forest. When you reach the paved road again, turn right. Just before the path winds uphill, look for another dirt path to the left. Follow this downhill through more woodland and past a small pond until you reach the paved road again. The Lilac Garden is to your right (it is in full bloom in March and April). To return to the entrance, follow the paved road past the Japanese teahouse and Zen garden.

▶ NEARBY ACTIVITIES

Descanso Gardens hosts the Pasadena POPS Orchestra as part of an annual summer concert series. Concerts take place on the main lawn in the middle of the gardens. For more information, go online to www.descansogardens.org or www.pasadenapops.org.

If you want to avoid fees or are seeking a more challenging hike in the area, you might want to check out the network of trails in the San Rafael Hills above Descanso Gardens. Drive south past the garden entrance to Chevy Chase Drive. Turn right, then make another right on Hampstead Road. This takes you to the entrance to Cherry Canyon Open Space access road. From here, you can access a number of trails that ascend to mountain and valley views. For more information, go to lacanadaflintridgetrailscouncil.org.

DEUKMEJIAN WILDERNESS PARK:
DUNSMORE CANYON AND LE MESNAGER LOOP TRAILS

▶ IN BRIEF

This meticulously maintained park in the northernmost section of Glendale is one of the city's best-kept secrets. The hike described here ascends 700 feet to a shady streambed, then loops around to terrific views of the Verdugo Mountains and the foothill communities of La Crescenta and Tujunga.

▶ DESCRIPTION

This 700-acre park operated as a vineyard and winery in the early 1900s. One of the trails is named for the former owner, a French emigrant and Los Angeles businessman named George Le Mesnager. The city of Glendale purchased the site in 1988 and named it after former California governor George Deukmejian, who grew up in the area. Its 4-mile trail system opened in 1995, and the park underwent an extensive renovation in 2004 that added restrooms, a paved parking lot, and an amphitheater. A stone barn from the property's winemaking days sits near the trailhead.

The park is also used to access Mount Lukens, the highest peak within Los Angeles city limits, via the Rim of the Valley Trail. It is bordered on the north, west, and east sides by the Angeles National Forest.

To get to the Dunsmore Canyon trail, follow the paved fire road north of the parking lot. In the spring, the path is flanked by California poppies.

▶ DIRECTIONS

From downtown Los Angeles, take the Glendale Freeway (2) north to the 210 (Foothill Freeway) west and exit at Pennsylvania Avenue. Turn right, then make a left on Foothill Boulevard and a right on Dunsmore Avenue. Follow Dunsmore north until it ends. Turn right on Markridge and make an immediate left into a landscaped driveway that ends at the parking lot.

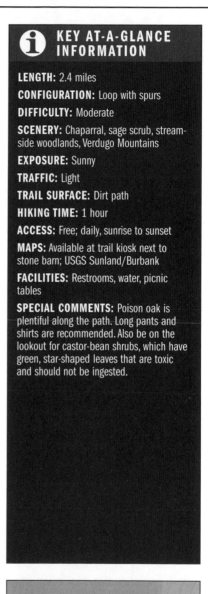

ℹ KEY AT-A-GLANCE INFORMATION

LENGTH: 2.4 miles

CONFIGURATION: Loop with spurs

DIFFICULTY: Moderate

SCENERY: Chaparral, sage scrub, streamside woodlands, Verdugo Mountains

EXPOSURE: Sunny

TRAFFIC: Light

TRAIL SURFACE: Dirt path

HIKING TIME: 1 hour

ACCESS: Free; daily, sunrise to sunset

MAPS: Available at trail kiosk next to stone barn; USGS Sunland/Burbank

FACILITIES: Restrooms, water, picnic tables

SPECIAL COMMENTS: Poison oak is plentiful along the path. Long pants and shirts are recommended. Also be on the lookout for castor-bean shrubs, which have green, star-shaped leaves that are toxic and should not be ingested.

UTM Trailhead Coordinates for Deukmejian Wilderness Park

UTM Zone (WGS84)   11S

Easting   384551

Northing   3790552

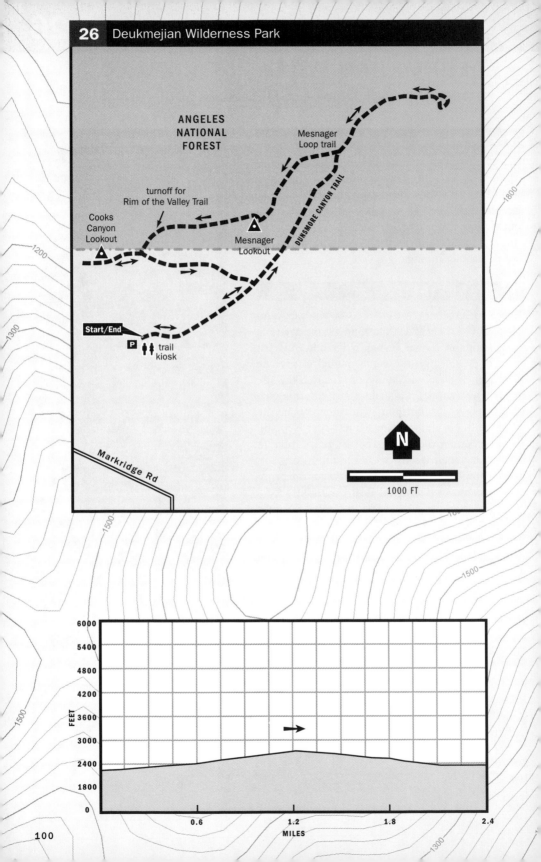

ANGELES
NATIONAL
FOREST

Mesnager
Loop trail

turnoff for
Rim of the Valley Trail

Cooks
Canyon
Lookout

DUNSMORE CANYON TRAIL

Mesnager
Lookout

Start/End

P trail
kiosk

Markridge Rd

N

1000 FT

A plaque marking the property's previous use as a winery is on your left. It also claims to be one of the hideouts of Tiburcio Vasquez, the notorious Mexican-born outlaw who committed a series of robberies and murders, then hid in the southern California foothills until he was captured and hanged in 1875.

When the paved path ends, turn left and follow the dirt path uphill. Before heading uphill, you can walk a few hundred feet behind you (toward the stone barn) to a kiosk that includes a map of the park and information on trail conditions and the park's wildlife, which includes rattlesnakes, squirrels, rabbits, and coyotes. Part of the Crescenta View trail, for instance, was closed due to landslides when I visited in April 2005. It has since reopened

The trail parallels a debris basin and the seasonal Dunsmore Canyon stream on the right as it begins its steep climb upward. There is no shade whatsoever on this path, so be sure to bring a hat and plenty of sunscreen. Expect it to be relentlessly hot in the summer months. The views include chaparral-covered slopes and seasonal fields of lupine and golden currant. Behind you is the 210 Freeway and the foothill communities of La Crescenta and Tujunga, all of which get increasingly distant as you continue your climb.

At about 0.75 miles, you come to a water drainage area, and the path curves around to the right and continues uphill. Soon you'll come to a wooden gate on the right. You're at an elevation of about 2,900 feet here and facing spectacular views of the foothill communities and the Verdugo Mountains. Follow the narrow gravel path past the gate as it descends to a shady oasis that overlooks the stream. There are no benches, but the concrete dam provides plenty of comfortable (sort of) places to rest and have a drink or snack. If it's hot, be sure to dunk your feet in the crystal-clear water.

From here, retrace your steps downhill to the signed turnoff for the Mesnager Loop Trail on the right. The path winds upward immediately and is prettily framed by brush and sage scrub. It is narrower and slightly steeper than the Dunsmore Canyon Trail. At about 1.3 miles, you'll come to a signed turnoff for the Mesnager Lookout Trail. Follow the path to the left up a steep incline to two small wooden benches and panoramic views of the La Crescenta Valley and Verdugo Mountains. If it's a cool day, this is another great spot to stop and rest, though there's not much room for more than a couple of people. I did this hike on a cool Saturday morning and saw only a handful of people anyway, mostly locals walking their dogs or hikers looking to access Mount Lukens via the park's Rim of the Valley Trail.

To continue the hike, turn around and hop back on the Mesnager Loop Trail as it heads west on a gradual decline. There's a little shade along this portion of the hike from low-lying trees, and the Verdugos come in and out of view as the path continues downward.

At 1.5 miles, you will reach the signed turnoff for the Rim of the Valley Trail, a rigorous 3.2-mile hike that climbs 2,500 feet in elevation to the Mount Lukens summit.

For this hike, continue straight on the Mesnager Loop Trail past rows of tall grass, wildflowers, and a grove of eucalyptus trees until you reach another signed turnoff. Take the narrow path right to another lookout area marked by a couple of large sandstone rocks (no benches this time). From here you can see the main entrance to the park below you, as well as the now-ubiquitous Verdugo Mountains. Retrace your steps downhill and back to the Mesnager Loop trail. The path descends steeply here, and the main park entrance is in clear view. The path then links back up with Dunsmore Canyon trail, which you want to follow to the right and back to the parking lot.

▶ NEARBY ACTIVITIES

Montrose Shopping Village is a small pedestrian-friendly shopping district with lots of cute mom-and-pop shops and restaurants. A few standouts: Zeke's Barbecue for North Carolina pulled pork, Tom's Toys for puzzles and board games, and the Paper Rabbit for unusual cards and stationery. From the park entrance, turn left on Markridge and follow about a miles to New York Avenue. Turn right, then make a left on Foothill Boulevard. Take Foothill about 2 miles to Ocean View Boulevard. and turn right, then proceed two miles to Honolulu Avenue. Most of the shops are along Honolulu east and west of Ocean View Boulevard.

DEVIL'S GATE TRAIL TO JPL

▶ IN BRIEF

Rife with resident and visiting birds and large boulders, this flat trail skirts a former reservoir on the north end of Pasadena's Arroyo Seco riverbed and ends at the outskirts of NASA's Jet Propulsion Laboratory.

▶ DESCRIPTION

Devil's Gate is Los Angeles County's oldest reservoir, though it hasn't been functional for decades. Its dam was deemed seismically unsafe in the 1970s, and heavy rains have left it looking more like a no-man's-land full of silt and debris than a water basin. Its name was changed from Oak Grove Park to Hahamongna Watershed Park in the 1990s (*hahamongna* is a Gabrielino Indian word meaning "fruitful valley"), but it is widely referred to as Devil's Gate. The natural area around the reservoir was turned into a recreational area in 1993. It has a soccer field, picnic area with barbecue pits, and an 18-hole disc golf course.

I hiked this trail not long after moving to the nearby community of Altadena. I had passed the park, which straddles the towns of La Cañada Flintridge, Altadena, and Pasadena, dozens of times on my way to and from the shops on Foothill Boulevard, but it didn't seem very inspiring from the road. All I could see was a narrow strip of picnic tables, and the parking lot never

▶ KEY AT-A-GLANCE INFORMATION

LENGTH: 2.2 miles

CONFIGURATION: Out-and-back

DIFFICULTY: Easy

SCENERY: Arroyo rocks, San Gabriel Mountains

EXPOSURE: Sunny

TRAFFIC: Light

TRAIL SURFACE: Dirt and boulders

HIKING TIME: 40 minutes

ACCESS: Free; open daily sunrise–sunset

MAPS: USGS Pasadena

FACILITIES: Restrooms are padlocked, but there are portable toilets nearby; water, picnic tables

SPECIAL COMMENTS: Don't be surprised if you see a Frisbee-like object or two whiz by as you make your way from the parking lot to the trailhead. This park is home to the world's first disc golf course, established in 1976, according to the Professional Disc Golf Association.

▶ DIRECTIONS

From the I-5 freeway heading north, take the Glendale Freeway (2) north to the 210 Freeway east toward La Cañada Flintridge. Exit at Berkshire Avenue/Oak Grove Drive and turn left onto Berkshire. Make another left onto Oak Grove Drive, then a right into the parking lot of the Hahamongna Watershed Park. The lot is directly across the street from La Cañada High School. There is a two-hour parking limit during the day.

UTM Trailhead Coordinates for
Devil's Gate Trail to JPL

UTM Zone (WGS84)   11S

Easting   391514

Northing   3783927

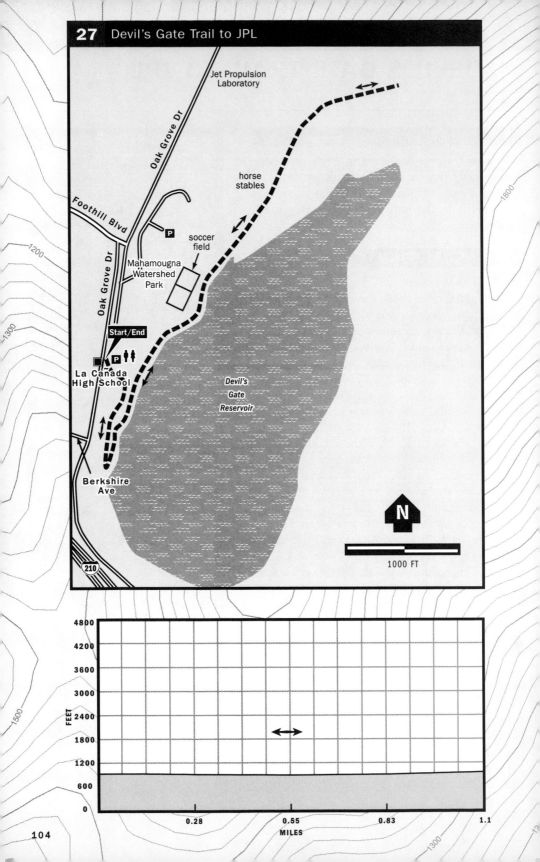

seemed to have more than a handful of cars at a time. Little did I know that below the parking lot sat a recreational oasis: a lush green soccer field, more picnic areas, and access to a flat trail that draws birders, dog walkers, and families. The trail also provides a close-up peek at the sprawling campus of NASA's Jet Propulsion Laboratory (JPL), the high-security spacecraft research hub that most people only ever glimpse from the highway. It is also host to more than 140 species of birds, according to the Pasadena Audubon Society, which leads monthly bird-watching walks around the basin.

From the upper parking lot, hop on the trail shaded by oak and sycamore trees just behind the padlocked restrooms and hitching post, a nod to the horse stables nearby. You may also access the trail at the fire road gate in the lower parking lot. The dirt path from the upper lot heads south into a shady glen, then curves down and to the left at the end of a short flight of wooden steps. From here, reverse course and follow the rough gravel trail north. You'll pass a soccer field on the left at 0.4 miles and see the overgrown basin that makes up what's left of the Devil's Gate Reservoir to the right. At the soccer field, follow the right-hand path, which starts to get sandy, then veer left toward the distant buildings of the JPL. The San Gabriel Mountains will stretch out in front of you as the path widens and continues north along a chain-link fence and past horse stables. The path is completely exposed from this point on, so bring hats or sunscreen and plenty of water. Even on weekends, this path never seems very crowded.

As you approach the edge of the JPL campus, the path turns rocky and curves to the right toward the basin. This trail isn't landscaped, but it is attractive in its own rough way. Wildflowers, thistle, and other low-lying shrubs mix with coastal sage scrub and large boulders, all complemented by the backdrop of the San Gabriels. As you walk northeast, see a yellow fire gate in front of you, but the road that leads to it has been washed out. From here, you can turn back and retrace your steps to the parking lot or poke around the rocks a bit longer (I saw quite a few parents with kids doing this). If you look beyond the fire gate, you may see hikers and mountain bikers heading north down another trail. This is known as the Arroyo Seco Trail (p. 84), a very popular trail that begins on the northeast side of Devil's Gate.

▶ NEARBY ACTIVITIES

The Jet Propulsion Laboratory offers free walking tours of its facility for individuals or groups. You must call ahead and make a reservation, and tours often fill up months in advance. Highlights of the 2.5-hour tour include a multimedia presentation called *Welcome to Outer Space* and a visit to the JPL's space flight operations and spacecraft assembly areas. For more information, go online to www.jpl.nasa.gov/pso/pt.cfm.

Trader Joe's, a local grocery chain with on Foothill Boulevard, is a good place to stock up on picnic provisions. It's about a mile away from the park on Foothill Boulevard.

DUARTE RECREATIONAL TRAIL

KEY AT-A-GLANCE INFORMATION

LENGTH: 3.2 miles

CONFIGURATION: Out-and-back

DIFFICULTY: Easy

SCENERY: San Gabriel Mountains, residential homes and streets

EXPOSURE: Sunny

TRAFFIC: Moderate

TRAIL SURFACE: Paved path

HIKING TIME: 1 hour

ACCESS: Free, always open

MAPS: USGS Azusa

FACILITIES: Restrooms, and playground and picnic areas are located at the eastern end of the path in Royal Oaks Park

SPECIAL COMMENTS: Dogs, bicycles, and horses are welcome on this well-maintained trail, which features ample water fountains, benches, and kiosks with plastic bags.

UTM Trailhead Coordinates for
Duarte Recreational Trail

UTM Zone (WGS84)   11S

Easting   409880

Northing   3778493

IN BRIEF

Popular with runners and power walkers, this paved, flat trail is flanked by wildflower-covered hills and the San Gabriel Mountains to the north and Royal Oaks Drive to the south.

DESCRIPTION

The 1.6-mile Duarte Recreational Trail follows the path of the Pacific Electric Railway, a mass transit system that connected Los Angeles and Orange counties using streetcars, buses, and light rail cars during the first half of the twentieth century. The city of Duarte purchased the land from the railroad after the trains stopped running and created a path based on a concept developed by the not-for-profit Rails to Trails Conservancy. It also marks the dividing line between the cities of Duarte, a dense mix of residential and commercial districts, and Bradbury, a bedroom community of horse ranches and sprawling mountain homes to the north. You can access the trailhead from the corner of Buena Vista Drive and Royal Oaks Avenue, or on the eastern end at Royal Oaks Park and Vineyard Avenue.

The path's western entrance begins with a yellow sign featuring a picture of a nun that warns visitors of SISTERS XING—either city planners have a sense of humor or there is a convent nearby. On your left is a dirt trail for horses that parallels the paved path. On the right are the rows of royal oak trees that earned the street its name and a long

DIRECTIONS

Take the 210 freeway east past Pasadena and exit at Buena Vista Avenue in Duarte. Turn left and go several miles north to Royal Oaks Drive. The trail begins at the northeast corner of Buena Vista and Royal Oaks. Street parking (see signs for restrictions) is available along Royal Oaks Drive.

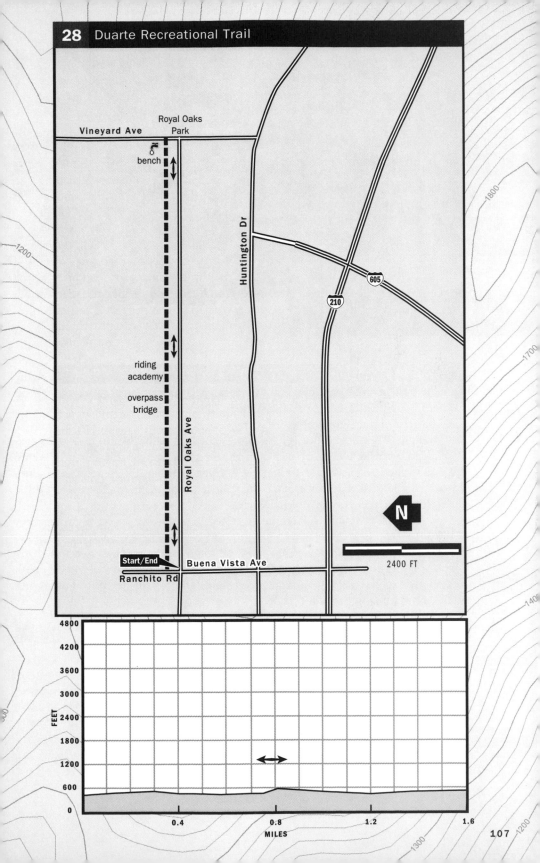

The western entrance of the Duarte Recreational Trail

stretch of lush green grass. Drought-resistant evergreens also line the path, helping block the traffic noise from Royal Oaks Drive. Expect to see many serious runners on this path, along with duos of power walkers, parents with strollers, and the occasional bicyclist or horseback rider.

At about 0.5 miles, you will pass under a pedestrian bridge. In the spring, yellow and purple wildflowers are in bloom on the green hills to the north. The trail dips below the road here and feels more secluded. At the intersection of Chimes Avenue, you'll come to a horse ranch on your left, one of many that make up the equestrian-minded community of Bradbury.

After about 1.4 miles, you'll come to a bench and water fountain on the right. To the left are the sports fields and playgrounds of Royal Oaks Elementary School. The trail ends at Vineyard Avenue, at more benches sitting under a cluster of shady royal oak trees. Across the street is Royal Oaks Park, a nicely maintained city park with tennis and basketball courts, a playground, and restrooms. Turn around and retrace your steps on the trail.

▶ NEARBY ACTIVITIES

Racing enthusiasts will want to pay a visit to Santa Anita Park, the Depression-era thoroughbred racetrack in nearby Arcadia that was home to Seabiscuit, the long-shot racehorse whose victories captivated America in the 1930s. After the 2003 film was released, the park added free tram tours based on the life its famous resident. It is open to the public from December through April. For more information, go on-line to www.santaanita.com. Afterward, have dinner at the Derby, the historic restaurant once owned by Seabiscuit jockey George Woolf. With its red leather booths, racing memorabilia, and meat-and-potatoes menu, it feels like you've stepped into a time warp.

EATON CANYON: STREAM TRAIL

▶ IN BRIEF

This flat, rocky trail parallels a seasonal stream and will appeal to families and explorer types who don't mind scrambling over boulders and forging their own way from time to time.

▶ DESCRIPTION

I intended to hike the 4-mile waterfall trail when I arrived at Eaton Canyon Natural Area in Altadena on a sunny Saturday in April. When I checked in at the nature center, however, I learned that the northern part of this popular path was closed due to mudslides and washouts caused by the January and February rains, and there were no plans to begin assessing and repairing the damage until late spring. Because the park was packed with cars, I decided to investigate what all these people were doing there anyway. As it turns out, there was a rattlesnake festival going on in the nature center, and it was brimming with reptile-loving kids and their parents. But a decent number of visitors were also making their way to the stream that leads to the waterfall. Thanks also to the earlier rains, it was going at full force and made a great place to splash around and have a picnic on the surrounding boulders. You can also forge a decent 2-mile hike along the western side of the stream; it requires some scrambling over boulders and debris left from the rains, but is relatively easy to navigate using the parallel stream as your guide. This path has little shade and is best done in the late spring or early summer, before the weather gets too hot.

Before setting off, stop at the nature center for a trail map and a guide to the canyon's native

① KEY AT-A-GLANCE INFORMATION

LENGTH: 2.4 miles

CONFIGURATION: Out-and-back

DIFFICULTY: Moderate

SCENERY: Stream, San Gabriel Mountains

EXPOSURE: Mostly sun, some shade

TRAFFIC: Heavy on weekends

TRAIL SURFACE: Packed dirt and boulders

HIKING TIME: 1 hour

ACCESS: Daily, sunrise to sunset

MAPS: Available at nature center; USGS Mount Wilson

FACILITIES: Restrooms, water, picnic area

SPECIAL COMMENTS: Trails with the Eaton Canyon Natural Area were hard hit by the 2005 rains; be sure to check conditions before you go. Docents staff the nature center daily 8 a.m.–5 p.m., phone (626) 398-5420.

UTM Trailhead Coordinates for Eaton Canyon: Stream Trail

UTM Zone (WGS84)   **11S**

Easting   **398931**

Northing   **3782750**

▶ DIRECTIONS

From the 210 (Pasadena Freeway), take the Altadena Drive exit and follow it north. The park entrance is on the right, just past the intersection of Altadena Drive and New York Avenue.

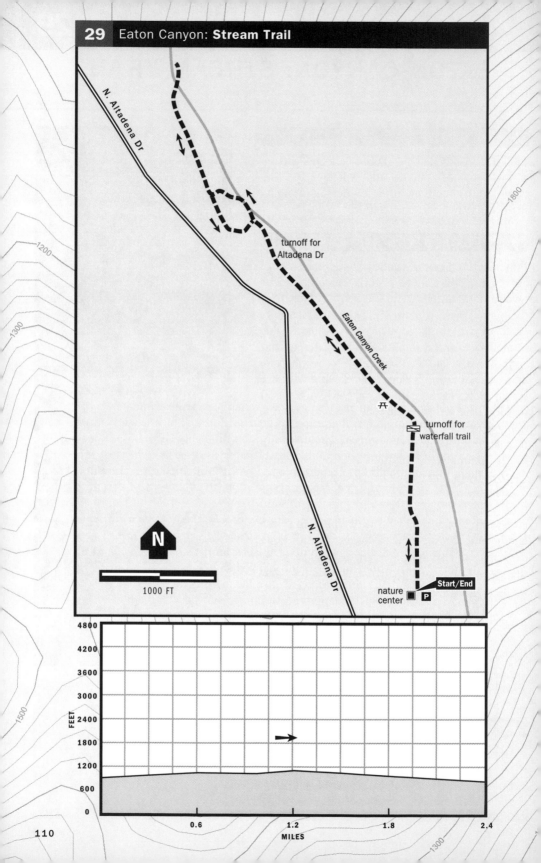

N. Altadena Dr

turnoff for
Altadena Dr

Eaton Canyon Creek

turnoff for
waterfall trail

N. Altadena Dr

N

1000 FT

nature
center

Start/End

P

1800

1200

1300

1500

1200

1300

4800
4200
3600
3000
2400
1800
1200
600
0

FEET

0.6   1.2   1.8   2.4
MILES

plants, which include honeysuckle, laurel sumac, coast live oak, toyon, yucca, prickly pear cactus, and Matilija poppy. Eaton Canyon was badly burned in a brush fire in 1993 and the slopes and flats are still recovering. A fire ecology brochure available at the nature center explains how the area's native plants regrew following the fire.

From the far north end of the parking lot, pass through a gate and head straight ahead toward a landscaped picnic area. You'll glimpse some private homes on your left. To the right is the dirt path that leads to the waterfall. At the end of the picnic area, the path turns to dirt and is attractively framed in the spring by buckwheat, sage, and golden currant. I also saw scads of painted-lady butterflies here; the profusion of wildflowers brought on by heavy rains tends to attract large quantities of the orange-and-black creatures as they migrate from Mexico. After about 0.3 miles, the stream will come into view, as will the looming San Gabriel Mountains, which make a nice backdrop for most of the hike. You can follow a rock-strewn path down to the right to access the stream immediately (as the majority of visitors tend to do) or take the narrow dirt path on the left above the stream to continue the hike. It gets shady here with oak trees and starts to get less crowded as people turn off the path and stake out places along the stream to picnic, sunbathe, or just hang out.

After scrambling over boulders for about a quarter of a mile, you'll find yourself back on a narrow dirt trail skirting the riverbed. You will also pass a turnoff for an access path leading to a small parking lot on Altadena Drive. Continue along the dirt path as it winds back toward the stream. You'll need to navigate more boulders here as the stream diverges into a Y. This is a good turnaround point, or you can continue boulder-hopping to the bridge that leads to the waterfall.

▶ NEARBY ACTIVITIES

Café Culture, about a mile south of the Eaton Canyon Park entrance, is a jack-of-all-trades kind of place. Besides strong coffee and an assortment of teas, it serves salads, sandwiches, and smoothies and sells everything from lip gloss to used books. It even has belly-dancing classes on some evenings. Upon leaving Eaton Canyon, turn right on Altadena Drive and head south about a mile. Café Culture is on the left at 1359 North Altadena Drive. It has a small parking lot.

ECHO MOUNTAIN VIA SAM MERRILL TRAIL

KEY AT-A-GLANCE INFORMATION

LENGTH: 5 miles

CONFIGURATION: Out-and-back

DIFFICULTY: Strenuous

SCENERY: Native plants, trees; panoramic views

EXPOSURE: Mostly sunny

TRAFFIC: Heavy on weekends

TRAIL SURFACE: Packed dirt

HIKING TIME: 3.5 hours

ACCESS: Free; open daily sunrise–sunset

MAPS: At kiosk beyond trailhead; USGS Pasadena/Mt. Wilson

FACILITIES: None

SPECIAL COMMENTS: Bring plenty of water and sunscreen, as there is little shade on this trail.

UTM Trailhead Coordinates for
Echo Mountain via Sam Merrill Trail

UTM Zone (WGS84)   11S

Easting   395842

Northing   3785368

▶ IN BRIEF

This path dips briefly into a shaded canyon and past a dry riverbed, then begins to climb via long switchbacks up Echo Mountain to an altitude of 1,400 feet. The reward is the ruins of a turn-of-the-twentieth-century mountain resort with sweeping views of downtown Los Angeles and the San Gabriel Valley.

▶ DESCRIPTION

Stone pillars and an old iron gate mark the entrance to this former estate in Altadena, a laid-back community just north of Pasadena. The grounds are now a part of the Angeles National Forest, and a plaque at the entrance dedicates the property as "a quiet place for people and wildlife forever." This is one of my favorite trails in Los Angeles County—the hikers are friendly and polite, the views are spectacular, and it offers a history lesson to boot. The looping switchbacks make the hike seem longer than it actually is. Save for a few red-tailed hawks, I have never seen much wildlife here, but the Pasadena Audubon Society considers the area a bird-rich refuge. It's a prime spot for the group's annual Christmas bird count; among the species members spotted and logged in recent years are fox sparrows, great horned owls, and European starlings.

From the gate at Lake and Alta Loma, follow the rutted driveway east about 200 yards until it begins to curve north. (If you stay on the driveway, you'll wind up at a rusted old water tank—this is

▶ DIRECTIONS

From the 210 Freeway in Pasadena, exit at Lake Avenue and drive north 3.4 miles to Loma Alta Drive. Park on Lake or Loma Alta. The trailhead begins at the intersection of Lake and Loma Alta at the iron gate marked COBB ESTATE.

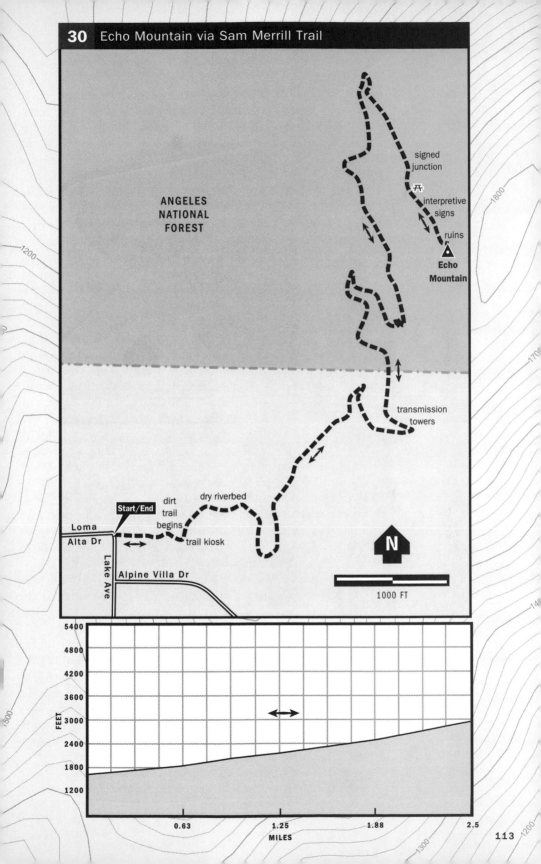

ANGELES
NATIONAL
FOREST

signed
junction

interpretive
signs

ruins

**Echo
Mountain**

transmission
towers

dry riverbed

Start/End

dirt
trail
begins

Loma
Alta Dr

Lake Ave

trail kiosk

Alpine Villa Dr

N

1000 FT

5400
4800
4200
3600
3000
2400
1800
1200

FEET

0.63   1.25   1.88   2.5
MILES

Stone pillars mark the entrance to the Sam Merrill Trail.

not a bad walk, but it's nothing compared to the stunning views offered by the Merrill Trail. Turn off the driveway onto a dirt trail and walk a few yards to a kiosk with a hand-drawn map and some old photos and information on the history of the area. Here you can also sign a guest book, which lets park rangers know who is on the trail.

Mount Lowe Railway was a top tourist attraction in southern California from 1896 to 1936, designed by Thaddeus S.C. Lowe, a professor, inventor, and Civil War balloonist. Millions of visitors rode the cable incline railway to a luxury resort complex that sat atop Echo Mountain and looked out over the then-bucolic Los Angeles basin. The resort burned in the early 1900s; 30 years later, Altadena residents built a trail along the same route the railway had followed. During the next decade, a retired Altadena resident named Samuel Merrill overhauled and maintained the path. After he died in 1948, the trail was named after him.

From the kiosk, you'll want to follow the Lower Sam Merrill Trail, which dips north into Las Flores Canyon by way of a narrow dirt path lined with cactus, brush, and boulders. After about 0.5 miles, reach a dry riverbed and concrete debris dam (you may see a few picnickers or sunbathers camped out here). Once on the other side of the canyon, the trail winds south and turns into long switchbacks that begin the 2-mile climb up Echo Mountain. The trail is shaded at first by forest, but it won't be long before you glimpse views of Altadena rooftops and the Los Angeles basin beyond. It's tempting to linger, but the views only get better as you ascend.

You're halfway to the top when you reach a flat area with three electrical transmission towers and panoramic valley-to-ocean views. To the left and below is the rusted water tower that the old driveway leads to (you may be tempted to smirk at the hikers who chose this path over Merrill Trail; go ahead—they can't see you).

Some people turn back here, satisfied with the vistas and the mile-plus uphill workout. If you want to continue to the top of the mountain, keep following the switchbacks for another half-mile until you reach a junction with wooden markers. Bear right on the Echo Mountain Trail and continue to follow the old railbed to the ruins of the resort. You'll pass a huge wheel cog on the left that once hauled the cable cars up the incline, as well as several signs with photos and text explaining the construction of the railway and resort. There is also an original megaphone from the resort's heyday, encouraging visitors to use it and see how Echo Mountain got its name. The final stop is a wide, flat area covered with a maze of stone ruins of the old hotel. There are few trees up here, but it's a nice spot to rest for a while on a cool day and enjoy the view.

From here, most hikers turn back and retrace their steps along the switchbacks to the Sam Merrill Trail. Hardier souls can hike another steep half mile to Inspiration Point, where there are more great views and an enclosed pavilion.

If you do this hike in the summer, you'll want to get an early start, before the sun rises from behind the northern ridge of the San Gabriels. There is very little shade, and water and sunscreen are a must. If you're hiking in the winter or spring, it's pleasant to time it so you're descending as the sun begins to set; just make sure to give yourself enough time to get back to Lake Avenue before dark.

▶ NEARBY ACTIVITIES

Lake Avenue, between the 210 freeway and the trailhead, is home to several venerable southern California eateries. The Hat, 491 North Lake, established in 1951, is known for its terrific pastrami dip sandwiches. Roscoe's Chicken 'n' Waffles, 830 North Lake, serves juicy fried chicken and has a devoted following. For those watching their cholesterol, the cozy Coffee Gallery at 2029 North Lake, which sells pizzas, sandwiches, and beverages, might be a better choice.

GARCIA TRAIL TO AZUSA PEAK

KEY AT-A-GLANCE INFORMATION

LENGTH: 2.2 miles

CONFIGURATION: Out-and-back

DIFFICULTY: Strenuous

SCENERY: Wildflowers, chaparral, valley and mountain views

EXPOSURE: Sunny

TRAFFIC: Moderate

TRAIL SURFACE: Loose dirt

HIKING TIME: 1 hour

ACCESS: Free; open sunrise–sunset, daily

MAPS: Posted at trailhead; USGS Azusa

FACILITIES: Picnic table

SPECIAL COMMENTS: A new home development called Rosedale is in the works across the street from the Garcia Trail. A sign posted at the trailhead warned hikers of occasional closings due to construction, but the city of Azusa has no plans to shut down the trail permanently. For updated information, go to www.rosedaleazusa.com/updates.html.

UTM Trailhead Coordinates for
Garcia Trail to Azusa Peak

UTM Zone (WGS84)   11S

Easting   417918

Northing   3778819

IN BRIEF

The steep single-track trail gains 1,100 feet in just over 1 mile, ending at the Glendora Ridge Motorway, a dirt fire road that runs east to west. Highlights include an unusually diverse array of spring wildflowers and sweeping views of the San Gabriel Valley.

DESCRIPTION

Many trails in the San Gabriel Mountains take their names from the early settlers who owned or maintained property in the foothills. This is the case with Garcia Trail, according to a history of the hiking and riding trails in the foothill community of Glendora by William Cullen. According to Cullen, the trail is believed to have been built by a man named Garcia, who lived in a small house under a eucalyptus tree in the canyon next to the fire station. Most likely, he worked for Azusa Foothill Ranch or the McNeil family, owner of the property. Today, the city of Azusa owns the land, and the trail is maintained by a professor and

DIRECTIONS

From Pasadena, take I-210 freeway east to Azusa Avenue and follow it north to Sierra Madre Avenue. Turn right on Sierra Madre Avenue and drive about 1 mile until you see Los Angeles County Fire Station no. 97 on the left (the address is 18453 Sierra Madre Avenue). Park along the street and walk up a grassy area to the left of the fire station to get to the trailhead.

Alternate Directions: At press time, Sierra Madre Boulevard west of the Garcia Trail was scheduled to be closed between January and April 2006 due to widening linked to a new home development. To avoid this, you can take the I-210 to Grand Avenue, turn right (north) and follow it to Sierra Madre Avenue. Turn left and park along the street east of the fire station.

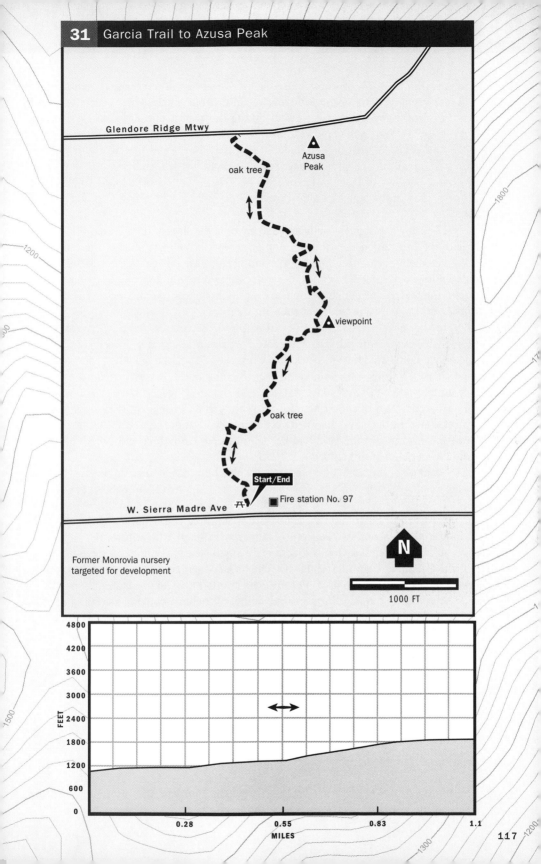

Glendore Ridge Mtwy

oak tree

Azusa Peak

viewpoint

oak tree

Start/End

W. Sierra Madre Ave   Fire station No. 97

Former Monrovia nursery
targeted for development

N

1000 FT

4800
4200
3600
3000
2400
1800
1200
600
0

FEET

0.28   0.55   0.83   1.1
MILES

student volunteers from nearby Azusa Pacific University. I first learned about the trail and its sweeping views of the San Gabriel Valley from a newspaper article written by the president of the university. He said hiking this trail in the early morning hours is a great way to "watch the city wake up."

This is also a great hike to make in the early evening as the city lights are starting to come on. Just be sure to time it so you don't find yourself heading downhill in the dark. Because of its high exposure, the Garcia Trail is best hiked in the cooler months. July and August can be brutally hot, unless you arrive very early in the morning.

Look for the signed trailhead just beyond the grassy picnic area on the west side of the fire station. A primitive map is posted at the start. Follow the dirt trail as it immediately begins to climb up the mountain past tall grass, coastal sage scrub, and wildflowers. After 0.25 miles, the trail passes under a large oak tree that provides one of the few patches of shade on the trail. Some hikers like to stop and rest here to muster up more energy for the remaining trek.

In the spring, a dazzling display of plant life frames the trail: yucca, orange monkey flowers, blue lupine, buckwheat, California dodder (witch's hair), wild cucumber, laurel sumac, and black and white sage. There are also nice views of chaparral-cloaked hills as you ascend higher up the mountain. Just shy of half a mile, look to your left for a clear view of what used to be the Monrovia Nursery, a 500-acre commercial garden that operated here for 50 years before selling to a developer. The area is now slated to become a planned community with more than 1,000 homes. When I last visited, most of the land had been bulldozed. Construction of model homes is slated to begin in spring 2006.

From here, the trail continues to switchback up the mountain. Be alert for other hikers making their way down. The path is narrow, so one of you will have to move to the side to let the other pass. I was surprised to pass a dozen or so hikers on my way up when I hiked this trail on a hazy Saturday morning. They ran the gamut from single dog walkers to serious runners to families with small kids in tow.

At about 0.5 miles, you will come to a small clearing with good views of the valley (the elevation is about 1,400 feet). This is a convenient place to stop and rest and take a long swig of water, as you've still got another 600 feet to climb.

At about 0.7 miles, turn around and look behind you for sweeping views of the San Gabriel Valley and beyond. On a clear day, the city seems to stretch on forever.

As you begin the final ascent up to the ridge, you will see evidence of the damage caused by 2005's heavy rainstorms, though the trail is still quite passable. Portions of the trail are narrower from being washed out, a couple of trees have been uprooted, and dirt from mudslides covers parts of the path. It's a good idea to use extra caution here.

Just before the ridge comes into view, you will pass under another old oak tree, a good place to take a last swig of water before reaching the top. Azusa Peak will come into view to the northeast. The Garcia Trail ends at the unmarked Glendora Ridge Motorway, a dirt east–west road that extends from Azusa to Glendora. Before heading back, savor the great views of the San Gabriels and snowcapped Mount Baldy to the north.

If you're energized from the exercise and want to extend the hike, you can climb an additional 0.2 (steep) miles to Azusa Peak for more sweeping views, or follow the fire road east for several miles to Glendora Mountain Road. Or you can call it a day and head back down the mountain to your car. Watch for other hikers on the way down.

▶ NEARBY ACTIVITIES

Doughnut lovers drive from all over L.A. to get the seasonal strawberry and peach doughnuts served by Donut Man, a 24-hour takeout-only shop. From the trailhead, take Sierra Madre Boulevard about 2 miles to Lorraine Avenue, turn right and drive about 1.3 miles to Route 66 East. Turn right and follow 0.2 miles to Donut Man on the right. Phone: (626) 335-9111.

View of the San Gabriel Valley from the Garcia Trail

LA CAÑADA FIRE ROAD TO GABRIELINO TRAIL

 KEY AT-A-GLANCE INFORMATION

LENGTH: 3.4 miles

CONFIGURATION: Out-and-back

DIFFICULTY: Moderate

SCENERY: Mountains, Arroyo Seco stream

EXPOSURE: Sunny

TRAFFIC: Light

TRAIL SURFACE: Paved and packed dirt

HIKING TIME: 1 hour, 10 minutes

ACCESS: Free; always open

MAPS: USGS Pasadena

FACILITIES: Water, restrooms at Gould Mesa Campground, picnic areas

SPECIAL COMMENTS: This is a less congested and steeper route to the Angeles National Forest than the Gabrielino/Arroyo Seco Trail (p. 86). There is little shade until you reach the stream, so bring sunscreen.

UTM Trailhead Coordinates for La Cañada Fire Road to Gabrielino Trail

UTM Zone (WGS84) 11S

Easting 390380

Northing 3787492

▶ IN BRIEF

This is an alternate way of reaching the Arroyo Seco stream that hugs the popular Arroyo Seco/Gabrielino Trail. It takes you behind an upscale hillside neighborhood and an electricity substation, then quickly disappears into nature as it switchbacks downhill to a streamside campground. It is quieter and more exposed than the first stretch of the Arroyo Seco Trail in Altadena.

▶ DESCRIPTION

The Gabrielino Trail is one of several in the Angeles National Forest designated as a multiuse national recreation trail. It follows the route of an original 1920s road that ran from Pasadena north up the canyon past wilderness resorts and old rustic cabins. The road lost its appeal after the Angeles Crest Highway was built, but today it has reinvented itself as a multiuse trail for hikers, horseback riders, mountain bikers, and birders.

This hike gains you access to the Gabrielino Trail from the Angeles Crest Highway via a well-maintained fire road the skirts the back of the town of La Cañada-Flintridge. Most hikers access via the trailhead near the NASA Jet Propulsion Laboratory. This trail is a quieter alternative to that and allows you to skip the first couple of miles of the Gabrielino Trail, which are often

▶ DIRECTIONS

From downtown Los Angeles, take the Golden State Freeway north to the Glendale Freeway (2) and head north. The road turns into the Angeles Crest Highway at Foothill Boulevard in La Cañada Flintridge. From Foothill Boulevard, continue about 2 miles on the Angeles Crest Highway (you'll pass the La Cañada Country Club on the right) until you see a pullout parking area on the right. Park in the lot and look for the fire-road gate at the north corner.

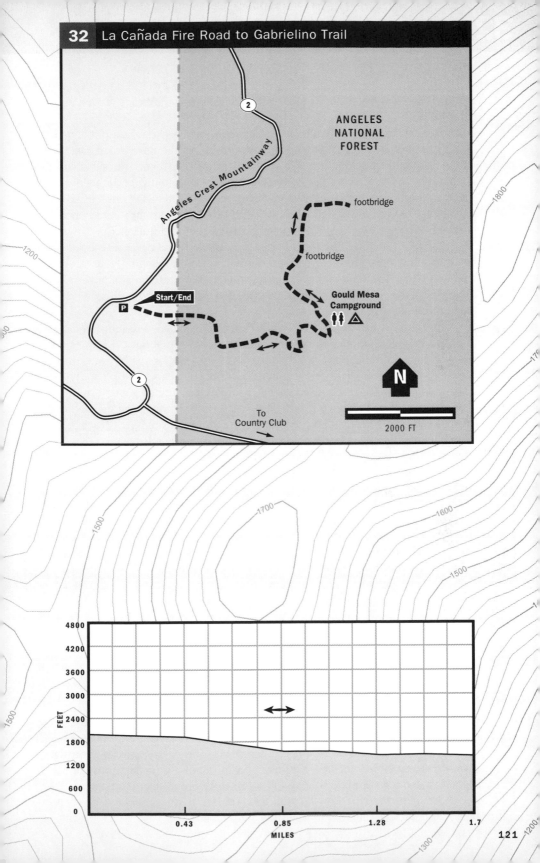

2

ANGELES
NATIONAL
FOREST

footbridge

footbridge

Angeles Crest Mountainway

**Gould Mesa
Campground**

Start/End

P

2

To
Country Club

N

2000 FT

4800

4200

3600

3000

2400

1800

1200

600

0

FEET

0.43   0.85   1.28   1.7

MILES

crowded, and head straight for the bucolic segment of the trek. This path also allows you to access the forest 24/7, unlike most other forest trailheads, which are closed between sunset and sunrise.

From the parking pullout area, look for the sign for the Gabrielino Trail. Walk around the fire-road gate at the north end and follow the paved road east. You will pass a sign marked 2N69, and a couple of large private homes on left. Landscaped wildflowers and succulents flank the path here, helping mitigate the ugliness of the transmission towers that are also part of the scenery. After 100 yards or so you will pass a huge electricity substation on the right. It's loud, unsightly, and impossible to ignore, but once you're past it, the path turns greener and quieter.

At about 0.4 miles, the trail turns to dirt and starts to descend via wide switchbacks into the forest. You may hear a seasonal stream gurgling on your left, and you will start to get some nice views of chaparral-covered mountains straight ahead. To the right are the rooftops of some of La Cañada's more expensive hillside homes, but they quickly disappear from view.

For the next half a mile the trail hugs the canyon wall and remains exposed to the hot sun as it continues to descend into the forest. At about 0.75 miles the path winds around to the left and briefly turns shady before passing by a clearing with a couple of pieces of rusted-out machinery, a couple of dilapidated picnic tables, and piles of cut logs. Don't be discouraged by this view; things soon turn shady and much more scenic. Just after 1 mile, you will pass a sign marking the border to the Angeles National Forest. Continue on a gradual decline as the path reaches the final stretch before it connects with the Gabrielino Trail at 1.1 miles.

You will come to a T and a sign for Gould Mesa Campground. Beyond that is the Arroyo Seco stream, which will be a welcome sight if it's a hot day. To the right are bathrooms and a water fountain. You want to hang a left here and follow the path north toward Oakwilde Campground. At 1.3 miles, the trail crosses over a wooden footbridge, then winds a bit closer to the stream and passes the Nino Canyon picnic area on the left. This is a great place to stop for a snack, read a book, or just hang out under the shade of oak and alder forest with the background of a gurgling stream. I only saw a handful of people on this stretch of the trail (Gould Mesa to Nino Canyon) when I was here on a Saturday afternoon, in contrast to the dozens of recreation seekers I passed on the busier southern portion of the Gabrielino Trail.

At 1.6 miles the trail crosses another wooden footbridge and soon reaches a stream crossing. This is another good place to stop and rest on one of the many big boulders that frame the stream, From here, you can cross the stream and add another 1.5 miles to the hike by continuing to Oakwilde Campground. Or you can turn around and retrace your steps back to the fire road and La Cañada-Flintridge. Just be sure to reserve some water for the uphill trek back.

▶ NEARBY ACTIVITIES

Foothill Boulevard, east of the Angeles Crest Highway in La Cañada-Flintridge, has several grocery stores, including a Trader Joe's. The La Cañada-Flintridge Farmer's Market is also a good place to stop for supplies before a hike. It's held every Saturday morning at the corner of Foothill and Beulah. If you're looking for a sit-down meal, Dish, at 734 Foothill Boulevard, is a good bet.

LEGG LAKE LOOP TRAIL

▶ IN BRIEF

Ducks, geese, and two attractive recreational lakes dominate the scenery of this easy loop trail in a nature park near the western edge of the San Gabriel River.

▶ DESCRIPTION

Legg Lake and North Legg Lake are two of four bodies of water within the 400-acre Whittier Narrows Natural Area Park. The park was run by the Audubon Society from 1939 until 1970, when it was purchased by the Los Angeles County of Parks and Recreation. Spring and fall are the best times to visit because the weather is nicest and the trees are in bloom.

The loop trail begins at the northern edge of the parking lot. You'll immediately see (and hear) the lake's resident ducks and geese trying to cadge some crumbs from picnickers gathered at tables and on blankets on the lawn in front of you. Follow the gravel trail to the right as it runs parallel with the north side of the lake. Known as North Legg Lake, this is the bigger of the two lakes within the recreation area; on weekends it is often filled with paddleboats, though no swimming or wading is allowed. You'll also hear traffic noise from the nearby freeway as you begin walking, but a parking lot and the cackling of seagulls and other birds tends to buffer it.

Besides ring-necked ducks, Canada and snow geese, and California gulls, other birds commonly

ⓘ KEY AT-A-GLANCE INFORMATION

LENGTH: 2.4 miles

CONFIGURATION: Loop

DIFFICULTY: Easy

SCENERY: Native plants, birds

EXPOSURE: Mostly sun, some shade

TRAFFIC: Heavy on weekends

TRAIL SURFACE: Gravel path

HIKING TIME: 1 hour

ACCESS: Open sunrise–sunset, daily; $3 parking fee on weekends and holidays

MAPS: USGS El Monte

FACILITIES: Restrooms, water, picnic tables, boat rentals

SPECIAL COMMENTS: Legg Lake is located within the Whittier Narrows Recreation Area and open daily from sunrise to sunset. Its picnic tables and lake banks fill up with families and anglers on weekends, but the hiking trails are wide and well-maintained and never seem overly crowded.

▶ DIRECTIONS

From downtown L.A., take I-5 south to the Pomona freeway (CA 60), and head east. Exit at Santa Anita Avenue, turn right, and follow the signs to South El Monte and the Whittier Narrows Recreation Area. The parking lot is on your right. Parking is also available in two large lots off Rosemead Boulevard.

UTM Trailhead Coordinates for Legg Lake Loop Trail

UTM Zone (WGS84) **11S**

Easting **402480**

Northing **3766742**

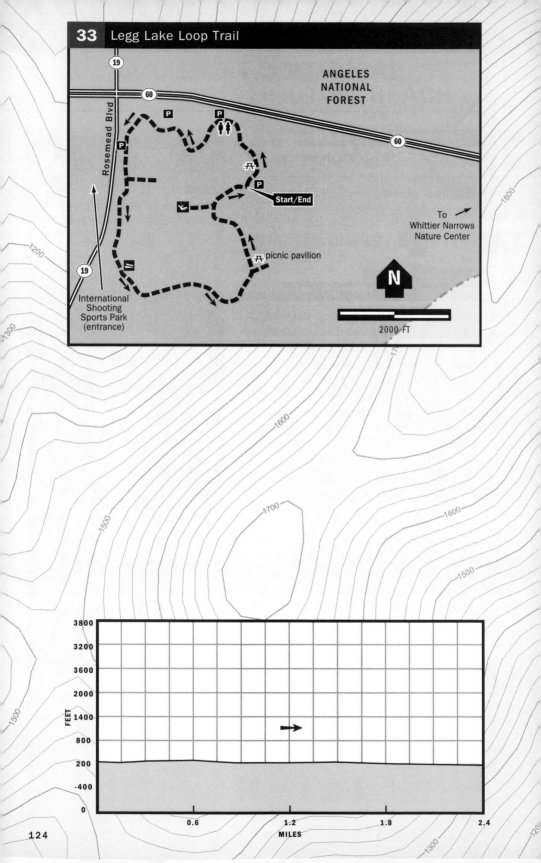

ANGELES
NATIONAL
FOREST

Rosemead Blvd

Start/End

To
Whittier Narrows
Nature Center

picnic pavilion

International
Shooting
Sports Park
(entrance)

N

2000 FT

3800

3200

3600

2000

1400

800

FEET

200

-400

0

0.6   1.2   1.8   2.4
MILES

spotted around the lakes are mourning doves, coots, hummingbirds, swallows, killdeer, and double-crested cormorants. Cottontail rabbits, raccoons, and California ground squirrels are also abundant. On the human side, expect to see a mix of joggers, bicyclists, families with kids, lone power walkers, and strolling couples.

Continue following the trail west as it winds past restrooms and heads south at a parking lot along Rosemead Boulevard. At the edge of the parking lot, veer to the left slightly at a sign that says BIKE ROUTE, then continue straight between the recycling bins on the right and two electric transmission towers on the left. If you make a sharp left, you'll find yourself on a shorter trail leading back to the Santa Anita parking lot. At about 1.1 miles you'll come to a palm tree and another turnoff for a path that leads to a large playground and eventually back to the parking lot. Continue straight on the loop trail as it becomes nicely shaded by palms and drought-resistant pines. You'll soon spot Legg Lake (and more quacking ducks and geese) on your left. There are more restrooms here and a concrete platform for launching model boats. The trail runs very close to the lake at this point; it's a nice spot to stop and soak up the view. This area of the park tends to be less crowded than the northern end, especially on weekdays. As the trail curves west around the lake, you'll spot a refinery on your right. In the foreground are a few makeshift stables and their equine residents munching grass just beyond a chain-link fence. From here, you can access the bike path of the upper San Gabriel River to the south.

At 1.8 miles, you'll come to a Y in the path with a picnic pavilion directly in front of you. The right trail is the most direct route back to the parking lot, but I recommend opting for left one, because it is more scenic. Among the things you'll see on this route: some modest fitness equipment, a pretty green bridge that overlooks North Legg Lake, and a few kid-friendly climbing structures. You'll also pass more picnic tables and another path on the left that leads to the playground in the middle of the park. Continue to the right past a grove of palm trees and a long boat ramp, then more picnic tables, and soon you'll see the parking lot in the distance. Just before the end of the loop is a kiosk that rents bikes and boats on weekends.

▶ NEARBY ACTIVITIES

Whittier Narrows Nature Center, 1100 Durfee Road, is a rustic cabin with interpretive displays of native plants and wildlife, a well-stocked library of history and nature books, and a tiny live zoo of Western toads, lizards, a great blue heron, and even an untethered horned owl. Off the parking lot is the entrance to a mile-long nature trail that's popular with school groups. It's open from 8 a.m. to 5 p.m. From the Santa Anita Avenue parking lot, turn right and follow Santa Anita Avenue 0.4 miles to Durfee Road. Turn left on Durfee and drive 0.5 miles to nature center on the right.

Anyone in search of food might consider heading just up the road to Monterey Park, a residential neighborhood with some of the best Chinese restaurants in the city. A couple of good ones: Ocean Seafood, at 145 N. Atlantic Boulevard, known for its huge 800-seat dining room and fresh fish menu, and NBC Seafood, at 404 S. Atlantic Boulevard, which draws big dim sum crowds on weekends.

LOWER ARROYO
SECO PARK TRAIL

KEY AT-A-GLANCE INFORMATION

LENGTH: 4 miles

CONFIGURATION: Out-and-back

DIFFICULTY: Easy

SCENERY: Historic bridges, flood-control channel, shady streambed

EXPOSURE: Sunny

TRAFFIC: Moderate

TRAIL SURFACE: Dirt and gravel

HIKING TIME: 1 hour, 45 minutes

ACCESS: Free; the park is open daily sunrise–sunset

MAPS: USGS Pasadena

FACILITIES: None

SPECIAL COMMENTS: No bikes are allowed, and all dogs must be on a leash, though few dog owners seem to follow this rule. Horseback riders also frequent the trail, as evidenced by the droppings that can be found along the path.

UTM Trailhead Coordinates for
Lower Arroyo Seco Park Trail

UTM Zone (WGS84) 11S

Easting   392455

Northing   3776560

▶ IN BRIEF

This historic Pasadena hike parallels the Arroyo Seco flood-control channel for its first mile, then winds under a grand old bridge before reaching a natural stream and turning bucolic and shady. It ends near Brookside Park, home to an aquatics center, a kids' museum, and the Rose Bowl stadium. Its loose dirt path and flat surface make it a popular spot for early-evening joggers and dog walkers from the surrounding Pasadena neighborhoods.

▶ DESCRIPTION

The trail begins at a sign marked HORSEBACK RIDING AND HIKING TRAIL. Follow the loose dirt trail as it winds along the east side of the concrete flood-control channel. The west side of the flood channel is also a trail, but it tends to be muddier than its eastern counterpart; the two trails eventually merge into one after they cross under the Ventura Freeway bridge. Expect to see a number of joggers,

▶ DIRECTIONS

From downtown Los Angeles, take the Pasadena Freeway north to Marmion Way/Avenue 64. Bear left and continue to York Avenue. Turn right on York, then make a left onto San Pascual Avenue and drive about 0.7 miles to Lower Arroyo Seco Park. Park on the street or in the dirt lot next to the baseball field (or across from the field if all the spaces are taken) and walk north past San Pascual Stables to the trailhead. There is also a parking lot near the trailhead, but it's for stable patrons only.

Alternate Directions: From the Ventura Freeway, exit at Orange Grove Boulevard and drive south to California Boulevard. Turn right, then make an immediate left on Arroyo Boulevard. Bear right onto San Pascual Avenue (just south of San Rafael Avenue) to the park entrance.

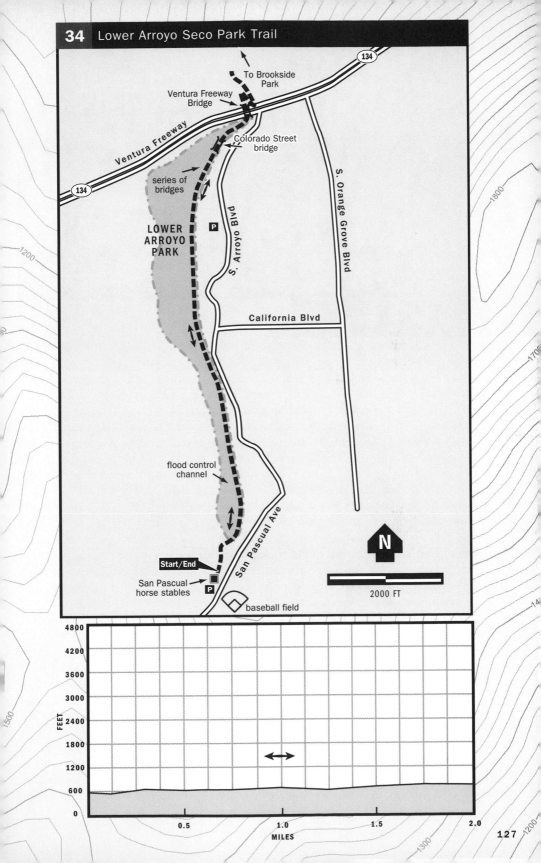

To Brookside Park

Ventura Freeway Bridge

134

Colorado Street bridge

Ventura Freeway

series of bridges

134

LOWER ARROYO PARK

P

S. Arroyo Blvd

S. Orange Grove Blvd

California Blvd

flood control channel

San Pascual Ave

N

Start/End

San Pascual horse stables

P

baseball field

2000 FT

4800
4200
3600
3000
2400
1800
1200
600
0

FEET

0.5   1.0   1.5   2.0

MILES

View of the historic Colorado
Street Bridge from the trail

attracted by the loose dirt and flatness, on this part of the path. I also encountered many dog walkers here during the early spring evening that I hiked this trail.

The path is flanked by some native trees, such as oak and sycamore, but the dominant scenery during the first half of the hike is the concrete flood-control channel that was built in 1940s by the U.S. Army Corps of Engineers after a major flood devastated the area in 1938. Canyon walls loom on each side of the channel, and if you look up and to the left, you will see some of Pasadena's finer homes peeking out from behind them. The neighborhood to the west is the exclusive San Rafael area of Pasadena; the homes here are more reminiscent of Beverly Hills estates than the Craftsman bungalow structures for which the city is known. At about 0.6 miles you will pass on the right another testament to the path's use as an equestrian trail—a large horse statue fashioned out of sticks. Continue walking straight along the channel. This is arguably the least attractive part of the hike—a chain-link fence borders either side of the channel, and the plant life is limited to random shrub clusters and an occasional oak or sycamore tree.

Look up and to the east and you will see the top of a castle-like building jutting out from the trees. This is the former Vista del Arroyo Hotel, a posh Spanish Colonial Revival resort that thrived in the 1930s. It was used as a military hospital during World War II, then was restored by the government in the 1980s, and is now a U.S. Court of Appeals and federal building.

At about 1.3 miles, you will pass another small bridge on the left that crosses the flood channel; to the right is a path that leads to the park's upper parking lot. Continue straight on the trail as it heads beneath a series of bridges. The first one is the most interesting, both architecturally and anecdotally. Listed on the National Register of Historic Places, the 150-foot Colorado Street Bridge was built in 1913 to make it easier for horse-drawn wagons to cross the Arroyo Seco, and it has served as a scenic gateway to central Pasadena ever since. As the legend goes, a construction worker helping build the bridge tumbled over the side and into a vat of wet concrete below. Assuming it was futile to try to save him, his coworkers left his body in the quick-drying material. Some claim you can still hear his desperate cries and attribute them to the bridge's reputation as a popular suicide spot. Between 1919 and 1937, close to 100 people reportedly jumped to their deaths from the bridge.

After passing below the Colorado Street Bridge, the path winds under the utilitarian Ventura Freeway bridge and heads uphill briefly before dropping into a shady glen with a small stream on the left. The final 0.3 miles of the hike is serene and bucolic, despite its proximity to a major commuting thoroughfare. After passing a private home on the right, the dirt path ends at a white picket fence, and you will find yourself facing Arroyo Boulevard. Look north and you will see the parking lot for Brookside Park, Pasadena's largest park. It is about a half-mile walk along the side of the boulevard to the park's picnic area from here. Another quarter-mile leads to the Rose Bowl stadium. Or you can turn around and follow the flood-control channel back to the main parking lot.

▶ NEARBY ACTIVITIES

There's more to Brookside Park than picnic tables. The well-regarded Kidspace Museum reopened here in 2005 after operating out of a junior high school gymnasium for 25 years. Situated on 3.4 acres across from the Rose Bowl stadium, it features a nature exchange, a mini-model of Pasadena's Arroyo Seco, a tricycle racetrack, and other kid-friendly activities. For more information, go online to www.kidspace-museum.org. Next door, the Rose Bowl Aquatic Center has a state-of-the-art lap pool and lots of water-based activities for kids and adults, including swim lessons and a polo league. It's open daily. Nonmembers may use the center for a day-use fee of $10. For more information, go to www.rosebowlaquatics.org.

MILLARD CANYON: FALLS TRAIL

KEY AT-A-GLANCE INFORMATION

LENGTH: 1 mile

CONFIGURATION: Out-and-back

DIFFICULTY: Moderate

SCENERY: Oak and alder forest, waterfall

EXPOSURE: Shady

TRAFFIC: Heavy on weekends

TRAIL SURFACE: Paved sidewalk and dirt path

HIKING TIME: 45 minutes

ACCESS: California Adventure pass required to park in lot; see front of book for information on how to purchase one. Chaney Trail closed to public 8 p.m.– 6 a.m. , otherwise always open.

MAPS: USGS Pasadena

FACILITIES: Restrooms, water available at Millard Campground, a short walk from the parking lot

SPECIAL COMMENTS: It's best to avoid this trail after heavy rains, when its multiple stream crossings become treacherous with slippery rocks and rough waters.

UTM Trailhead Coordinates for Millard Canyon: Falls Trail

UTM Zone (WGS84) 11S

Easting   394410

Northing   3786745

IN BRIEF

This half-mile (one-way) hike through an oak and alder forest requires lots of boulder hopping across a wide stream. The reward is a cool, tranquil 60-foot waterfall and grotto. It's a nice hike to do on a hot summer day, though the waterfall is more like a trickle at this time of year.

DESCRIPTION

Millard (pronounced Mill-ARD) Canyon is named for Henry Millard, a beekeeper who reportedly lived in the canyon with his wife and child from 1862 to 1872. The area near northwest Altadena is known today for its popular five-site campground and 50-foot waterfall. It is also the site of Dawn Mine, which was worked for gold from the late 1800s until the 1950s but never really produced anything of significance.

To get to the waterfall trailhead, walk past the fire-road gate at the east end of the parking lot and follow the dirt path as it parallels a stream to the left. There is a private home on your right, one of several in this area that dates back to the early part of the twentieth century, when land could be leased from the U.S. Forest Service for less than $20 a year.

The first stretch of the path is exposed and sunny, but it soon turns shady and you will find yourself in the thick of an oak and alder forest. After

DIRECTIONS

From the 210 Freeway in Pasadena, exit at Lake Avenue and follow it north to the end. Turn left onto Loma Alta Drive and follow it about a mile to Chaney Trail (there is a yellow flashing light at the intersection). Make a right on Chaney and follow it uphill past wide canyon and valley views, then down the hill to the Millard Canyon parking lot. The trailhead is beyond the fire-road gate at the east end of the lot.

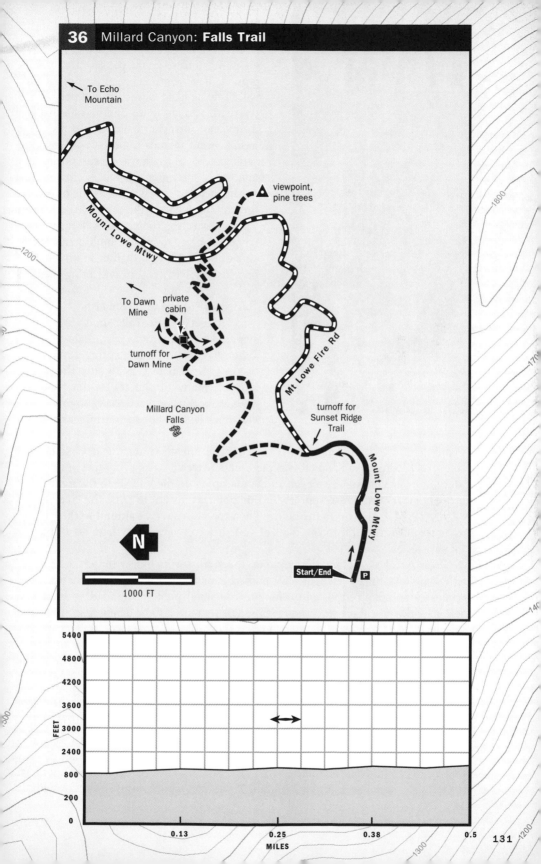

To Echo Mountain

viewpoint, pine trees

Mount Lowe Mtwy

To Dawn Mine

private cabin

turnoff for Dawn Mine

Mt Lowe Fire Rd

Millard Canyon Falls

turnoff for Sunset Ridge Trail

Mount Lowe Mtwy

Start/End

P

N

1000 FT

FEET

5400
4800
4200
3600
3000
2400
800
200
0

0.13   0.25   0.38   0.5

MILES

Millard Canyon Falls

about 0.2 miles, you'll pass Millard Campground. If it's a weekend, all five of its sites will likely be filled with tents and people. On the right is an outhouse, and beyond that is a dilapidated Airstream trailer that looks like it hasn't been moved in decades. After the campground, the path reaches the stream. You may see some mountain bikers crossing the stream here to access the El Prieto Trail to Brown Mountain. As the story goes, El Prieto Canyon was the home of a former slave named Robert Owen who built a cabin here and worked as a wood cutter in an effort to buy his family's freedom and bring them to Los Angeles from Texas. *El Prieto* means "black" or "dark one" in Spanish.

To get to the Falls Trail, follow the signed path on the right past a sign-in kiosk. When I was here in late spring 2005, there was a campaign in gear to stop the graffiti marring many of the trail's thick-trunked trees. Hikers were asked to report any suspicious behavior or abuse they might have witnessed while on the trails.

The stream is on the left as the dirt path skirts a canyon wall and crosses the boulder-strewn stream a couple of times. At about 0.3 miles you will see a deck and landscaping on the hillside to the right. Soon a sprawling dark-red house appears. At this point, you want to cross the creek again, as if you were heading up to the house. Then the path swerves around to the left and the house is on the cliff to the right of you. It's still very shady here—a brilliantly cool oasis of oak and alders.

Because of all the boulder-hopping, this path seems longer than it actually is. Just when you think you might have missed it or taken a wrong turn, the waterfall appears—a sun-dappled vision gushing into a small pool surrounded by boulders. Look up and you will see several huge boulders that seem to be dangling from the top of the waterfall. I overheard more than one person joke that they wouldn't want to be hanging out here during an earthquake, given the precarious nature of the rocks.

There are no warning signs, but take care not to climb up over or around the falls. There have been quite a few accidents as a result. The path pretty much ends here and the only way back is to retrace your steps along the stream.

After passing the campground, I felt as if I were the only one on this path. Then just before reaching the waterfall, I came on a group of high school–age kids, lolling about on the boulders. A few more steps and I found another group of young adults—a couple of them cooling their heels in the grotto by the waterfall. Soon a middle-aged couple had wandered over to the pool and staked out a prime spot near the cascade. There was room for everyone; it was just a big contrast from the solitude

I had witnessed on the path. It's definitely worth planning to spend a little time hanging out by the waterfall before turning back.

▶ NEARBY ACTIVITIES

Lake Avenue, between the 210 freeway and the trailhead, is home to several venerable southern California eateries. The Hat, 491 North Lake, established in 1951, is known for its terrific pastrami dip sandwiches. Roscoe's Chicken 'n' Waffles, 830 North Lake, serves juicy fried chicken and has a devoted following. For those watching their cholesterol, the Coffee Gallery at 2029 North Lake, which sells light snacks and beverages, might be a better choice.

MILLARD CANYON: SUNSET RIDGE TRAIL

KEY AT-A-GLANCE INFORMATION

LENGTH: 4 miles

CONFIGURATION: Out-and-back

DIFFICULTY: Strenuous

SCENERY: Waterfalls, forested canyon, views of San Gabriel Valley and Los Angeles basin

EXPOSURE: Mostly shade, some sun

TRAFFIC: Light

TRAIL SURFACE: Dirt path, paved fire road

HIKING TIME: 2 hours

ACCESS: Free; Chaney Trail closed to public 8 p.m.–6 a.m.

MAPS: At kiosk 100 yards beyond trailhead; USGS Pasadena

FACILITIES: None

SPECIAL COMMENTS: Heavy rains and other weather conditions sometimes force the closure of Millard Campground and the road leading to the lower parking lot. Check the sign at the bottom of the road before heading uphill. Also, watch out for large patches of poison oak along this trail.

UTM Trailhead Coordinates for
Millard Canyon: Sunset Ridge Trail

UTM Zone (WGS84)   11S

Easting   394295

Northing   3786563

▶ IN BRIEF

Bordered by fern- and flower-draped rock walls, this Angeles National Forest trail begins on the Mount Lowe Fire Road and quickly descends into a serene forested canyon, then climbs uphill via switchbacks to good views of the San Gabriel Valley and Los Angeles.

▶ DESCRIPTION

This trail begins at an elevation of 2,000 feet and climbs about 800 more feet to panoramic views of the San Gabriel Valley and beyond. This is another hike I discovered accidentally. I had planned to hike Millard Canyon via the Dawn Mine Trail, but I happened to show up on a school holiday when the streamside trail was crowded with a large group of giddy teenagers. They were harmless and amiable enough—it was just that I was in the mood for a quiet hike that day. So I decided instead to follow the signs for Sunset Ridge Trail, which I had passed on my way to the stream, and see what that was all about. It turned out to provide just the solitude I was looking for. This path is near my home, and I finished the hike vowing to make it a regular part of my walking/exercise agenda.

To get to the trailhead, follow the fire road east past the locked gate to a sign-in stand and a watering trough made out of local arroyo rocks.

▶ DIRECTIONS

From the Foothill freeway (210), exit at Lake Avenue and head north to the end. Turn left onto Loma Alta Drive to Chaney Trail. Turn right on Chaney and drive north about 2 miles until you reach a locked fire-road gate. Park on the side of the road. A California Adventure Pass is required to park here, as well as in the larger parking lot at the bottom of the canyon. (To purchase, see pages xii–xiii for details.)

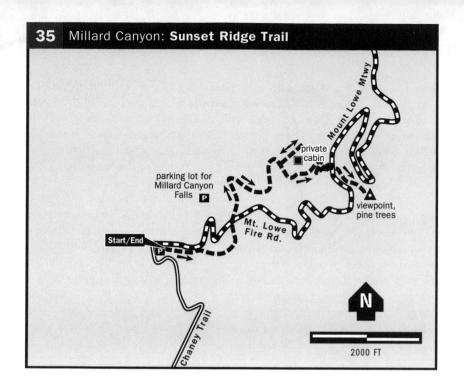

parking lot for
Millard Canyon
Falls **P**

Mount Lowe Mtwy

private
■ cabin

▲ viewpoint,
pine trees

Start/End
P

Mt. Lowe
Fire Rd.

N

2000 FT

Chaney Trail

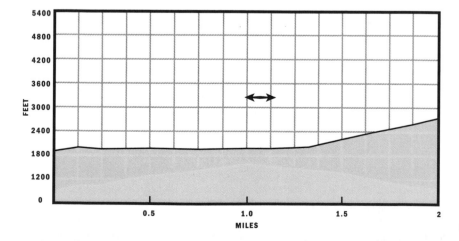

There is also an interpretive sign with a hand-drawn map and information on Mount Lowe Railway, a top tourist attraction in southern California from 1896 to 1936. Millions of visitors rode the cable incline railway to a luxury resort complex that sat atop Echo Mountain and looked out over the then-bucolic Los Angeles basin. The resort burned in the early 1900s; a century later, the area surrounding it is a popular trail system that leads to the remains of the old resort, among other destinations throughout the Angeles National Forest.

Across from the kiosk, you will see a narrow dirt path on the left side of the fire road near a brown post marked ALTADENA CREST TRAIL; this descends to Millard Campground. Continue straight on the fire road. This is the shadeless portion of the trail; it also has impressive wide-open views of the foothill community of Altadena and the Los Angeles basin. At about 0.4 miles, bear left on a dirt path marked Sunset Ridge Trail. The path quickly turns shady and secluded as it begins a gentle descent north, then east along Millard Canyon's southern wall. You will glimpse (and hear) the 50-foot Millard Canyon waterfall on the left. In the spring, gorgeous yellow wildflowers cover the rocky hills that border the right side of the path. This is a good hike if you're looking for a brief escape from everyday stress and pressures. The green mountains and sounds of nearby waterfalls have a calming effect, and make you feel like you're far deeper into the wilderness than you actually are.

At about 0.9 miles, the Sunset Ridge Trail branches off to the right and immediately ascends into dense woodland. If you follow the path straight, you'll pass a private mountain cabin and beyond that, a boulder-strewn stream that leads to an old gold mine that operated from the late 1800s to the middle of the twentieth century. Continue on the Sunset Ridge trail as it climbs in long and short switchbacks up the fern-draped canyon wall. The path turns steep, narrow, and pleasantly shady with occasional patches of sunlight. I only encountered one other hiker on this leg of the path, a man who was enthusiastically photographing the abundant spring wildflowers along the route. Among the native plants that bloom here in late winter and spring are black and white sage, white and purple California lilac, Indian paintbrush, buckwheat, and laurel sumac.

Sounds of the canyon stream serenade you as you continue walking uphill. After about half a mile of climbing, two more waterfalls come into view through the trees. Known as Punchbowl and Saucer Falls, these cascades are located on the other side of the canyon and tough to access up close. Better views of the falls await as you continue climbing the switchbacks to an elevation of 2,800 feet.

At about 1.9 miles, you will come to a level dirt clearing with good views of the of the San Gabriel Valley and Los Angeles basin. Resist the temptation to stop, and continue a few more steps to a turnoff for a trail that leads uphill to a couple of big-cone pine trees and even better views. There are no benches, but it's a good place to rest and mark the halfway point of this quiet and contemplative hike.

From here, you can rejoin the Mount Lowe fire road by following the main path another 0.2 miles and loop back to the trailhead, or retrace your steps back down the canyon. The shadier out-and-back option is a wiser choice during the hot summer months.

MONROVIA CANYON PARK: BILL CULL TRAIL

▶ IN BRIEF

Canopies of coast live oak, big-leaf maple, and sycamore trees line this pleasant trail, which is named after a volunteer and follows a stream and manmade dams to a 50-foot waterfall that runs year-round.

▶ DESCRIPTION

Located on the southern fringe of the Angeles National Forest, 80-acre Monrovia Canyon Park is run by the city of Monrovia and was the site of a resort lodge used by city dwellers as a weekend getaway between 1911 and 1945. In addition to hiking trails, it has several shady picnic areas and a nature center that hosts education programs and guided hikes. The waterfall trail, either via the Bill Cull Trail or the nature center parking lot, has an elevation gain of 600 feet and is shorter and more crowded than the Overturff Trail. The waterfall trail seems to attract a good deal of solo hikers. I once encountered a couple in office attire (he in a tie, she in sweater and slacks), squeezing in a quick brush with nature during the weekday lunch hour.

The trail can be accessed via the nature center or from the Bill Cull trailhead at the park's entrance station. The Bill Cull trailhead begins just beyond the entrance station on the left. The trail is fairly easy to follow on its own, but small signs are posted along the way directing you toward the waterfall. Follow the narrow dirt path as it winds uphill along a sunny slope and

ⓘ KEY AT-A-GLANCE INFORMATION

LENGTH: 2.6 miles

CONFIGURATION: Out-and-back

DIFFICULTY: Moderate

SCENERY: Dense woodland, waterfall

EXPOSURE: Shady

TRAFFIC: Moderate

TRAIL SURFACE: Dirt path

HIKING TIME: 1.5 hours

ACCESS: Gate open 8 a.m.–5 p.m. Wednesday–Monday; closed Tuesday; $5 parking fee

MAPS: Available at entrance gate and nature center; USGS Azusa

FACILITIES: Restrooms, water fountains, picnic areas

SPECIAL COMMENTS: Dogs are allowed in the park, but they must be kept on leashes. The 7.2-mile Ben Overturff trail, named for the Monrovia contractor who built a resort here in the early 1900s, is closed indefinitely due to mudslides caused by the 2005 storms. Park officials instead recommend following Sawpit Canyon Fire Road, which parallels the Overturff Trail and leads to same place—the remains of the lodge at Deer Park. It's always a good idea to call ahead to check conditions: (626) 256-8282.

▶ DIRECTIONS

Exit the 210 freeway in Monrovia at Myrtle Avenue and drive north through Old Town Monrovia to Foothill Boulevard. Turn right, then make a left on Canyon Boulevard and follow it for about 1 mile to the park entrance. Park in the lot just below the entrance station.

UTM Trailhead Coordinates for Monrovia Canyon Park: Bill Cull Trail

UTM Zone (WGS84) 11S

Easting 408675

Northing 3781807

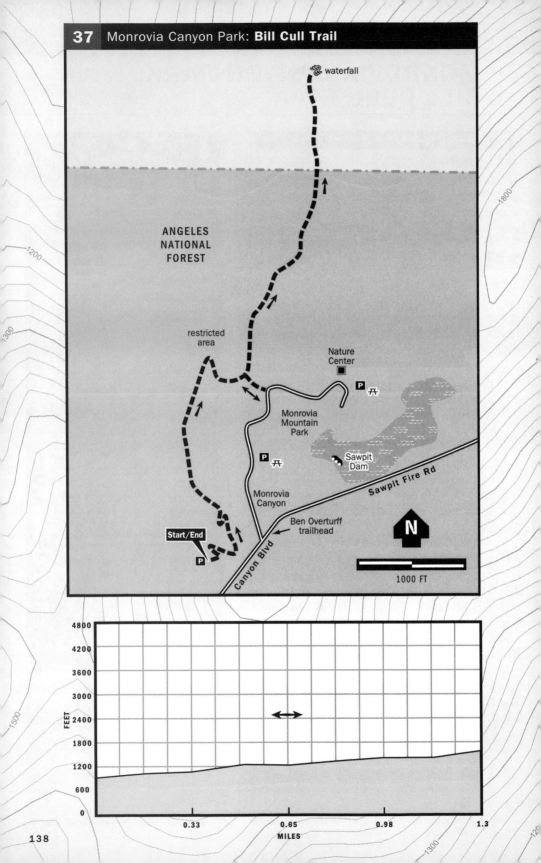

waterfall

ANGELES
NATIONAL
FOREST

restricted
area

Nature
Center

P

Monrovia
Mountain
Park

Sawpit
Dam

Sawpit Fire Rd

P

Monrovia
Canyon

Ben Overturff
trailhead

Canyon Blvd

Start/End

P

N

1000 FT

4800
4200
3600
3000
2400
1800
1200
600
0

FEET

0.33   0.65   0.98   1.3
MILES

parallels a stream below. In the late winter and spring, you can also expect to see an abundance of yellow and purple wildflowers. Watch for poison oak, which is plentiful here. At 0.2 miles, the path curves around to the right (you'll see a sign warning of a restricted area if you go straight) and continues on a gradual incline through dense groves of white alder, maple, sycamore, and coast live oak trees. I've spotted the occasional opossum and lots of gray squirrels and salamanders here; the park is also home to mountain lions, Southern Pacific rattlesnakes, deer, coyotes, and gray foxes. At about 0.5 miles, you'll pass the first of several manmade dams along the trail on your right. A little farther along, the trail crosses the stream (it's narrow and there are big rocks that make crossing easy) and you'll come to a short flight of stone steps. Follow these straight, then head left to continue toward the waterfall. If you turn right, you'll find yourself at a picnic area and parking lot in the middle of the park.

Along the Bill Cull Trail

From here, the path continues to the left of the stream and descends into a shady clearing strewn with large rocks. Continue walking as the path weaves back and forth on both sides of the stream. At about 1.3 miles, you'll reach the waterfall, which is usually gushing at full force. The boulders flanking the waterfall make for a good place to stop and enjoy a sack lunch. Or take a few moments for reflection before retracing your steps back to the parking lot.

▶ NEARBY ACTIVITIES

Before heading out of the park, stop by the Nature Center for displays of flora and wildlife native to the park and pay homage to the redwood statue of Sampson the Hot Tub Bear. As the story goes, Sampson, an old black bear, spent several months hanging out in a hot tub in the area until he ingested a plastic bag and was captured by local officials. He got used to being cared for by people and couldn't be released back into the wild. Monrovia residents made him a cause célèbre and donations poured in to save him from being put to sleep. He ended up at the Orange County Zoo (in a cage that featured a hot tub) and lived out the rest of his days there until he died in 2001. The statue was erected in 2003 as a paean to all animals that have died needlessly.

Old Town Monrovia's main street, Myrtle Avenue, is lined with antiques shops, sidewalk cafés, and mom-and-pop restaurants. On Fridays from 4 to 8 p.m. there's a farmer's market along Myrtle Avenue.

ROSE BOWL LOOP

KEY AT-A-GLANCE INFORMATION

LENGTH: 3.1 miles

CONFIGURATION: Loop

DIFFICULTY: Easy

SCENERY: San Gabriel Mountains, Rose Bowl Stadium

EXPOSURE: Sunny

TRAFFIC: Heavy

TRAIL SURFACE: Paved

HIKING TIME: 1 hour, 10 minutes

ACCESS: Free; open daily

MAPS: USGS Pasadena

FACILITIES: Public restrooms, water

SPECIAL COMMENTS: Avoid visiting this area during stadium events, such as UCLA football games and the huge outdoor flea market that takes place on the second Sunday of every month. Traffic and parking nightmares are likely. Go to www.rosebowl-stadium.com for an events schedule. In warmer months, plan your hike for the morning or evening, or bring plenty of water. This park can get very hot.

UTM Trailhead Coordinates for Rose Bowl Loop

UTM Zone (WGS84) 11S

Easting 392354

Northing 3780112

▶ IN BRIEF

Each morning, joggers, power walkers, and parents with strollers pack this flat, paved trail, which loops around the Rose Bowl stadium and an 18-hole golf course. The historic stadium and the dramatic backdrop of the San Gabriel Mountains make this path stand out from your standard neighborhood exercise route.

▶ DESCRIPTION

The Rose Bowl stadium was built in 1921 and hosted its first football game (the University of California Bears versus the University of Southern California Trojans) on October 28, 1922. Since then, it has turned into Pasadena's most recognized attraction, hosting the annual New Year's Day football game, as well as five NFL Super Bowl Games, UCLA football home games, and Major League soccer games. In the early 1990s, the city of Pasadena painted a pedestrian lane on the asphalt around the stadium and adjacent golf course. Today, it is a popular exercise route for bicyclists, strollers, walkers, joggers, and inline skaters. The best time to go is weekday mornings, when there is ample parking and there are no events to get in the way of a good uninterrupted walk or jog.

Don't expect an abundance of nature along this route; you are likely to see more cars than birds, though the path is sporadically shaded by

▶ DIRECTIONS

From downtown or points south, take the 110 north to Pasadena. Exit at Orange Grove Boulevard and turn left. Make another left on Holly Street, then right onto Arroyo Boulevard. Park in Lot K on the west side of the loop.

From the San Fernando Valley, take the 134 East to the 210 West Exit at Seco Street and turn left. Make a right on North Arroyo Boulevard. Park in Lot K.

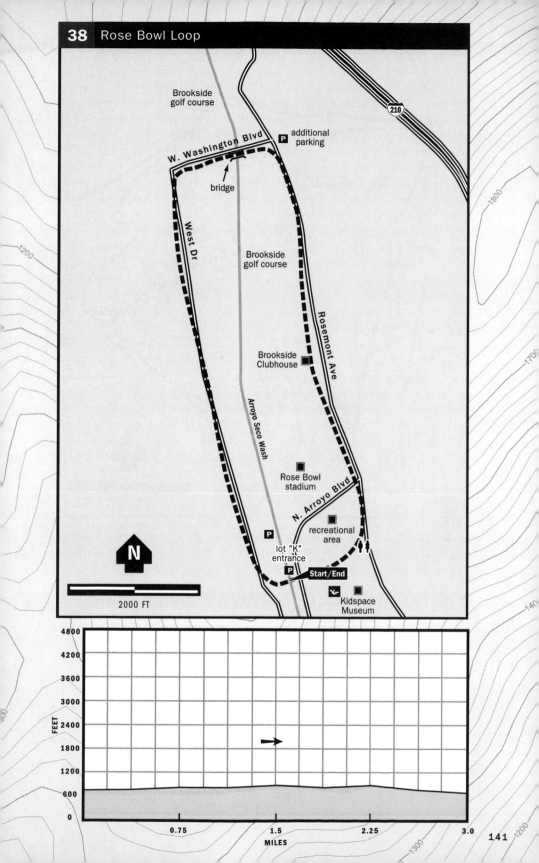

Brookside
golf course

W. Washington Blvd

additional
parking

210

bridge

West Dr

Brookside
golf course

Rosemont Ave

Brookside
Clubhouse

Arroyo Seco Wash

Rose Bowl
stadium

N. Arroyo Blvd

recreational
area

N

2000 FT

lot "K"
entrance

Start/End

Kidspace
Museum

1800

1700

1200

1400

1300

1200

FEET

4800

4200

3600

3000

2400

1800

1200

600

0

0.75

1.5

2.25

3.0

MILES

huge old oak and sycamore trees that skirt the golf course. It is most popular with residents of Pasadena and other surrounding communities, but it's worth a visit even for those from outside the area. On most days, everything seems to be in Technicolor, from the blue sky to the golf-course greens to the rainbow of roses that line the road to the stadium.

This path is accessible from any point along the loop, but most people pick it up at Lot K on the southwest corner. The pedestrian lane instructs users to follow it counterclockwise, but more people opt to take it clockwise, perhaps because the views of the San Gabriels are better.

From Lot K, follow the path as it curves north along West Drive. Soon you'll pass a small parking lot and the turnoff for Salvia Canon Road on the left, and you will see the Rose Bowl stadium on the right. After about half a mile, you will reach the edge of Brookside Golf Club, a two-course golf complex established in 1942. It gets shadier here, thanks to a few gnarled old oak and sycamore trees, and you may even spot a few squirrels and blue jays romping around. The golf course is surrounded by a chain-link fence.

Continue straight along West Drive. At about 1.3 miles, West Drive ends and the path curves to the right along Washington Boulevard. Another 18-hole golf course is on your left; it's also part of the Brookside Golf Club. You will cross a small bridge just before the path curves around again to the right and heads south back toward the stadium. At the intersection of Washington Boulevard and Rosemont Avenue, there is another small parking lot for loop patrons. This portion of the loop is more exposed to the sun than the west side. Also heed the signs for flying golf balls!

At 2.2 miles, the first golf course ends and the scenery gets less attractive. You'll pass the Brookside clubhouse on the right and a members-only parking lot. Continue along the pedestrian lane to the left of the chain-link fence. The 210 Freeway is on the left, but it's well hidden by a shrub-covered hillside. Soon you'll reach the east side of the stadium, followed by a well-kept grassy area that hosts pick-up soccer games and casual recreational activities like kite-flying and Frisbee-tossing. As the path curves around to the right and enters the final stretch, Brookside Park will be across the street on your left.

▶ NEARBY ACTIVITIES

The well-regarded Kidspace Museum is situated on 3.4 acres across from the stadium, and it features a nature exchange, a mini-model of Pasadena's Arroyo Seco, a tricycle racetrack, and other fun kid-friendly activities. For more information, go to www.kidspacemuseum.org. Next door, the Rose Bowl Aquatic Center has a state-of-the-art lap pool and lots of water-based activities for kids and adults, including swim lessons and a polo league. It's open daily. Nonmembers may use the center for a day-use fee of $10. For more information, go to www.rosebowlaquatics.org.

SWITZER FALLS VIA BEAR CANYON TRAIL

▶ IN BRIEF

The first half of this hike is a pleasant meander along a boulder-strewn creek to the remains of a turn-of-the-twentieth century resort, then the trail edges upward along a rock wall before dropping back down into the canyon near a small pool fed by a 15-foot waterfall.

▶ DESCRIPTION

The falls and picnic area are named for Commodore Perry Switzer, who apparently founded a resort here in the 1880s and used to lead visitors from Pasadena to the campsite via burro. Today, the logistics required to get here are much easier. You simply drive up the breathtaking Angeles Crest Highway from the town of La Cañada-Flintridge and leave your car in a pullout just above the campground. The area is well known in hiking and picnicking circles, so don't expect much solitude on your hike. Not long after hiking this trail, I received a summer catalog from the local community college and featured in its non-credit outdoors section was a guided Saturday hike to Switzer Falls.

To get to the trailhead from the upper parking lot, walk past the fire-road gate and down the paved road. It's a 300-foot drop in elevation from the lot to the trailhead—not so bad going down, but it can be rough going on the way back up

▶ DIRECTIONS

From the Foothill Freeway (I-210) in La Cañada-Flintridge, take Angeles Crest Highway (2) north and drive 10 miles to Switzer Falls picnic area on the right. Parking is available at pullouts at the top of the picnic area. There is also parking at the bottom of the picnic area, though this lot fills up quickly on weekends. The trail begins just beyond the footbridge on the west end of the bottom lot.

ℹ KEY AT-A-GLANCE INFORMATION

LENGTH: 5 miles

CONFIGURATION: Out-and-back

DIFFICULTY: Moderate to strenuous

SCENERY: Waterfall, stream lined with oak and alder forest, chaparral hillsides

EXPOSURE: Mostly shade, some sun

TRAFFIC: Heavy

TRAIL SURFACE: Dirt and rocks

HIKING TIME: 2 hours, 15 minutes

ACCESS: U.S. Forest Service Adventure pass required to park in lots; open daily 6 a.m.–10 p.m.; gate closes at 6 p.m.

MAPS: Posted at Clear Creek Ranger Station just west of Switzer Falls parking lot; USGS Condor Peak

FACILITIES: Picnic area, restrooms

SPECIAL COMMENTS: Slippery and unstable rocks around the bottom of Switzer Falls make it impossible to get too close. Instead, most hikers take in the main falls from a viewpoint high overhead and make do with stopping at the bottom of a smaller 15-foot waterfall located off the Bear Canyon Trail. Also expect to do some minor stream fording here; it's only a challenge if you find yourself here following heavy rains.

UTM Trailhead Coordinates for Switzer Falls via Bear Canyon Trail

UTM Zone (WGS84)   11S

Easting   394518

Northing   3792273

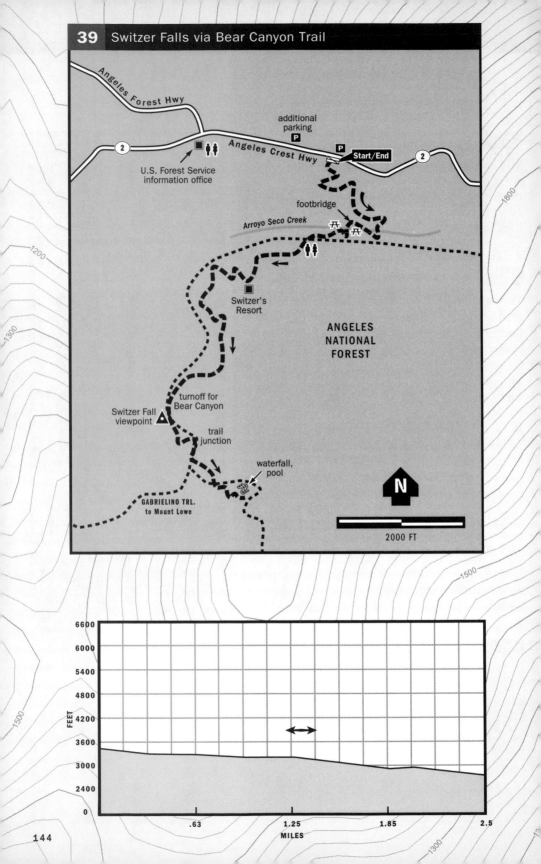

Angeles Forest Hwy

2

additional parking
P

P Start/End

2

U.S. Forest Service information office

footbridge

Arroyo Seco Creek

—1200—

Switzer's Resort

ANGELES NATIONAL FOREST

—1300—

turnoff for Bear Canyon

Switzer Fall viewpoint

trail junction

waterfall, pool

N

GABRIELINO TRL. to Mount Lowe

2000 FT

—1500—

—1500—

FEET

6600
6000
5400
4800
4200
3600
3000
2400
0

.63   1.25   1.85   2.5
MILES

—1300—

after a long hike. The road ends at the Switzer Falls picnic area. If it's a weekend, expect to see many people hanging out here. If it's a hot summer weekend, expect even more. The bottom of the canyon is an oasis of cool, with dense oak forest surrounding the gurgling Arroyo Seco creek. The fire road drops you at the west end of the parking lot. Look for the signed trail marker for the Gabrielino Trail/Switzer Falls and cross the narrow footbridge to get to the dirt path. On your right is the stream and a small clearing with a dozen or so picnic tables and barbecue grills.

Continue walking alongside the stream into a dense oak and alder forest. Beware the poison oak that lines the hillsides along this trail. The path is wide here and typically crowded with families, dogs, and frolicking kids, but the crowds thin out soon after you pass another restroom facility on the left at about 0.4 miles.

Once you've gone about a half-mile from the picnic area, expect easy back-and-forth boulder-hopping across the stream. The path is also paved for a short distance—expect a few minor potholes caused by winter rainstorms.

Just shy of a mile from the picnic area, you will begin to see the remains of Switzer's resort in the form of stone walls and cabin foundations. The resort was a top attraction for solace-seeking southern Californians in the early 1900s; it suffered damage from flooding in the 1930s and finally was demolished in the 1950s. At about 1.5 miles, you will come to a fork in the path and another Gabrielino Trail sign. Follow the trail to the right and cross the stream to get to Bear Canyon and a bird's-eye view of the falls. If you head straight on the narrower trail, you will soon run into a sign warning you to proceed to the bottom of the falls at your own risk. As an added incentive, it cites a statistic: 118 accidental falls occurred at the falls between 1975 and 1977. There is also a faded "you are here" map to give you an idea of how close you are to the bottom of the falls.

After crossing the stream, the trail begins a steep uphill climb along the west wall of the canyon. The trail is completely exposed here, so be prepared to fish a hat out of your backpack and shed a layer or two of clothing. To the left are views of the 50-foot Switzer Falls. There is no clearing or stopping area to enjoy the view, so it's best to keep walking and avoid gridlock with other hikers. A chain-link fence lines parts of the trail here and serves as protection from a precipitous drop into the canyon. At about 1.3 miles from the picnic area, you will come to a trail junction. Follow the left fork downhill toward Bear Canyon. The right-hand trail eventually ends up at the Mount Lowe Campground in Altadena.

After about 0.4 miles, the trail reunites with the Arroyo Seco creek and the shade that marked the first half of this hike. Turn left (upstream) and continue about 0.2 miles to a 15-foot waterfall running into a small pool surrounded by rock walls. Don't expect to have the pool to yourself; this area can be accessed via other Angeles National Forest trails and is often populated by mountain bikers and hiking groups on weekends. Find a vacant boulder and rest for while before retracing your steps back to the picnic area. If you parked in the upper lot, you may want to stop again at the picnic area before the steep shadeless climb back up the fire road.

STOUGH CANYON NATURE CENTER TRAIL

 KEY AT-A-GLANCE INFORMATION

LENGTH: 2.4 miles

CONFIGURATION: Out-and-back

DIFFICULTY: Moderate

SCENERY: Hills, valley views

EXPOSURE: Full sun

TRAFFIC: Light

TRAIL SURFACE: Dirt fire road

HIKING TIME: 1.75 hours

ACCESS: Free; trail open dawn-dusk

MAPS: Available at Stough Canyon Nature Center, next to trailhead; open 11 a.m.–5 p.m., Tuesday–Friday; 9 a.m.–5 p.m., Saturday and Sunday; USGS Burbank

FACILITIES: Restrooms, water fountains

SPECIAL COMMENTS: Free guided fitness hikes are offered every Tuesday and Wednesday, year-round, starting at 6:30 p.m. in the nature center parking lot.

UTM Trailhead Coordinates for Stough Canyon Nature Center Trail

UTM Zone (WGS84) 11S

Easting 379598

Northing 3786592

▶ IN BRIEF

This peaceful, sun-baked trail in the Verdugo Mountains follows a gradual incline along a well-maintained fire road to an elevation of 1,000 feet. Benches donated by local community groups dot the trail, so hikers can rest or just take some time to soak up the prime viewpoints.

▶ DESCRIPTION

I lived in Los Angeles for six years before discovering this uphill trail in the Verdugo Mountains above Burbank. It's popular with residents of the surrounding neighborhoods, but (undeservedly) doesn't have much recognition beyond the east San Fernando Valley. The Verdugos are a geologically detached part of the San Gabriel Mountains encompassing 9,000 acres; they are run by the Angeles District of the state park system and are home to chaparral, coastal sage brush, coast live oak trees, and toyon and lemonade berry bushes.

The modern nature center opened in 2001 and is a hub for maps, wildlife updates, and organized children's activities. It also hosts weekly group hikes for all ages and fitness levels (full moon, fitness, and Halloween are a few of the regular themes). Check the Web site for details: www.burbank.com/nature.shtml. Even if the center is closed, you can use the restrooms or view a detailed color map of the area near the entrance before beginning your hike.

▶ DIRECTIONS

From the I-5 freeway, exit at Olive Avenue and head northwest to Sunset Canyon Drive. Turn left on Sunset Canyon and continue to Walnut Avenue. Make a right on Walnut and follow it for 1.1 mile past the Starlight Amphitheatre and DeBell Municipal Golf Course until you reach the nature center's parking lot. The trailhead is to the left of the building.

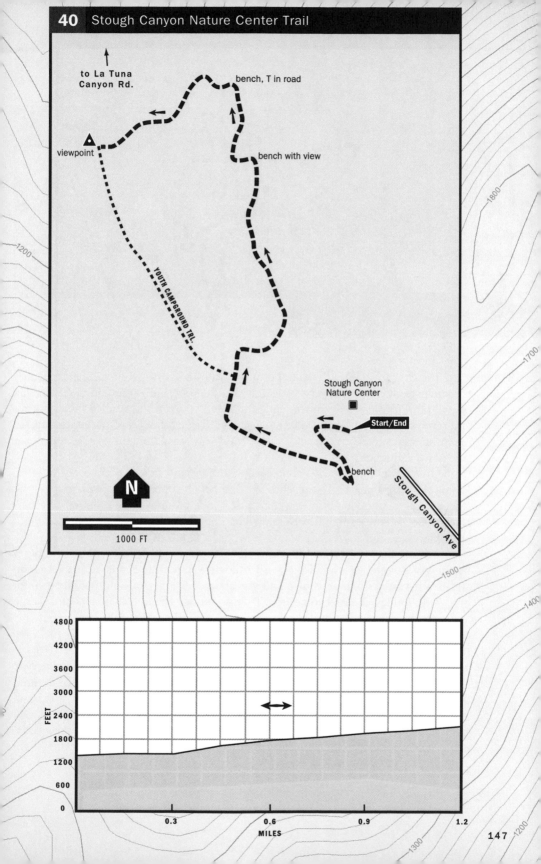

to La Tuna
Canyon Rd.

bench, T in road

viewpoint

bench with view

YOUTH CAMPGROUND TRL.

Stough Canyon
Nature Center

Start/End

bench

Stough Canyon Ave

N

1000 FT

On the way to Switzer Falls

    The Stough trailhead begins beyond a gate to the west of the nature center, climbing steadily uphill along a wide gravel path. Soon the parking lot and all signs of civilization will start to vanish, and you'll find yourself surrounded by chaparral- and scrub-covered hillsides. Don't be surprised if you pass a few random mountain bikers on their way downhill; this trail extends to La Tuna Canyon Road on the north side of the mountains and is a popular riding path. At about 0.25 miles, you'll come to the first of several benches donated by the Burbank Rotary Club. Continue following the trail uphill until it reaches another bench. Here, you'll come to a Y—the right side is a continuation of the fire trail. The left side is the beginning of a narrower, more strenuous uphill path known as the Old Youth Campground Trail. Both end up at the same point.

    As you continue to gain altitude along the fire trail, you'll come to another bench with sweeping views of the San Fernando Valley. This is a good place to stop and rest if you're tired, as you've still got about 0.5 miles of uphill climbing from here. At 0.9 miles, the trail comes to a T. This east–west road is known as the Saddle and extends from one end of the Verdugos to the other. The right path eventually connects with Wildwood Canyon Park and the Brand Park fire road to the east, whereas the left one leads to the neighborhoods of Sunland and Tujunga. This is another good place to stop and drink in 360-degree views of mountains and cityscape (from yet another bench) before heading west and continuing to climb. Keep in mind that this trail gets very hot in the summer; it's a good idea bring plenty of water and sunscreen even on cooler winter days. As you near the intersection with the Old Youth Campground Trail, you'll be able to see traffic from the 210 freeway in the distance and beyond that the (sometimes) snowcapped Mount Baldy. From here, you can retrace your steps back to the parking lot.

COAST
(Malibu, Pacific Palisades, Palos Verdes)

CHARMLEE WILDERNESS PARK LOOP TRAIL

KEY AT-A-GLANCE INFORMATION

LENGTH: 1.5 miles

CONFIGURATION: Loop

DIFFICULTY: Easy

SCENERY: Wildflowers, ocean views

EXPOSURE: Sunny

TRAFFIC: Light

TRAIL SURFACE: Dirt

HIKING TIME: 40 minutes

ACCESS: Daily 8 a.m.–sunset; $3 fee at self-pay kiosk

MAPS: Posted at kiosk near trailhead; USGS Triunfo Pass

FACILITIES: Picnic tables; park is open 8 a.m.–sunset. A small nature center open weekends 10 a.m.–noon and 2–4 p.m.

SPECIAL COMMENTS: Dogs must be kept on a leash. Keep in mind that this is rattlesnake territory; although this park is kid- and pet-friendly, be alert on the trails.

UTM Trailhead Coordinates for Charmlee Wilderness Park Loop Trail

UTM Zone (WGS84) 11S

Easting 326552

Northing 3770317

IN BRIEF

Despite a confusing lack of signage, this hike is a hassle-free trek past open meadows, coastal sage scrub, and seasonal wildflowers. Some of the unmarked trails lead to 1,300-foot bluffs and wonderful ocean views that extend as far as the Channel Islands.

DESCRIPTION

Once a cattle ranch, Charmlee Wilderness Park is now a 460-acre nature preserve operated by the city of Malibu. It includes a nature center, an 8-mile network of trails, and a shaded picnic area. Naturalists praise the park for its dozens of species of wildflowers, which include dove lupine, wild hyacinth, hummingbird sage, golden poppies, deerweed, sticky monkey flower, and coastal lotus. On the other hand, the park is also home to many nonnative trees such as eucalyptus, Italian pine, Mediterranean palm, and New Zealand *myoporum*. Even in the nonblooming fall and winter seasons, this is a good place to hike because of the park's stellar clifftop ocean views.

It's a good idea to look at a map before starting out, because the trail system is poorly marked. There is one posted at the trail kiosk near the picnic area. Maps are also available at the small nature center, but it is only open on weekends for a limited number of hours. Pick up the

DIRECTIONS

From the Ventura Freeway (101), take Westlake Boulevard south until it turns into Mulholland Highway. Bear left on Lachusa Road, then right on Encinal Canyon Road to the park entrance.

Alternate Directions: From the Pacific Coast Highway in Santa Monica, head north and turn right on Encinal Canyon Road; proceed 4 miles to the park entrance.

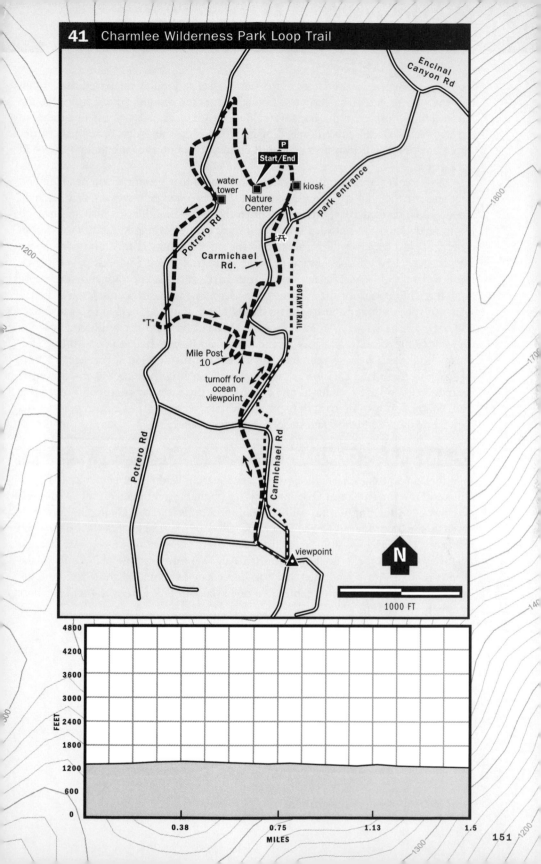

Encinal Canyon Rd

P
Start/End

water tower

kiosk

Nature Center

park entrance

Potrero Rd

Carmichael Rd.

BOTANY TRAIL

"T"

Mile Post 10

turnoff for ocean viewpoint

Potrero Rd

Carmichael Rd

viewpoint

N

1000 FT

FEET

4800
4200
3600
3000
2400
1800
1200
600
0

0.38   0.75   1.13   1.5
MILES

loop trail at the southwest corner of the parking lot and follow the paved road uphill past the nature center. The shadeless trail soon turns to dirt and curves around to the left, heading south toward a large water tank. If it's a clear day, you will be able to see the Pacific Ocean straight ahead of you. The loop trail skirts around the water tower, but you may detour up a small hill and walk around the tank for another good ocean view.

At 0.8 miles, the trail dips downhill and comes to a T. You want to head left and continue on the trail another 0.2 miles to a three-way intersection with a small wooden post marked 10. (I missed this turn the first time I did this hike and headed left instead of right. A left turn brings you back to the parking lot and makes for an easy 1.5-mile hike.) A right turn extends the hike by about 1 mile and adds about 200 feet in elevation loss and gain. The right trail takes you past a wide-open meadow to an old concrete reservoir. From here, you want to descend south to a stunning clifftop view of the Pacific. On a clear day, you can see as far as Catalina Island to the south and the Channel Islands to the north. It's a good spot to linger and soak up the scenery. From here, you can head back up the hill and across the east side of the meadow and pick up the unmarked Botany Trail at the northeast end. This will take you back to the picnic area near the parking lot. A big sign near the entrance to the picnic area warns visitors to refrain from picking the wildflowers. I encountered only one couple (having a picnic) on the Saturday afternoon I hiked this trail. Granted, it was a record-hot spring day, but I expected more people, given the park's proximity to Malibu and the San Fernando Valley.

▶ NEARBY ACTIVITIES

Visit the Santa Monica Recreation Area's headquarters and visitor center at 401 West Hillcrest Drive in Thousand Oaks to stock up on maps, get updated trail conditions, and check out rotating art and wildlife exhibits. Also featured is *Mountains, Movies & Magic*, a film coproduced by the Discovery Channel that highlights the history and resources of the Santa Monica Mountains. To get there from western Mulholland Highway, take Westlake Boulevard north to the Ventura Freeway (101) and exit at Moorpark Road. Turn right, then make an immediate left onto Hillcrest Drive and follow it 0.7 miles to the visitor center. It's open daily from 9 a.m. to 5 p.m. For more information, call (805) 370-2301.

PALOS VERDES: PORTUGUESE BEND TRAIL

▶ IN BRIEF

Gorgeous views of the Pacific Ocean dominate this well-tended Palos Verdes Peninsula trail frequented by hikers, mountain bikers, and horseback riders.

▶ DESCRIPTION

The Palos Verdes Peninsula is a 26-square-mile area located in the southwest corner of Los Angeles County. Its name means "green sticks" in Spanish. The upscale community has managed to keep big hotels and industry at bay since limited residential development began in the 1920s, and the whole area has a peaceful, rural feel that vanished long ago from most other southern California coastal areas.

There aren't many landmarks on this trail; its best feature by far is the ocean views that weave in and out of the path. On a clear day, you'll be able to spot Catalina Island and some of the northern Channel Islands. The trailhead begins at the end of Crenshaw Boulevard just beyond Burrell Lane. Walk around the gate to a packed-dirt fire road flanked by yellow wildflowers and coastal sage scrub. The backyards of several private homes are on your right beyond a chain-link fence; to the left and in front of you are sweeping views of the Palos Verdes coastline and rolling green hills dotted with distant houses. The trail descends gradually from an elevation of 1,200 feet to 500 feet. I did this hike on a weekday afternoon and saw more mountain bikers than hikers. I found out later that bikers love the

❶ KEY AT-A-GLANCE INFORMATION

LENGTH: 4 miles

CONFIGURATION: Out-and-back

DIFFICULTY: Strenuous

SCENERY: Ocean views, chaparral-covered hills

EXPOSURE: Sunny

TRAFFIC: Moderate

TRAIL SURFACE: Dirt path

HIKING TIME: 2 hours

ACCESS: Free; open daily

MAPS: USGS Torrance

FACILITIES: None

SPECIAL COMMENTS: The peninsula's first upscale resort and spa, Terranea, is expected to open in 2007 on prime oceanfront property along Palos Verdes Drive. Hike this trail before its pristine ocean view is altered forever.

▶ DIRECTIONS

From the San Diego Freeway (405), exit at Crenshaw Boulevard in Torrance and follow it to its end at Del Cerro Park. There is free parking in the park's lot from sunrise to sunset or on the street just before the trailhead.

UTM Trailhead Coordinates for Palos Verdes: Portuguese Bend Trail

UTM Zone (WGS84) 11S

Easting 373379

Northing 3736124

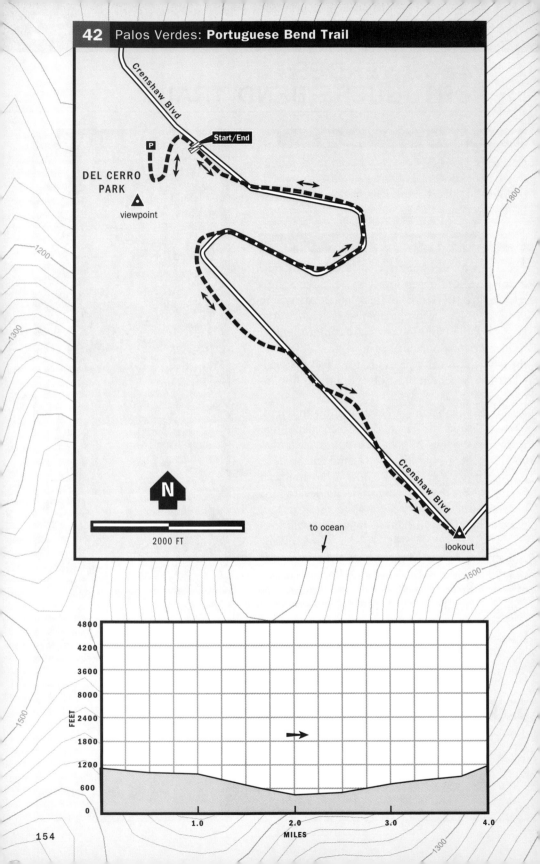

Crenshaw Blvd

P

Start/End

DEL CERRO PARK

△ viewpoint

N

2000 FT

to ocean

Crenshaw Blvd

△ lookout

FEET

4800

4200

3600

8000

2400

1800

1200

600

0

1.0   2.0   3.0   4.0
MILES

many physically challenging single-track paths that spin off the fire road near the trailhead. The main path is wide enough, though, so that their presence isn't distracting. You also can expect to spot a good number of horseback riders, especially at the lower end of the path; the Portuguese Bend Riding Club is nearby and its students and instructors use the trail for lessons and excursions.

At about 0.7 miles, the trail starts to level off and head away from the ocean, shrouded by dense foliage on the left and chaparral-covered hills on the right. The trail becomes smoother with fewer water drainage ruts at about 1.3 miles, and you'll be able to see Palos Verdes Drive, a relatively busy road that runs parallel with the ocean, in the distance to your right. As you approach the 2-mile marker, the trail climbs upward for another 0.5 miles to a small overlook with views of the Pacific. From here, you can retrace your steps for the uphill climb back to Del Cerro Park or continue on the path to a residential street that will eventually lead back to the trailhead. I prefer the out-and-back option for its ocean and hills scenery.

Cap this hike with one last spectacular view of the Pacific by walking up the grassy hill from the Del Cerro parking lot to a bench that overlooks portions of the path you just traversed.

▶ NEARBY ACTIVITIES

The Wayfarers Chapel, a glass church designed by architect Lloyd Wright (son of Frank) is arguably the Palos Verdes Peninsula's biggest tourist attraction and an easy drive from Del Cerro Park. Surrounded by gardens and a small forest of redwood trees, the chapel is made of clear glass and framed by aged redwood timbers. Among the celebrities married here: Brian Wilson, Dennis Hopper, and Jayne Mansfield. It was also recently featured on the television show *The O.C.* The chapel and grounds are open daily from 9 a.m. to 5 p.m. From Crenshaw Boulevard, turn left on Crest Road, then make another left on Hawthorne Boulevard and follow it to its end. Turn left on Palos Verdes Drive. Wayfarers Chapel is on the left at 5755 Palos Verdes Drive, across from Abalone Cove Shoreline Park.

PASEO MIRAMAR TRAIL TO PARKER OVERLOOK

KEY AT-A-GLANCE INFORMATION

LENGTH: 5.5 miles

CONFIGURATION: Out-and-back

DIFFICULTY: Moderate

SCENERY: Wildflowers, chaparral, ocean and city views

EXPOSURE: Sunny

TRAFFIC: Heavy

TRAIL SURFACE: Packed dirt

HIKING TIME: 2 hours

ACCESS: Free; open daily sunrise–sunset

MAPS: USGS Topanga

FACILITIES: None

SPECIAL COMMENTS: This trailhead begins in a dense residential neighborhood high in the hills of Pacific Palisades. Parking is allowed on the street, but heed the restrictions or your car may be towed.

UTM Trailhead Coordinates for
Paseo Miramar Trail to Parker Overlook

UTM Zone (WGS84)   11S

Easting   356277

Northing   3768863

▶ IN BRIEF

Coastal views and chaparral dominate the scenery for most of this popular Topanga State Park hike, which winds uphill along a wide, well-maintained fire road to a clearing with unbeatable views of the Pacific Ocean.

▶ DESCRIPTION

To get to the Paseo Miramar trail, you must pass through an upscale Pacific Palisades neighborhood. The road is narrow, so be wary of other cars and bicycles that might suddenly spring up on the other side of a curve. Except for one sign that points you in the direction of the trail as you head up the hill, this hike isn't well advertised. So it's all the more surprising to reach the trailhead and find a dozen or more cars parked on the street just south of it. Part of Topanga State Park's 26-mile coastal trail network, this hike is popular with mountain bikers, horseback riders, large chatty groups, UCLA students, solace seekers—you name it. The *Los Angeles Times* even ranked it number one on a 2005 list of ten essential L.A. hikes. If you don't mind the crowds and frequent whiz of mountain bikers flying

▶ DIRECTIONS

From Santa Monica, head north on Pacific Coast Highway and turn right at Sunset Boulevard. Make a left at Paseo Miramar and follow it uphill until it dead-ends at the trailhead. Make a U-turn at the trailhead and park on the west side of the street.

Alternate Directions: Take the 405 Freeway to the Sunset Boulevard exit and follow it south several miles until just before it intersects with Pacific Coast Highway. Make a right on Paseo Miramar and follow it uphill until it dead-ends at the trailhead. Make a U-turn at the trailhead and park on the west side of the street.

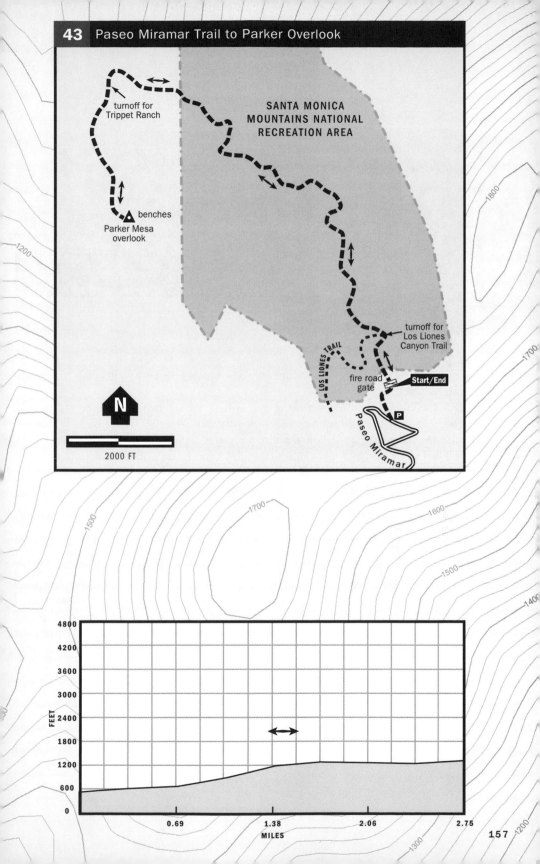

SANTA MONICA
MOUNTAINS NATIONAL
RECREATION AREA

turnoff for
Trippet Ranch

benches
Parker Mesa
overlook

turnoff for
Los Liones
Canyon Trail

LOS LIONES TRAIL

fire road
gate

Start/End

P

Paseo Miramar

N

2000 FT

1200

1800

1700

1700

1600

1500

1400

1500

1300

1200

FEET

4800
4200
3600
3000
2400
1800
1200
600
0

0.69   1.38   2.06   2.75

MILES

Resting and soaking in the view at Parker Overlook

past, it's an excellent way to introduce energetic out-of-towners to one of the more beautiful sides of L.A.

The limited number of parking spaces near the trailhead may force you to park nearby. Expect it to add up to a half mile of uphill climbing to the hike. When you get to the fire-road gate, follow the dirt path as it begins a gradual ascent past chaparral and views of the wealthy hillside neighborhoods of Pacific Palisades to the east. Soon you will be able to see the crescent-shaped coastline of Santa Monica to the south. It's just a small hint of the spectacular views to come.

Most of the trail is exposed from this point on, but salty ocean breezes help make this a comfortable year-round hike. Bring plenty of water and sunscreen, and don't expect to pass any rest areas on the way to the overlook. At about 0.25 miles, the Pacific Ocean comes into wide view on the left and pretty much stays with you for the rest of the hike. On a clear day, the deep blue horizon is stunning.

At about 0.5 miles, you will truly begin to feel like you have left civilization far behind as the trail heads deeper into the mountains. The ocean weaves in and out of view on the left. To the east, you can see as far as downtown Los Angeles, fog permitting. After about a mile of nonstop climbing, the path levels for a bit, allowing for a chance to catch your breath and revel in the scenery. In the spring and early summer, mustard, California dopper (witch's hair), purple lupine, and other wildflowers stretch for what seems like miles on either side of the path.

The trail continues flat, winding along a mountain ridgeline, then dips downhill into a rare patch of shade provided by a few coast live oak trees. Soon you will reach a wide grassy meadow and pass through another small cluster of oaks, manzanita, and chemise. At 1.8 miles, the trail begins another steep ascent as it heads northwest. You still have another 200 feet of elevation gain ahead of you, but the toughest climb is over.

At about 2 miles, you will come to a right-hand turnoff for a dirt trail leading to Trippet Ranch, a popular Topanga State Park base for hikers and bikers (it's another 2.7 miles from here). Continue straight on the gently uphill path toward Parker Mesa Overlook as it heads due south toward the ocean. There are more nice views of the Santa Monica Mountains on the right. Savor the panoramic ocean-city-mountain views as you approach the final stretch of the hike to the overlook. After a brief final climb, the trail gives way to Parker Mesa Overlook, a wide clearing with two large wooden benches with front-row views of the Pacific. If it's a clear, sunny day, don't expect to get a seat. These prime seats are often filled by hikers and bikers resting and soaking up the view. Take a break wherever you can and rehydrate before heading back to your car.

After a rest, head back to the trailhead the same way you came. The ocean and mountain views you get on the way back are just as excellent as those on the first half of the hike.

▶ NEARBY ACTIVITIES

The nearby Self-Realization Fellowship Lake Shrine is a nondenominational spiritual sanctuary with 10 acres of gardens, a spring-fed lake, and a meditation temple. Visitors are welcome; it's a nice spot to have a picnic, read a book, or just clear your head for a moment. It is located at 17190 Sunset Boulevard, just across the street from the turnoff for Paseo Miramar, and is open Tuesday through Sunday. For more information, go to www.lakeshrine.org.

SOUTH COAST BOTANIC GARDEN

KEY AT-A-GLANCE INFORMATION

LENGTH: 1.8 miles

CONFIGURATION: Loop with some backtrack

DIFFICULTY: Easy

SCENERY: Native plants, manmade lake

EXPOSURE: Sunny

TRAFFIC: Moderate

TRAIL SURFACE: Paved

HIKING TIME: 1 hour

ACCESS: $7 entrance fee; gates are open 9 a.m.–5 p.m. daily

MAPS: Available at ticket kiosk; USGS Torrance

FACILITIES: Restrooms, water

SPECIAL COMMENTS: For additional information, go to www.palosverdes.com/botanicgardens.

UTM Trailhead Coordinates for South Coast Botanic Garden

UTM Zone (WGS84) **11S**

Easting **375150**

Northing **3738924**

▶ IN BRIEF

This easy path winds past categorized gardens of drought-tolerant plants, flowering fruit trees, herbs, and roses. Its location on a former landfill and cutting-edge cultivation methods attract horticulturalists and land reclamation specialists along with garden-club groups and birders.

▶ DESCRIPTION

From 1929 to 1956, this 87-acre garden operated as an open pit mine for diatomite, a porous mineral mass used in filtration systems and insulation. When production declined, Los Angeles County bought the land and turned it into a sanitary landfill for trash. Once it reached capacity, the city agreed to plant a garden on top of it, despite its dubious location. Today, the garden has more than 150,000 plants from around the world, including eucalyptus from Australia, Chinese gingkos, Canary Island palms, and California redwoods. It's not as pristine and lush as other Los Angeles–area gardens (Descanso Gardens and the Huntington Library come to mind), but it will probably appeal to anyone who wants to combine a walk with a horticulture lesson. Weekdays are less crowded, but they also mean you're likely to encounter service trucks and noisy maintenance work along the paths.

Walk through the visitor center courtyard to the beginning of the loop trail. On the right is a fuchsia garden and a children's garden with teddybear topiaries, a doll house, and ceramic gnomes. The rose garden will be directly in front of you. Follow the path clockwise toward the gazebo and events meadow on the left. You'll soon be flanked

▶ DIRECTIONS

From the San Diego Freeway (I-405), exit at Crenshaw Boulevard and head south 8 miles to the South Coast Botanic Garden. Entrance is on the left.

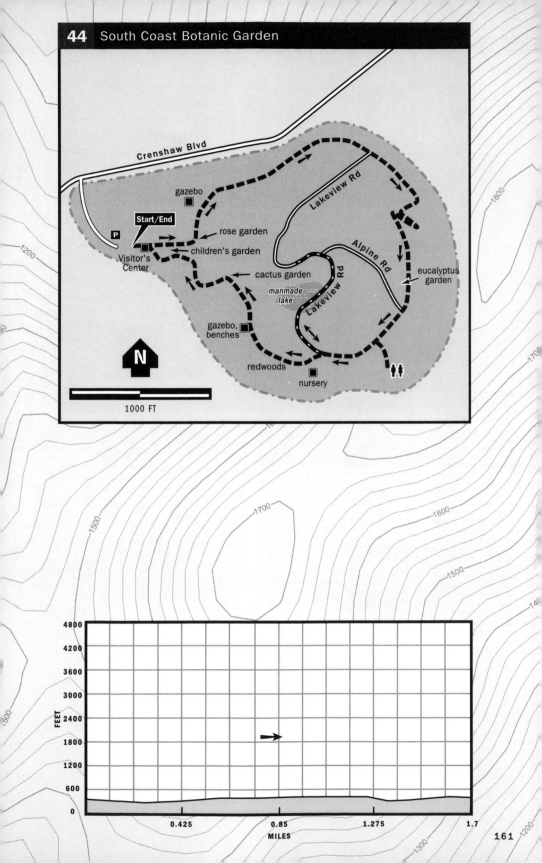

Crenshaw Blvd

gazebo

Start/End

rose garden

Visitor's
Center

P

children's garden

cactus garden

Lakeview Rd

Alpine Rd

eucalyptus
garden

manmade
lake

Lakeview Rd

gazebo,
benches

redwoods

nursery

N

1000 FT

4800
4200
3600
3000
2400
1800
1200
600
0

FEET

0.425   0.85   1.275   1.7
MILES

on either side by rows of evergreen (*Pittosporum*), ficus, and magnolia trees. At about 0.5 miles, you'll pass the first of two turnoffs for Lakeview Road. Continue straight on the main path, past gingko trees, chinaberries, and pygmy palms and a flame tree from eastern Australia. I found this area (the Plant Collections section of the park) to be the least interesting part of the gardens—few of the plants are labeled, and there seemed to be a lot of digging and plowing going on. There is also a turnoff for restrooms here on the left at about 0.8 mile into the loop. After a little more than a mile, you'll see the second turnoff for Lakeview Road on the right. It's worth a brief detour to see the manmade lake and accompanying ducks. Keep in mind, though, that no food is allowed in the gardens, except in designated picnic areas.

As the loop starts to wind back to the entrance, you'll come upon the color-theme gardens—arranged by blue-lavender flowering plants, white-flowering trees and shrubs, and blue-green and gray foliage. Also worth a look is the cactus garden on your left. It's known for its wide selection of cacti, Euphorbias, aloes, and Haworthias from Africa, South America, Mexico, and the United States. You will then pass smaller arrangements of herbs, bulbs, and California native plants before the path empties you back to the visitor center.

TEMESCAL RIDGE TRAIL

▶ IN BRIEF

This heavily traveled trail near the Pacific Coast Highway begins with a 1,000-foot ascent that gives way to panoramic ocean-and-city views, then descends into a sycamore-shaded canyon to a seasonal waterfall.

▶ DESCRIPTION

During the 1920s and 1930s, Temescal Canyon was the western headquarters for Chautauqua assemblies, the educational gatherings that featured concerts, lectures, and stage performances. The property was purchased by the Presbyterian Church in the 1940s and used as a retreat until 1995, when the Santa Monica Mountains Conservancy bought it and turned it into a park with hiking trails and picnic areas. The cabins and retreat facilities are now used as a summer camp for kids.

Do this hike on a weekday if you prefer solitude; the park is packed with a variety of people on weekends, from marathon trainers to extended families to fit parents with babies in tow. This is a great year-round hike because of the shade provided by the dense woodland that makes up a large part of the trail.

To get to Temescal Ridge, follow the signs for Sunset Trail, which begins just beyond the restrooms in the lower parking lot of Temescal Canyon Park. The dirt path descends into a wooded canyon of oak, maple, and sycamore trees

▶ DIRECTIONS

From the Pacific Coast Highway, turn east on Temescal Canyon Road and drive to the end. Parking is available in fee lots or on Temescal Canyon Road and Sunset Boulevard.

Alternate Directions: From the 405 Freeway, exit at Sunset Boulevard and follow about 8 miles to the entrance for Temescal Canyon Park. Turn right into parking lot or park on the street.

🛈 KEY AT-A-GLANCE INFORMATION

LENGTH: 3.7 miles

CONFIGURATION: Loop

DIFFICULTY: Strenuous

SCENERY: Chaparral-covered hills, panoramic ocean and city views, waterfall

EXPOSURE: Sun and shade

TRAFFIC: Heavy

TRAIL SURFACE: Dirt path

HIKING TIME: 2 hours

ACCESS: $5 parking fee at self-pay stations, or park along Sunset Boulevard or Temescal Canyon Road; park open 5 a.m.–10 p.m. daily

MAPS: Available at kiosks in parking lots and at supply store; USGS Topanga

FACILITIES: Restrooms, water fountains, supply store with snacks and maps

SPECIAL COMMENTS: Dogs are only allowed on the lower half of this trail. Bring lots of water to help you through the steep first half and watch out for poison oak.

UTM Trailhead Coordinates for Temescal Ridge Trail

UTM Zone (WGS84)   11S

Easting   358818

Northing   3768983

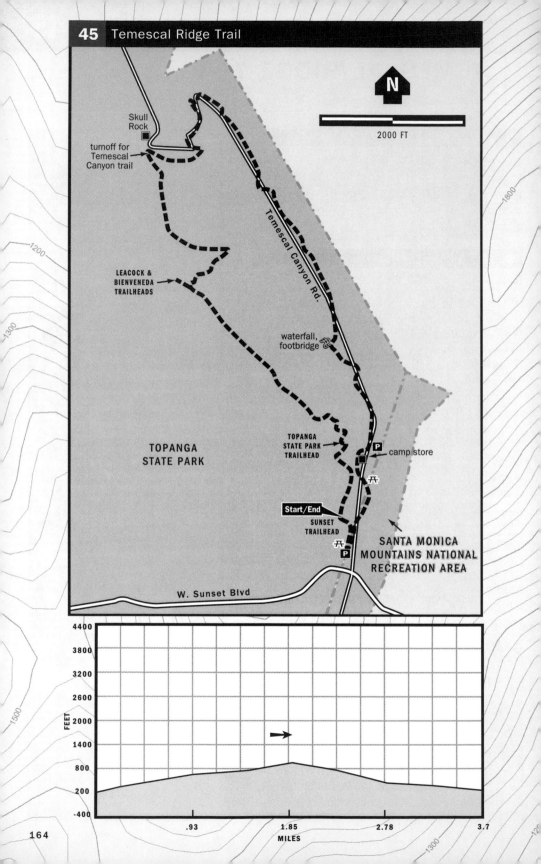

N

2000 FT

Skull
Rock

turnoff for
Temescal
Canyon trail

Temescal Canyon Rd.

1800

1200

LEACOCK &
BIENVENEDA
TRAILHEADS

1300

waterfall,
footbridge

TOPANGA
STATE PARK

TOPANGA
STATE PARK
TRAILHEAD

P camp store

Start/End

SUNSET
TRAILHEAD

P

SANTA MONICA
MOUNTAINS NATIONAL
RECREATION AREA

1500

W. Sunset Blvd

1300

FEET

4400
3800
3200
2600
2000
1400
800
200
-400

.93   1.85   2.78   3.7
MILES

and crosses a creek by way of a wooden footbridge. At about 0.5 miles, you'll come to a signed junction that marks the dividing line with Topanga State Park (this is where the no-dogs rule begins). Take the path to the left to get to Temescal Ridge. The trail to the right is an easier half-mile hike to the waterfall. You can also hike this trail counterclockwise and take the waterfall trail to Temescal Ridge. I prefer to end the hike at the waterfall.

The ridge path immediately starts to climb upward along a narrow ridgeline surrounded by tall chaparral, gaining 1,000 feet in elevation in just 1 mile. Expect to see the usual variety of Santa Monica Mountains animal life on this hike: toads, lizards, squirrels, rabbits, and the occasional mule deer or coyote.

After a few twists and turns, the trail levels at a crest with spectacular views of the southern California coastline: on a clear day, the views extend west to the ocean and Catalina Island, south to the Palos Verdes Peninsula and east to downtown. Continue past the trailheads for Leacock and Bienveneda Trails to a signed junction with Temescal Canyon. From here, you can take the half-mile trail uphill to Skull Rock, a lookout area with rock formations and even better views of downtown and the coastline, or follow the Temescal Canyon path as it begins a gradual descent through dense woodland back to the bottom of the canyon. At about 3 miles, you will reach a footbridge with a view of a small waterfall cascading over large boulders. After the winter rains, the water flow is pretty heavy; in the summer, it's not much more than a trickle. This is a good place to stop and rest or poke around a bit amid the rocks (there are a couple of smaller waterfalls upstream) before continuing the gradual 1-mile descent back to the parking lot.

▶ NEARBY ACTIVITIES

Consider hitting Will Rogers State Beach after the hike. It's a 2-mile stretch of sand, surf, playgrounds, and volleyball nets. From the parking lot, head straight on Temescal Canyon Boulevard to the intersection with Pacific Coast Highway. Turn left, then right into the day-use parking lot. If you're hungry, head north on Pacific Coast Highway a couple of miles to the Reel Inn for some fresh mahi-mahi or fish-and-chips. The ambience is surfer-casual, but the portions are ample, the prices reasonable, and the seafood top-quality. The restaurant is located at 18661 Pacific Coast Highway, just north of Topanga Canyon Boulevard.

WILL ROGERS STATE PARK: INSPIRATION POINT TRAIL

KEY AT-A-GLANCE INFORMATION

LENGTH: 2.2 miles

CONFIGURATION: Loop

DIFFICULTY: Easy

SCENERY: Coastal sage, live oak trees, panoramic views of mountains and sea

EXPOSURE: Sunny

TRAFFIC: Heavy

TRAIL SURFACE: Dirt and gravel path

HIKING TIME: 1 hour

ACCESS: $7 parking fee; open sunrise–sunset, daily

MAPS: Available at visitor center and parking kiosk; USGS Topanga

FACILITIES: Restrooms, water, picnic area

SPECIAL COMMENTS: The National Park Service began a major renovation of the main Rogers house in 2004 to repair drainage problems, add heating and cooling systems, and meet earthquake safety standards. It is expected to reopen in spring 2006.

UTM Trailhead Coordinates for Will Rogers State Park: Inspiration Point Trail

UTM Zone (WGS84) 11S

Easting 360343

Northing 3769251

IN BRIEF

Cool coastal breezes, an easy-to-navigate path, and sweeping views of the Pacific make this trail popular with families, visitors, and UCLA students. The polo field and the intact 1920s ranch house that once belonged to Will Rogers lend a historical element to the hike.

DESCRIPTION

The park was originally the private ranch of movie star Will Rogers and his family. After Rogers died in a plane crash in 1935, his wife, Betty, willed the property to the state of California with the condition that it continue to be used for equestrian activities. On any given weekend between April and October, you'll find polo games going on in the immaculate green field to the south of the hiking trails. The ranch also breeds and boards horses in the stables behind the main house.

In a way, this path represents the best and worst of Los Angeles. The panoramic views are unparalleled, and it's a great way for new transplants to convince their out-of-town friends and relatives that there's much more to L.A. than traffic and smog. But the trail to Inspiration Point is always crowded and tends to make me feel like I'm on a class field trip with an eclectic mix of people—from fit UCLA coeds and power walkers

DIRECTIONS

From the 405 freeway, exit at Sunset Boulevard and follow south 4.5 miles to Will Rogers Way. Turn right and follow Will Rogers Way 1 mile to the park's entrance. The lower lot is closest to the trailhead. The upper parking lot straddles the picnic grounds and the polo field to the south.

Alternate Directions: From Pacific Coast Highway, follow Sunset Boulevard east 1 mile to Will Rogers Way. Turn left and continue 1 mile to park entrance.

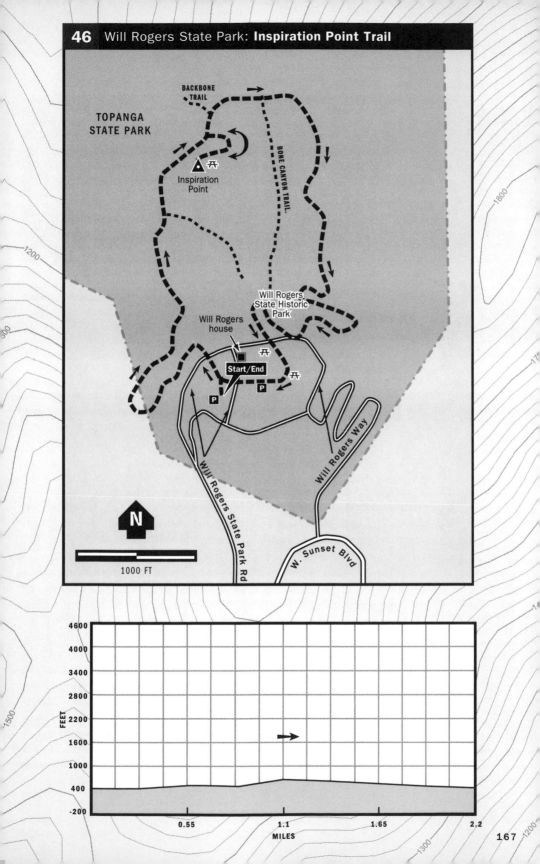

TOPANGA
STATE PARK

BACKBONE
TRAIL

BONE CANYON TRAIL

Inspiration
Point

Will Rogers
State Historic
Park

Will Rogers
house

Start/End

P

P

Will Rogers State Park Rd

Will Rogers Way

W. Sunset Blvd

N

1000 FT

1800

1200

1500

1300

FEET

4600
4000
3400
2800
2200
1600
1000
400
-200

0.55   1.1   1.65   2.2
MILES

Enjoy 360-degree views from atop
Inspiration Point.

to parents pushing jogging strollers and older couples in golf pants and sun visors. If you prefer tranquility on your hikes, plan to go early in the morning or on a weekday, or consider exploring one of the several narrow paths that extend off this trail and link up with the 55-mile Backbone Trail or empty back into the parking lot. It's difficult to get lost within this 186-acre park, thanks to plenty of sign markers and the lack of heavy forest or brush.

From the lower parking area, follow the trail upward along switchbacks bordered by a white fence. Soon you'll come to a T where a sign directs you to the left. (The right path leads to the stables and back to the upper parking lot.) Even though you're only at an elevation of 550 feet here, there are great views of the Pacific Ocean and the nearby neighborhoods of Pacific Palisades and Santa Monica. At about 0.5 miles, you'll come to another turnoff on the right that leads back to the parking lot. Keep going straight toward Inspiration Point as the trail continues north, bordered by coastal sage and scrub brush. After another 0.25 miles, you'll come to a short out-and-back trail that leads to Inspiration Point, a wide, flat expanse with picnic tables, trash cans, hitching posts, and 360-degree views that include the Pacific Ocean, the snowcapped San Gabriels, and Catalina Island to the south. It's usually fairly crowded up here, but most people tend to snap a few photos and then leave.

From here, retrace your steps back down the short path and follow the trail north. Soon you'll see a sign and trailhead for the Backbone Trail, a north–south trail that begins here and extends 55 miles to Point Mogu State Park in Malibu. This is also the border for the 11,000-acre Topanga State Park, another state park with an abundance of hiking trails. Continue on the Inspiration Point Trail as it begins to dip east and then south back to the parking lot. You'll see chaparral-covered hills to your left and pass a right turn for Bone Canyon Trail, another narrow trail that leads back to the stables and parking lot. Continue heading southeast as the trail winds past the tony mansions of Brentwood in the distance. You can also glimpse the Getty Center from here, its glass-and-chrome walls perched on a hill to the east. As the trail continues downward, a string of gnarled live oak trees lends the only shade of the entire hike. Soon you'll see the stables and grassy picnic area to your left, as the trail turns into a paved service road. Follow this south to the parking lot.

▶ NEARBY ACTIVITIES

Tours of the main 31-room ranch house, where Rogers and his family lived in the 1920s and 1930s, have been suspended until at least 2006, while it undergoes a major renovation to bring it up to speed on seismic safety and to install new heating and cooling systems. When the tours resume, it's well worth joining one. They're included in the $7 parking fee and give you a glimpse of the house as it was when Rogers lived there. Highlights include a collection of Indian rugs and baskets, a porch swing that sits smack in the center of the living room, and a mounted calf given to the legendary cowboy to encourage him to rope it instead of his friends. The visitor center, also closed for renovations, has maps, old photos, and a short film of Rogers's life. For more information, call (310) 454-8212.

If you find yourself here on a weekend between April and September, check out the polo games held every Saturday and Sunday on the field that Rogers once played with his pals Douglas Fairbanks and Tyrone Power. The field is the only outdoor regulation-size polo field in Los Angeles. For more information and a game schedule, go to www.willrogerspolo.org.

ORANGE COUNTY

BOLSA CHICA ECOLOGICAL RESERVE, HUNTINGTON BEACH

KEY AT-A-GLANCE INFORMATION

LENGTH: 3 miles

CONFIGURATION: Out-and-back

DIFFICULTY: Easy

SCENERY: Birds, marsh plants

EXPOSURE: Sunny

TRAFFIC: Moderate to heavy

TRAIL SURFACE: Paved

HIKING TIME: 1.5 hours

ACCESS: Daily 6 a.m.–8 p.m.; closed Mondays

MAPS: Available at the Bolsa Chica Wetlands Interpretive Center, 3842 Warner Avenue; USGS Seal Beach

FACILITIES: Portable toilets in parking lots

SPECIAL COMMENTS: The not-for-profit Bolsa Chica Conservancy began a major multiphase restoration project in late 2004, so access to some of the paths is restricted. For more information, contact the conservancy at (714) 846-1114

UTM Trailhead Coordinates for Bolsa Chica Ecological Reserve, Huntington Beach

UTM Zone (WGS84)   **11S**

Easting   **401783**

Northing   **3730678**

▶ IN BRIEF

Despite being sandwiched between the busy Pacific Coast Highway and a field of active oil derricks, the Bolsa Chica Ecological Reserve is a valuable wetland that is considered one of the best birding spots in the state. Several miles of paved paths around a water inlet make this a haven not only for birders but also for power walkers and families.

▶ DESCRIPTION

Developers and environmentalists recently settled a three-decade battle over the future of the Bolsa Chica Ecological Reserve. The marshland was once destined for a housing and commercial development with manmade marinas and canals, but environmental groups took the landowner to court and launched a Save Bolsa Chica grassroots campaign. The result: About 1,200 acres of the marsh have been set aside as open space and wildlife habitat, and a major rehabilitation project to remove defunct oil wells (Huntington Beach was once the seventh largest oil drilling area in the United States). The project, expected to be completed in 2008, will also rehabilitate plant life and build nesting areas for migratory birds. A housing development is still slated for about 100 acres that border the reserve, but its size has shrunk from nearly 6,000 homes to a more manageable 400.

To access the trailhead from Warner Avenue, park in the interpretive center lot and walk east along Warner Avenue to a wood kiosk that marks

▶ DIRECTIONS

From the 405 Freeway, take the Bolsa Chica exit south to Warner Avenue. Turn right on Warner Avenue and follow it west to Pacific Coast Highway. Turn left just before the road ends into the interpretive center parking lot, or turn left on Pacific Coast Highway and follow it 1 mile to a second parking lot on the left.

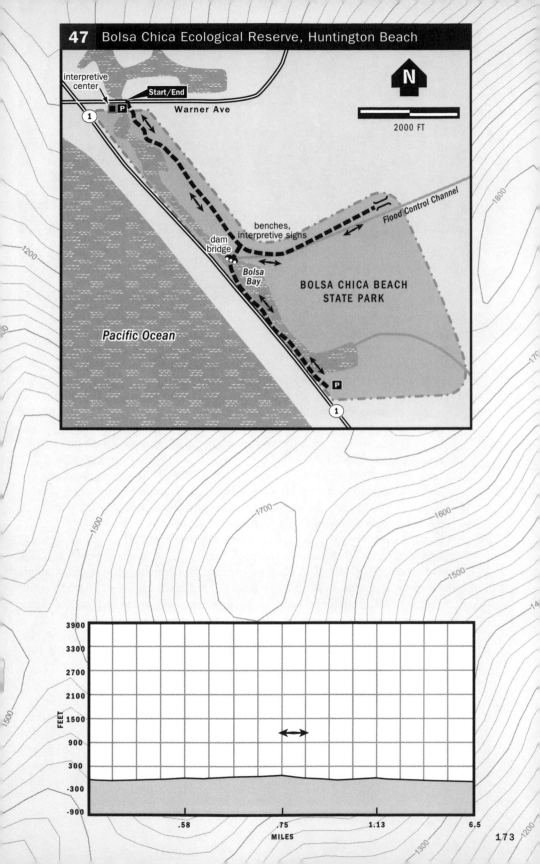

interpretive center

Start/End

Warner Ave

N

2000 FT

1

Flood Control Channel

1800

1200

benches, interpretive signs

dam bridge

Bolsa Bay

BOLSA CHICA BEACH STATE PARK

Pacific Ocean

1700

1

1500

1700

1600

1500

1500

1400

3900

3300

2700

2100

1500

FEET

900

300

-300

-900

.58   .75   1.13   6.5

MILES

1300

1200

Birds thrive within the Bolsa Chica wetlands.

the trailhead. The path follows a straight, exposed path south along the eastern side of the inlet. I recommend bringing sunscreen and binoculars on this hike. Even if you're not a serious birder, you may get the urge for a close-up view of the animal and plant activity taking place in and around the reserve.

At 0.6 miles, you'll come to a wooden fence and a group of interpretive signs that detail the reserve's wildlife and history. The salt marsh was once a popular hunting ground for Native American tribes. In the late 1800s, it was transformed into the Bolsa Chica Gun Club, a duck and fowl hunting club that dammed the original inlet, upsetting the tidal flow that brought marine life into the marsh. Later, a portion of the wetlands was used by World War II troops to watch for enemy attacks.

Today, despite its past, the reserve serves as a playground for 200 species of birds, including great blue herons, peregrine falcons, stilts, egrets, brown pelicans, and western sandpipers. Its plant life features cordgrass, prickly pear cactus, California buckwheat, tall eucalyptus, monkey flowers, and black sage. Just past the interpretive signs, you'll come to an overlook with benches and more interpretive signs. This is a popular stopping point for birding. Just beyond this, you'll come to steps that lead to a footbridge dividing the two lagoons. It is a good place to spot ducks, geese, pelicans, egrets, common loons, and herons as they wait in prey of a fish dinner. (The inlet is stocked with sea bass, halibut, and littleneck clams.)

From the footbridge, you can head east on a trail that straddles more marshland, or cross to the western side of the inlet and follow that south about a mile to a second parking lot. The latter option is the more popular one, especially for birders, although I found its proximity to the highway traffic distracting. The eastern trail is quieter and more pristine and just as abundant with birds and plant life, although some hikers may find the view of oil derricks in the distance just as distracting. At about 1.5 miles, you'll reach a bridge. Expect to see a few casual bicyclists around here, as bikes are allowed on these trails and there is access from a residential development that borders the reserve.

From the bridge, you may turn back here and retrace your steps or turn right or left to loop back to the footbridge. These alternate trails were closed temporarily when I did this hike in January, so I returned to the interpretive center the same way I had come. Before I did this hike, I thought of Huntington Beach as a traffic-choked Orange County suburb of surfer shops and tract homes. I came away with a newfound appreciation for its ability to keep development at bay from this fragile coastal habitat.

▶ NEARBY ACTIVITIES

Bolsa Chica State Beach, directly across the street from the ecological reserve, is a popular place for swimming, sunning, and surf-fishing for perch, corvina, croaker, and sand shark. Also popular during the summer is bare-handed fishing for California grunion, a species that only spawns on southern California beaches. The beach extends 3 miles from Seal Beach to Huntington Beach City Pier. A bikeway connects it with Huntington State Beach, 7 miles south.

CRYSTAL COVE STATE PARK: EL MORO CANYON ROAD TRAIL

KEY AT-A-GLANCE INFORMATION

LENGTH: 3.8 miles

CONFIGURATION: Out-and-back

DIFFICULTY: Moderate

SCENERY: Spring wildflowers, ocean-view bluffs

EXPOSURE: Sunny

TRAFFIC: Moderate

TRAIL SURFACE: Dirt path

HIKING TIME: 2 hours

ACCESS: $8 fee; gate open 6 a.m.–sunset

MAPS: Available at park office; USGS Laguna Beach

FACILITIES: Restrooms, water fountains; campsites

SPECIAL COMMENTS: After a long battle, residents of the adjacent El Moro mobile home park agreed in late 2005 to vacate the state-owned property to make way for a 60-site campground. At press time, the park was expected to be fully vacated by March 2006.

UTM Trailhead Coordinates for Crystal Cove State Park: El Moro Canyon Road Trail

UTM Zone (WGS84)   11S

Easting   423592

Northing   3714295

IN BRIEF

Bring lots of sunscreen for this tranquil, treeless hike through coastal sage scrub, grassland, and wildflower-covered hills.

DESCRIPTION

Crystal Cove State Park consists of 2,200 acres of campsites and hiking, bicycling, and horseback-riding trails. For years, it was used by the San Juan Capistrano Mission as grazing land for livestock. The land was sold to agriculture pioneer James Irvine in 1964. Irvine sold the land to the state in 1979, and it was incorporated into the California State Park System. Its location, just off the Pacific Coast Highway between the upscale towns of Newport Beach and Laguna Beach, is tough to beat—though some people may be annoyed by the newly built cluster developments that hover on either side of the park in stark contrast to the nature within it.

The trailhead for El Moro Canyon starts just beyond the stop sign at the park's entrance next to El Moro school. This is a good, mostly flat hike on its own, or you can use it to access other steeper trails within Crystal Cove State Park. There are helpful trail maps along the way with YOU ARE HERE signs, but I also recommend picking up a map from the park headquarters. A hat, sunscreen, and water are a must for this largely exposed hike.

Don't park in the school parking lot; you will likely get a ticket. Look for the fire-road gate near the entrance and take the dirt path beyond that. The path, flanked by coastal sage scrub year-round

DIRECTIONS

From the I-5 freeway, take the Laguna Beach exit and head south until the road ends at Pacific Coast Highway. Make a right and proceed north about 3 miles to the park entrance on the right.

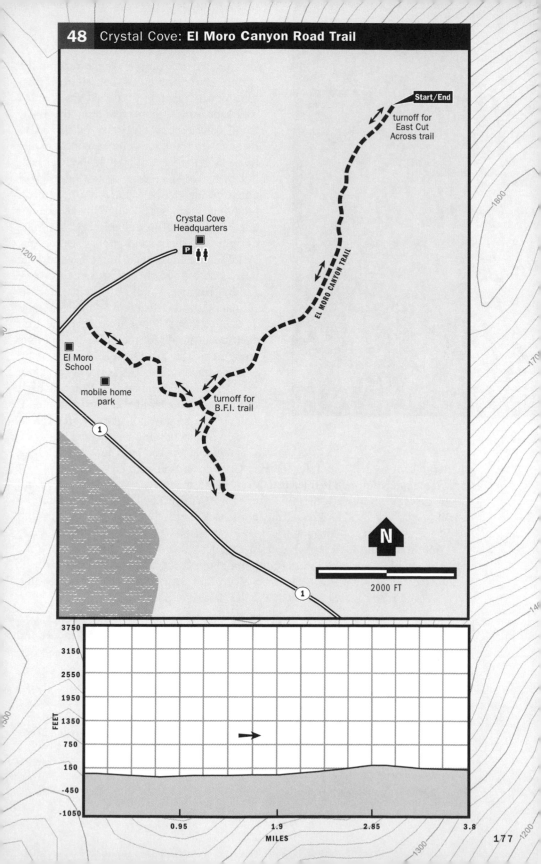

Start/End

turnoff for
East Cut
Across trail

Crystal Cove
Headquarters

P

EL MORO CANYON TRAIL

El Moro
School

mobile home
park

turnoff for
B.F.I. trail

1

N

1

2000 FT

3750
3150
2550
1950
1350
750
150
-450
-1050

FEET

0.95   1.9   2.85   3.8
MILES

Spring wildflowers cover the hillsides of Crystal Cove Park.

and yellow and purple wildflowers in the spring, starts out on a slight incline then dips down, passing a baseball field and a well-kept mobile home park on the right. You'll catch occasional views of the ocean through the buildings. You can hear traffic noise from the Pacific Coast Highway at first, but that soon fades away. A nice selection of native plants can be found within the park, including black sage, laurel sumac, lemonade berry, coastal wood fern, artichoke thistle, blue elderberry, and prickly pear cactus. Wildlife that make their home here include deer, bobcats, roadrunners, quail, ravens, turkey vultures, and two kinds of rattlesnakes, the red diamond and the Western.

At about 0.3 miles, you'll come to a right-hand turnoff for the BFI trail. Continue straight on the flat El Moro Canyon path, which parallels a small stream. This path can get a little muddy in winter. When I hiked this trail in January, it was closed to mountain bikes because of muddy conditions caused by recent rains, but pedestrian traffic was fairly heavy. The path continues straight another mile or so to a turnoff for the East Cut Across Trail, also known as "I Think I Can." It's a steep dirt path that leads to Moro Ridge, where there are picnic tables and coastal views. Continue a little farther on Moro Canyon Road and you'll come to a turnoff on the left for Poles Road. This loops back via the No Dogs Allowed Road to the ranger station and parking lot.

Another option is to retrace your steps back down Moro Canyon Road to the trailhead for BFI trail, a half-mile strenuous climb that leads to good views of the Pacific Ocean and Moro Ridge Road. At Moro Ridge, the dirt trail ends and you'll reach a paved road that leads to picnic tables and a couple of campsites.

▶ NEARBY ACTIVITIES

After your hike, walk across Pacific Coast Highway to the 3-mile stretch of beach that is also part of Crystal Cove State Park. Highlights include a broad bay that consistently ranks among the cleanest beaches in southern California, a multiuse coastal trail and a 1,140-acre protected underwater park that welcomes snorkelers and scuba divers. If you're in need of a refreshment, don't miss the well-regarded Shake Shack, a bright yellow roadside stand overlooking the cove that has served terrific frothy drinks and sandwiches for 50 years.

FULLERTON PANORAMA TRAIL

▶ IN BRIEF

This sterile, hassle-free trail begins at the edge of a golf course and climbs steadily to views of Orange County and the Santa Ana Mountains, then enters a residential neighborhood.

▶ DESCRIPTION

The trailhead starts at the western end of the parking lot. Follow the path to the right as it dips toward the golf course. Despite the signposts labeling the path a nature trail, the first thing you'll see as you begin to walk is an active oil pump (labeled Hole 75) on the right, framed by green hills and the San Gabriel Mountains in the distance. Soon you'll come to a gravel pathway on the left marked EQUESTRIAN TRAIL. Follow that upward past a couple of turnoffs for small overlooks on the right. They look out over the Coyote Hills Golf Course. To the left are views of the Santa Ana Mountains and the Orange County cities of Orange, Santa Ana, Tustin, and Irvine. Interpretive signs point out that two birds dwell here: the coastal cactus wren and California gnatcatcher.

After about 0.5 miles you'll come to a gate as the path enters a residential neighborhood. The trail's "panoramic" views end here, because a string of large two-story homes rings the path on both sides. The second leg of the trail is

▶ DIRECTIONS

Take the 60 Freeway east to I-57 South. Exit at Yorba Linda Boulevard and head west. Make a right on N. State College Boulevard, and another left onto Bastanchury Road. Turn left almost immediately into the Summit House restaurant parking lot. If you see the entrance for Coyote Hills Golf Course, you've gone too far. The trail begins at the far western side of the parking lot. Look for a sign that reads FULLERTON PANORAMA NATURE TRAIL.

ⓘ KEY AT-A-GLANCE INFORMATION

LENGTH: 3 miles

CONFIGURATION: Out-and-back

DIFFICULTY: Easy

SCENERY: City and mountain views, golf course, residential homes

EXPOSURE: Sunny

TRAFFIC: Light

TRAIL SURFACE: Gravel and dirt

HIKING TIME: 1.5 hours

ACCESS: Free; open daily dawn–dusk

MAPS: USGS La Habra

FACILITIES: Public restrooms at baseball field at trail's halfway point

SPECIAL COMMENTS: For a list of all Fullerton hiking trails, go to www.ci. fullerton.ca.us/comm_serv/parks/ traillist.html

UTM Trailhead Coordinates for Fullerton Panorama Trail

UTM Zone (WGS84)   11S

Easting   417326

Northing   3751141

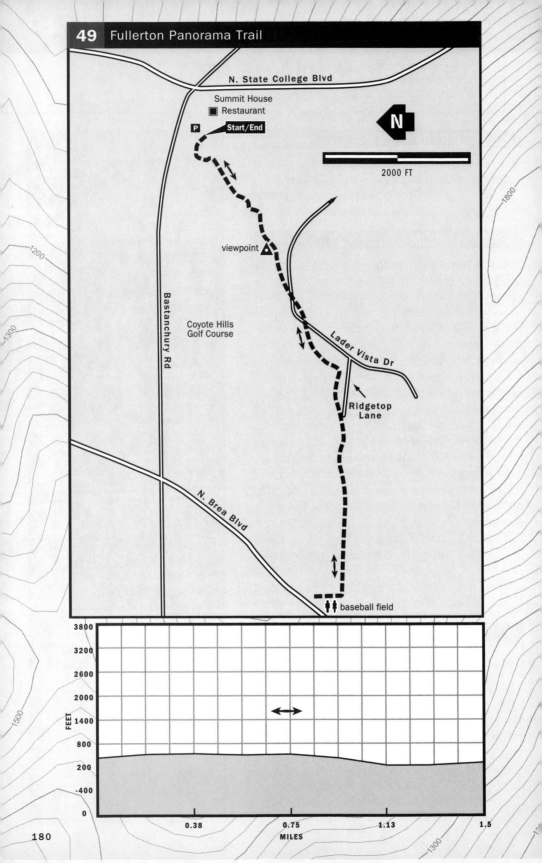

N. State College Blvd

Summit House
■ Restaurant

P

Start/End

N

2000 FT

viewpoint

Bastanchury Rd

Coyote Hills
Golf Course

Lader Vista Dr

Ridgetop
Lane

N. Brea Blvd

baseball field

3800
3200
2600
2000
1400
800
200
-400
0

FEET

0.38   0.75   1.13   1.5
MILES

somewhat anticlimactic, as you leave the views behind and enter a manicured suburban environment.

When you reach Ridgetop Lane, cross the street and follow the trail to the right along a white fence. At 1.3 miles, the paved path turns into dirt and begins a gradual incline through dense forest along a green chain-link fence. The golf course is on your right and private homes are to the left.

The trail ends at Brea Boulevard, near another oil pump and a small parking lot next to a baseball field with public restrooms. From here, you can retrace your steps back to the Summit House parking lot.

▶ NEARBY ACTIVITIES

The Summit House Restaurant serves hearty English pub food like prime rib and fish-and-chips in a comfortable atmosphere. There's no dress code, but keep in mind that you might find yourself in the middle of a swanky wedding party, especially on a weekends. It's open for lunch and dinner.

The Richard Nixon Library and Birthplace is another nearby attraction. Just follow Yorba Linda Boulevard east instead of west from I-57. For more information, go to www.nixonfoundation.org.

HACIENDA HILLS TRAIL

KEY AT-A-GLANCE INFORMATION

LENGTH: 3.6 miles

CONFIGURATION: Loop

DIFFICULTY: Moderate

SCENERY: Mountains, trees

EXPOSURE: Sun and shade

TRAFFIC: Moderate

TRAIL SURFACE: Gravel, dirt path

HIKING TIME: 2.25 hours

ACCESS: Free; trail closed sunset–sunrise

MAPS: Available at 7th Avenue kiosk or www.habitatauthority.org/trailaccess.html; USGS El Monte

FACILITIES: Restroom at parking lot at 7th and Orange Grove Avenues

SPECIAL COMMENTS: Time your visit so it doesn't coincide with the evening rush hour; traffic heading east on the Pomona freeway (SR 60) can be heavy.

UTM Trailhead Coordinates for Hacienda Hills Trail

UTM Zone (WGS84)   11S

Easting   407834

Northing   3763864

IN BRIEF

This dirt path loop is a gradual climb through cool forest and sun-baked switchbacks to 1,000-foot elevation and views of downtown Los Angeles, the coastal plains of Orange County, and the wooded community of La Habra Heights.

DESCRIPTION

The Hacienda Hills Trail is part of the Skyline Trail in the Puente-Chino Hills Wildlife Corridor, an unbroken chain of plant and wildlife habitat that extends about 30 miles from the Cleveland National Forest in Orange County to the west end of the Puente Hills in Los Angeles County. According to the Sierra Club, the hills represent the largest intact native habitat of its size in the urban Los Angeles basin. They are maintained by the Puente Hills Landfill Native Habitat Authority, a collaborative effort of Los Angeles County, the city of Whittier, and the Sanitation Districts of Los Angeles. which was created in 1984 to mitigate the effects of the nearby Puente Hills Landfill. The majority of hikers here seem to be residents of the Hacienda Heights area out for their weekend exercise jaunts, but it never seems overly crowded. Dogs are allowed, and mountain bikes are permitted in parts of the preserve.

This trail begins just beyond the gate of a chain-link fence at the west end of Orange Grove Avenue in a residential neighborhood. The gate is usually locked, but hikers can pass through an opening on the left side. You can also gain access

DIRECTIONS

From I-5, take the Pomona Freeway (CA 60) east to 7th Avenue/Hacienda Heights. Follow 7th Avenue about a mile until it dead-ends at Orange Grove. Turn right and park at the end of the street. The trailhead begins on the other side of the chain-link fence.

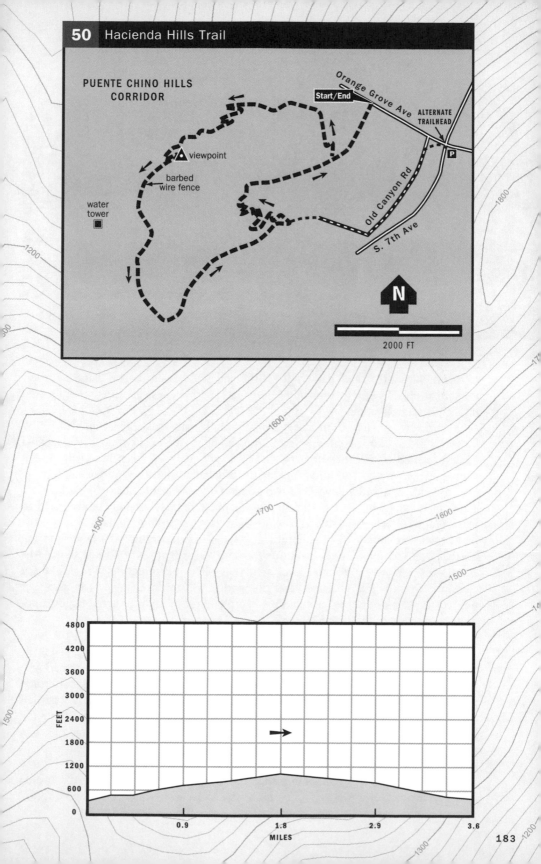

PUENTE CHINO HILLS
CORRIDOR

Orange Grove Ave

Start/End

ALTERNATE
TRAILHEAD

P

viewpoint

barbed
wire fence

Old Canyon Rd

water
tower

S. 7th Ave

1200

N

2000 FT

1800

1700

1600

1600

1700

1500

1600

1500

1500

4800

4200

3600

3000

2400

1800

1200

600

0

FEET

0.9   1.8   2.9   3.6
MILES

A view of the Hsi Lai Buddhist Temple from Hacienda Hills

to this trail from the small parking lot at the end of 7th Avenue. The Habitat Authority spiffed up this area in September 2005, adding benches, interpretive signs, and native-plant landscaping.

Begin by walking south along the chain-link fence past private homes. Wildflowers, cactus, and coastal sage scrub line the right side of the trail. There's also a piece of rusted-out farm equipment that looks like it hasn't been moved for half a century. Soon you'll come to a sign for the Habitat Authority Wilderness Preserve. Stay to your right and follow the dirt path as it dips west into shady forest before a series of uphill switchbacks. Look for the San Gabriel Mountains (snowcapped in winter) and inland urban sprawl to your right as you continue to ascend. Soon the flat, brown Puente Hills Landfill and a few radio towers will come into view to the north. Continue uphill on the path. Just beyond a sign that reads NO BIKES PAST THIS POINT, you'll come to a small level area that offers panoramic views of the San Gabriels, downtown Los Angeles, and the landfill. Off to the east, you can also spot the red pagodas of the Hsi Lai Buddhist Temple. Built in 1988, it is the largest Buddhist monastery in the United States.

This is a good spot to rest and drink some water before completing the loop. Despite the pockets of shade, much of this path is exposed to direct sunlight, so bring plenty of sunscreen and water. From here, the trail winds downhill to a barbed-wire fence and string of electric transmission towers. Bear left toward the water tower and follow the path south along the fence about 0.5 miles until you reach a Y. Head left (away from the brown sign marked multipurpose trail) as the trail winds back into the shady knoll that marked the beginning of the hike. At 2.5 miles, you'll come to a T in the path and a marker indicating that Orange Grove Avenue is to the left and 7th Avenue is to the right. Head left (unless you parked in the 7th Avenue lot) as the trail follows a few short switchbacks downhill and flattens into a wide, dirt path leading back to Orange Grove Avenue. Urban noises like leaf blowers and horns honking will start to intrude as you reenter the residential neighborhood.

OAK CANYON NATURE CENTER: BLUEBIRD AND WREN TRAILS

▶ IN BRIEF

Shrouded by oak forest and serenaded by a small stream, this family-friendly hike offers a cool escape on a hot and cloudless day.

▶ DESCRIPTION

Bordered by a golf course and several upscale gated communities, Oak Canyon Nature Center is a 58-acre park made up of three adjoining canyons that are tucked into the Anaheim Hills. Some of its hiking trails were damaged by the 2005 rainstorms that ravaged southern California, but the south side of the park remains open. Quails, scrub jays, raccoons, rabbits, and coyotes are among the wildlife that can be found here. Also located on site is an amphitheater and the John J. Collier Interpretive Center, a small museum with wildlife and natural history exhibits. Don't hesitate to ask the friendly front desk staff to recommend a hike or go over the park's conditions before hitting the trails. At press time, the Roadrunner Ridge and Quail trails were closed due to severe storm damage. Repairs were under way, but it wasn't clear when the trails would reopen.

Start off by taking the dirt path uphill to the western hillsides behind the nature center. The path then heads south and is surrounded by coastal sage scrub, tall grass, and oak trees. It was heavily overgrown when I was here in April, but I found it fairly easy to navigate, even while carrying my infant son in a Baby Bjorn. There are

▶ DIRECTIONS

From downtown Los Angeles, take the Golden State Freeway (I-5) south to the 91 Freeway east toward Riverside. Exit at Imperial Highway (CA 90) and head south to E. Nohl Ranch Road. Turn left, drive 1.7 miles and make a left onto Walnut Canyon Road. The park entrance is 0.5 miles ahead.

ⓘ KEY AT-A-GLANCE INFORMATION

LENGTH: 2 miles

CONFIGURATION: Out-and-back

DIFFICULTY: Easy with a few difficult spots

SCENERY: Oak forest, stream

EXPOSURE: Shady

TRAFFIC: Moderate

TRAIL SURFACE: Packed dirt and paved

HIKING TIME: 1 hour

ACCESS: Free; daily, 9 a.m.–5 p.m., April–October; daily, 9 a.m.–3 p.m., November–March

MAPS: Available at Nature Center; USGS Orange

FACILITIES: Restrooms, water

SPECIAL COMMENTS: No pets, horses, or bicycles are allowed in the park. Watch out for poison oak, especially after a bout of heavy rain, which tends to leave the trails overgrown

UTM Trailhead Coordinates for Oak Canyon Nature Center: Bluebird and Wren Trails

UTM Zone (WGS84)   11S

Easting   429952

Northing   3744509

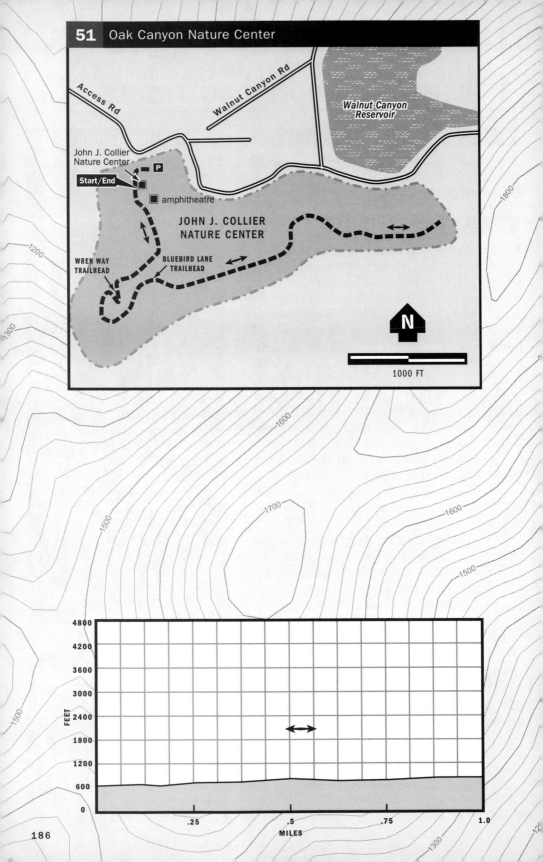

John J. Collier
Nature Center

Access Rd

Walnut Canyon Rd

Walnut Canyon
Reservoir

P

Start/End

■ amphitheatre

JOHN J. COLLIER
NATURE CENTER

WREN WAY
TRAILHEAD

BLUEBIRD LANE
TRAILHEAD

N

1000 FT

Thick stands of oak dominate the trails of Oak Canyon Nature Center.

a few small loop detours along this path, but they never wander very far from the main trail.

At about 0.3 miles, you will come to a sign for Wren Way. Follow the path up some rough steps to the right. At this point the trail turns to pavement and winds along a sunny ridge above the canyon. It also crosses a series of concrete gutters, which require some minor jumping (small children can be lifted across). If you look up, you will see some rooftops from homes that line the ridgetop surrounding the park. The trail quickly leads you back to nature, though, as you follow a short, steep flight of steps into the cool, leafy canyon and the path turns to dirt again.

At about half a mile, you will come to a Y. Take the right turnoff for Bluebird Lane and head uphill. Then the path levels (again, I found it to be overgrown and tricky to navigate) before heading downhill and turning into pavement again. It is very shady here and you can see and hear the stream on your left. At about 1 mile, the trail ends at a primitive fence made out of discarded telephone poles. A desk volunteer told me that some visitors like to extend the hike by crossing over the fence and following a narrow path northwest to a reservoir. From here, you can access a 3-mile loop trail that winds around the water. The path is easy to find, but it is thick with poison oak. If you're not dressed appropriately, I don't recommend the extension. From the fence, you can retrace your steps back to the parking lot. When the northeastern side of the park is open, you can also access the Roadrunner Ridge Trail from here and loop back to the parking lot, instead of going out and back.

▶ NEARBY ACTIVITIES

The nature center has all kinds of kid-friendly activities, such as Hikes for Tykes, crafts lessons, and storytelling hours. It also hosts 45-minute presentations for kids and adults on subjects like animal survival strategies and insect habitats. For more information, go to www.anaheim.net/ocnc/special.html, or call (714) 998-8380.

PETERS CANYON
LAKE VIEW TRAIL

KEY AT-A-GLANCE INFORMATION

LENGTH: 2.6 miles

CONFIGURATION: Loop

DIFFICULTY: Easy to moderate

SCENERY: Freshwater marsh, grassland, coastal sage scrub

EXPOSURE: Sunny

TRAFFIC: Moderate

TRAIL SURFACE: Paved

HIKING TIME: 1 hour, 15 minutes

ACCESS: $3 parking fee at self-pay kiosk, open daily 7 a.m.–sunset

MAPS: Available at kiosk near trailhead; USGS Orange

FACILITIES: Portable bathrooms in main lot, benches, water

SPECIAL COMMENTS: The park is open to hikers, joggers, mountain bikers, and equestrians. Pets are allowed but must be on a leash. For more information, go online to www.ocparks.com/peterscanyon.

UTM Trailhead Coordinates for Peters Canyon Lake View Trail

UTM Zone (WGS84)   11S

Easting   429408

Northing   3738480

IN BRIEF

This loop trail on the eastern edge of Orange County skirts a 55-acre reservoir past marshland, flowering cactus, and groves of willow, sycamore, and black cottonwood trees. Hundred-foot elevation gains at a couple of points make this a little harder than the average reservoir loop trail. The trail can be extended by several more miles by taking one of the handful of moderate-to-difficult trails that wind through the southern portion of the park.

DESCRIPTION

James Peters was a nineteenth-century farmer who grew barley and beans in the upper part of the property and lived near a eucalyptus grove in the lower reaches of his namesake canyon. Once owned by agriculture pioneer James Irvine, it was purchased by the Orange County Parks Department in 1992 and turned into a public park. During World War II, it was used as a training area for the U.S. Army, which staged mock battles there.

This hike circles a reservoir that was built in 1931 to regulate the flow of water taken from nearby Irvine Lake to conserve rainwater runoff and irrigate crops to the south of the park. Waterfowl that can be found here include mallards, snowy egrets, osprey, double-crested cormorants, and belted kingfishers. Other birds spotted include gnatcatchers, Cooper's and red-tailed hawks, and cactus wrens. A second reservoir was built in the lower half of the park in 1940; it is now dry and serves as a flood-control basin.

DIRECTIONS

From downtown Los Angeles, take the Golden State Freeway (I-5) south to Chapman Avenue in Orange. Follow Chapman east through Old Towne Orange to Newport Avenue. Turn right, then make a left onto Canyon View Avenue. The park entrance is 0.25 miles on the left.

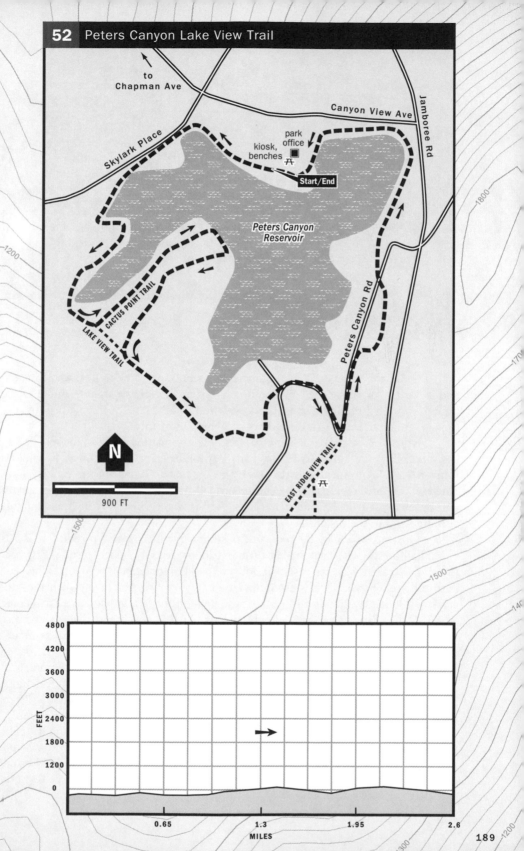

to Chapman Ave

Canyon View Ave

Jamboree Rd

Skylark Place

kiosk, benches

park office

Start/End

Peters Canyon Reservoir

CACTUS POINT TRAIL

LAKE VIEW TRAIL

Peters Canyon Rd

EAST RIDGE VIEW TRAIL

N

900 FT

FEET

4800
4200
3600
3000
2400
1800
1200
0

0.65   1.3   1.95   2.6
MILES

The Lake View Trail skirts a 55-acre reservoir.

Besides the reservoir, Peters Canyon has a running creek, a freshwater marsh, and a variety of trails used by mountain bikers, horseback riders, and exercise hounds from surrounding neighborhoods. It is meticulously maintained by the Orange County Department of Harbors, Beaches, and Parks.

The Lake View trailhead begins beyond the information kiosk in the main parking lot. Follow the single-track dirt path downhill and to the right as it parallels Canyon View Road, then hugs the reservoir. The first 0.5 miles of the trail is dominated by wildflowers, coastal sage scrub, and tall grass; the scenery then gives way to a freshwater marsh as the path moves closer to the water. The low-lying Anaheim hills surround you in the distance.

At just shy of a mile, the trail widens, and you will come to a turnoff for Cactus Point Trail on the left. Take the left turn and follow it past clusters of flowering cactus and a clear view of the reservoir and the parking lot from which you came. The path then rejoins the Lake View Trail. This is one of two points at which the trail gains a little in elevation. Continue past the dam on the left and soon you will come to a T. This is Peters Canyon Trail, which runs north to south and covers the entire length of the park. From here, you can either turn left and follow the trail as it continues to skirt the reservoir back to the parking lot, or turn right to access the park's backcountry trails. If you choose the latter, expect to encounter a good number of mountain bikers, who favor the challenging up-and-down terrain of the East Ridge View Trail, which loops south past a grove of eucalyptus trees and rejoins Peters Canyon Trail at the park's southernmost end.

If you take a left turn at Peters Canyon Trail, you will find that the trail ascends again about 100 feet, then winds past another viewpoint (with bench) at the 2-mile marker. After this, you will come to the least attractive part of the hike, as the trail edges away from the water and comes distractingly close to busy Jamboree Road on the right. At the junction with Canyon View Avenue, the path reverts briefly back to a single-track before depositing you in the main parking lot.

▶ NEARBY ACTIVITIES

After your hike, head to Old Towne Orange, a pedestrian-friendly square mile of restaurants and shops that bills itself as the antiques capital of California. To get there from Peters Canyon, turn left on Canyon View as you exit the park, then make a right on Newport and follow it to Chapman Avenue. Turn left on Chapman and follow it west until it runs right into the town center. For more information, go to www.oldtowneorange.net.

VENTURA CANYON AREA
(including Simi and Antelope Valleys)

ARROYO VERDE PARK LOOP (VENTURA)

KEY AT-A-GLANCE INFORMATION

LENGTH: 3.4 miles

CONFIGURATION: Figure 8

DIFFICULTY: Moderate

SCENERY: Chaparral, seasonal wildflowers, coastal views

EXPOSURE: Sunny

TRAFFIC: Moderate

TRAIL SURFACE: Packed dirt

HIKING TIME: 1.5 hours

ACCESS: Open daily; Monday–Saturday free; $1 parking fee on Sundays

MAPS: Available at kiosk just beyond the entrance gate. Also available online at www.ci.ventura.ca.us/resources/maps/arroyo_verde_trail_map.pdf; USGS Saticoy

FACILITIES: Restrooms, picnic areas, water fountains throughout park

SPECIAL COMMENTS: Rattlesnake warnings abound in this park; heed them, particularly during the hot summer months. This is also mountain lion country; several hikers spotted one in June 2004, according to a sign posted at the trailhead kiosk

UTM Trailhead Coordinates for Arroyo Verde Park Loop (Ventura)

UTM Zone (WGS84)   11S

Easting   294916

Northing   3796074

IN BRIEF

This hike near downtown Ventura runs parallel with a popular picnic area then quickly turns backcountry with rugged terrain and a 300-foot elevation gain that leads to nice views of the Pacific Ocean and Channel Islands.

DESCRIPTION

At first glance, Arroyo Verde Park looks like any manicured city park. A lush green lawn gives way to picnic areas, playgrounds, and a couple of baseball fields. Weekends draw families with young kids and hand-holding couples; it is also a popular place for outdoor birthday parties and as a photo backdrop for bridal and prom parties. But look beyond the edges and you'll see hints that there is more to this park than just pretty landscaping. High in the hills surrounding it, you will find hikers and runners making their way through dense chaparral and semi-rugged terrain to viewpoints that overlook the park and the Pacific Ocean.

The trails here don't have names. The map posted at the kiosk lists them in color code as Least Difficult, Difficult, and Most Difficult. Even after completing one, I'm not sure which one I did; I probably visited all three to some degree. I wouldn't worry about following a specific path too rigidly because except for elevation gains, the

DIRECTIONS

Take the 101 Freeway North to Victoria Avenue in Ventura, and drive north 2 miles to Foothill Road. Turn left on Foothill and follow to the park entrance on your right.

Alternate Directions: From the Pasadena area, take the Foothill Freeway (210) North to the Ronald Reagan Freeway (118) and head west toward Ventura. Take the 118 until it dead-ends at Foothill Road. Turn left on Foothill and follow it to the park entrance on right.

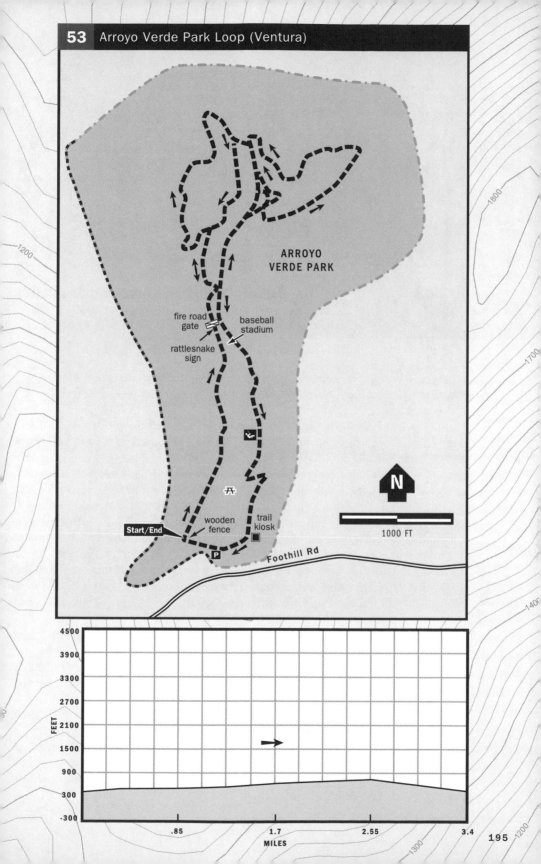

ARROYO
VERDE PARK

fire road
gate

baseball
stadium

rattlesnake
sign

N

1000 FT

Start/End

wooden
fence

trail
kiosk

P

Foothill Rd

A view of the Pacific Ocean from the hills of Arroyo Verde Park

scenery is basically the same throughout the park, and all trails eventually empty you back to the parking lot. The trails also get enough traffic that you never feel like you are completely alone.

I began my hike at the Hazel Snodgrass picnic area near the park entrance. There were plenty of open parking spaces throughout the park, even on a Saturday with a baseball game going on. From the park entrance, look for the brown wood fence and sign for Hazel Snodgrass; the trailhead is just beyond that. Follow the path north as it briefly dips, then flattens and winds through shady forest as it parallels the park's picnic areas. At about 0.7 miles, come to some steps that descend to the back parking lot. Look for the fire-road gate and rattlesnake warning sign, and take the path beyond it as it climbs uphill. From here, I made a series of lefts that took me on a loop through the park's northwestern side. Yellow and white wildflowers were everywhere (it was April), framing the bulk of the park's trail, giving way to chaparral slopes and views of the Pacific Ocean. Butterflies and bees crisscrossed the path often, so it is best to wear long pants if you find yourself here in the spring. Also bring plenty of sunscreen and a hat to protect yourself from the sun.

After completing the loop on the northwestern side, I found myself back at the fire-road gate. I wasn't quite ready to return to the car, so I reentered the backcountry area and started taking right turns on a trail that led east and uphill to more views of Ventura, the lower portion of the park, and the ocean. You can also see Anacapa and Santa Cruz islands, two of the five islands that make up the Channel Islands, a nearly isolated archipelago run by the National Park Service and known for their diversity of plant, animal, and marine life.

The views on the park's northeastern side weren't much different from the first loop, but the elevation was slightly higher at 750 feet. I also saw more people on this side of the park—mostly joggers and dog walkers who probably came from the surrounding residential neighborhoods.

Despite the lack of well-marked trails, I enjoyed spending an afternoon at Arroyo Verde Park. It's an easy getaway from L.A., especially if you take the less-crowded 118, yet the scenery and lackadaisical pace make it seem like it's much farther. My family and I like to visit Ventura a couple of times a year—we hit the beaches, which are always less crowded than our own, stroll the pedestrian-friendly Main Street, stop at a few produce stands (this is prime strawberry territory) and revel in the hassle-free parking. I will definitely be adding a stop at Arroyo Verde Park to the agenda.

▶ NEARBY ACTIVITIES

Ventura's Main Street, a couple of miles west of the park entrance, is a great place to hang out after a hike. The street between Ventura and Laurel avenues is lined with antiques and thrift shops, casual restaurants, and several good used bookstores. Don't miss the sublime burgers at Top Hat Burger Palace, a tiny outdoor stand at the corner of Main and Palm. A couple of other landmarks: the San Buenaventura Mission at 211 E. Main Street and the Ventura Theatre, an excellent live-music venue just off Main Street on Chestnut.

CORRIGANVILLE PARK LOOP TRAIL

KEY AT-A-GLANCE INFORMATION

LENGTH: 2 miles

CONFIGURATION: Loop

DIFFICULTY: Easy

SCENERY: Oak forest, sandstone rock formations, Santa Susana Mountains

EXPOSURE: Mix of sunny and shady

TRAFFIC: Light

TRAIL SURFACE: Dirt path

HIKING TIME: 50 minutes

ACCESS: Free; park open 6 a.m.–sunset

MAPS: USGS Simi Valley East

FACILITIES: Portable bathrooms, water, picnic tables

SPECIAL COMMENTS: The Hummingbird Trail (p. 205) can be accessed via a connector trail in Corriganville Park, though it requires crossing the freeway by way of an unattractive tunnel.

UTM Trailhead Coordinates for Corriganville Park Loop Trail

UTM Zone (WGS84)   11S

Easting   347854

Northing   3792728

IN BRIEF

This low-maintenance hike winds through an oak-shaded forest and the remnants of the park's heyday as a movie set, then follows a loop trail past dramatic sandstone rock formations. It's perfect for small children and out-of-town visitors who happen to be movie buffs.

DESCRIPTION

Founded by stuntman and B-movie actor Ray "Crash" Corrigan, Corriganville Park was one of the busiest movie sets in the country between the late 1930s and the 1950s. Among the hundreds of westerns and adventure films that shot scenes here were *The Adventures of Rin Tin Tin, Robin Hood, The African Queen,* and *Fort Apache.*

In 1949, Corrigan opened the property to the public as an amusement park featuring stunt shows, stagecoach rides, pony rides, and a working Western town. It was quite popular, attracting as many as 20,000 visitors on weekends. Major wildfires destroyed many of the sets in the 1970s, and the area languished until the city of Simi Valley purchased about 250 acres in 1988 and turned it into a regional park. Today it is used mainly as a hiking and jogging site, with an interpretive trail that chronicles the park's nature and wildlife as well as its former role as a movie set. The eastern part of the park is part of the Santa Susana Pass wildlife corridor, a tunnel designed to allow animals to migrate between the Simi Hills and the Santa Susana Mountains without having to cross the freeway.

DIRECTIONS

From downtown Los Angeles, take the Golden State Freeway (I-5) north to Highway 118 in Simi Valley. Just after crossing the Ventura County line, exit at Kuehner Drive, make a left and drive about a mile to Smith Road. Turn left, following the signs for Corriganville Park. Park in the large lot.

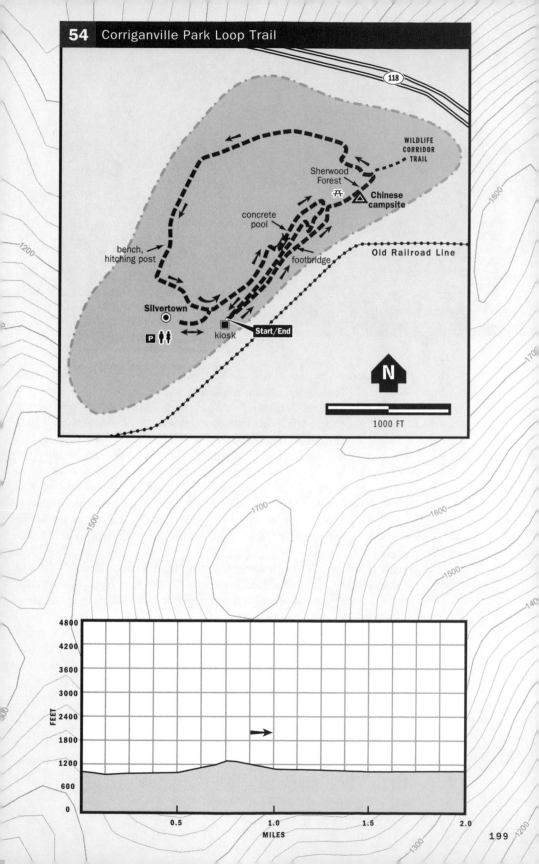

118

WILDLIFE
CORRIDOR
TRAIL

Sherwood
Forest

**Chinese
campsite**

concrete
pool

bench,
hitching post

footbridge

Old Railroad Line

Silvertown

P

kiosk

Start/End

N

1000 FT

1800

1200

1700

1600

1500

1700

1400

1500

FEET

4800

4200

3600

3000

2400

1800

1200

600

0

0.5

1.0

1.5

2.0

MILES

1300

1200

199

Sandstone rock formations dominate the second half of this hike.

To get to the Interpretive Trail, walk to the northeast end of the parking lot and look for the trail kiosk. There is a water fountain here and a current trail map on display, as well as an old brochure and map from the park's days as a western-themed amusement park. Follow the packed-dirt trail past coast live oak trees, purple elderberry plants, and a handful of picnic tables on the left. Numbered signs along the trail point out the natural and historic highlights of the area. The path parallels an old railroad line dating back to the late nineteenth century. On the right across from a bench is a preserved mound of rock material used during construction of a railway tunnel that connected Chatsworth with Simi Valley. Soon you'll cross a footbridge and a small stream. The next sign, at about 0.2 miles, marks the site of the camp where Chinese laborers stayed in the early 1900s during the construction of the railroad tracks and tunnel.

Just past the campsite, you will come to a sign for Sherwood Forest. The oak trees on the left were featured in the film *Robin Hood,* according to the interpretive sign. This is also a good point to observe birds native to Simi Valley, such as sparrows, roadrunners, wrens, and thrashers.

At about 0.25 miles, you will pass a picnic pavilion on your right and another kiosk with a map and interpretive sign detailing the area's wildlife, including gray squirrels, coyotes, skunks, jackrabbits, and rattlesnakes. Just past the kiosk, the trail splits. To the right is the rugged Wildlife Corridor Trail, which heads north under the freeway via a tunnel and links up with other trails within the Rancho Simi Recreation and Park District. Take the path to the left and cross a small bridge that straddles what appears to be a dilapidated concrete drainage tunnel (more on this later).

The environment immediately changes from dense woodland to arid, sunny desert. Follow the trail uphill toward the large sandstone rock formations and distant views of the Santa Susana Mountains that dominate the second half of this hike. You can also see and hear the 118 Freeway to the north, but I didn't find this to be overly distracting. In the spring, the boulders are attractively framed by colorful wildflowers. At about 0.6 miles, the still-shadeless path descends past rocky hills and more rock formations. There are few signs here, but the boulder caves surrounding the trail were apparently featured in many films and TV shows, including *The Fugitive* and *How the West Was Won.*

At about 0.75 miles, the path turns to pavement and there's a bench and hitching post on the left. Follow the road to the left as the pavement quickly turns back into dirt. To the right is a clearing below you. This is the remains of Silvertown, a cluster of building facades once used by filmmakers as a western-style Main Street. At about a mile, turn right and walk 50 yards to get a closer look at Silvertown. Wildfires destroyed most of the set in the 1970s, and all that remains today are a few building foundations and low-lying rock walls.

Retrace your steps back to the main path, which soon turns shady again and resumes its role as a interpretive nature trail. At 1.3 miles, the path curves to the right past some picnic tables. At the wooden-fenced bridge, turn to the north and look at the empty concrete tunnel under you. This was built specifically to shoot water scenes at Corriganville for films like *Robin Hood, The African Queen,* and *Jungle Jim.* Look for the square portholes on the sides of the walls; these were used as camera holes to capture the underwater shots. After the bridge, the path heads left under more shade trees and picnic tables, then curves back to the southwest to rejoin the interpretative trail and parking lot.

▶ NEARBY ACTIVITIES

The Oak Tree Restaurant, at 1555 Kuehner Drive, just before the turnoff for Corriganville Park, is a good place to fuel up for breakfast or lunch after your hike. It has an all-but-the-kitchen-sink menu—burgers, tuna sandwiches, quesadillas, and pancakes are just a few of the items—and plenty of indoor and outdoor seating. There's even an extensive list of specialty coffee drinks.

DEVIL'S PUNCHBOWL LOOP

KEY AT-A-GLANCE INFORMATION

LENGTH: 1.2 miles

CONFIGURATION: Loop

DIFFICULTY: Moderate

SCENERY: Rock formations, San Gabriel Mountains, juniper and pine trees

EXPOSURE: Sunny

TRAFFIC: Light

TRAIL SURFACE: Dirt path and boulders

HIKING TIME: 45 minutes

ACCESS: Free; gate open sunrise–sunset; nature center open daily 8 a.m.–4 p.m.

MAPS: Available at nature center and posted on outdoor kiosk; USGS Valyermo

FACILITIES: Restrooms, water, picnic tables

SPECIAL COMMENTS: Be sure to bring plenty of water and sunscreen if you hike this trail in the summer. Temperatures can hit the blistering three digits, and there is very little shade along the path. Spring and fall, when the temperatures range from 50–75°F, are the most popular times to visit.

UTM Trailhead Coordinates for Devil's Punchbowl Loop

UTM Zone (WGS84)   11S

Easting   421130

Northing   3808400

IN BRIEF

This loop trail descends 300 feet into a stunning bowl-shaped gorge formed by the collision of three earthquake faults millions of years ago. Green and snowcapped in winter, the San Gabriel Mountains add a dramatic border to the park's stark white cliffs and tortured terrain.

DESCRIPTION

This 1,300-acre park on the edge of the Mojave Desert gets its name from early Native Americans who lived in the area and believed the land was inhabited by mountain lion demons. Now a part of the Los Angeles County park system, the park is located where the San Andreas, Pinyon, and Punchbowl faults meet. The constant movement along the faults squeezes the underlying sandstone layers, pushing them upward, while wind and water erosion has sculpted the gorge into a breathtaking hodgepodge of peaks and pinnacles at an elevation of 4,700 feet. It is only an hour's drive from Los Angeles, but you will feel like you are a world away from the city a few minutes into the hike.

Below the Punchbowl rim, a juniper and piñon pine forest nourishes native mammals, reptiles, insects, and birds.

I arrived at the park on a late weekday afternoon and only had time to do the 1-mile loop trail before sundown. It's a decent workout and a good introduction to the area. The Burkhart Trail, for instance, is a steep 8-mile trek up switchbacks

DIRECTIONS

Take the I-5 Freeway north to the Antelope Valley Freeway (14). Get off at the Pearblossom Highway exit, turn left, and follow the signs to Pearblossom Highway (CA 138). Continue to Longview Road (also known as CR N6), turn right, and drive 7 miles. Turn left at Devil's Punchbowl Road and continue 1 mile to the park.

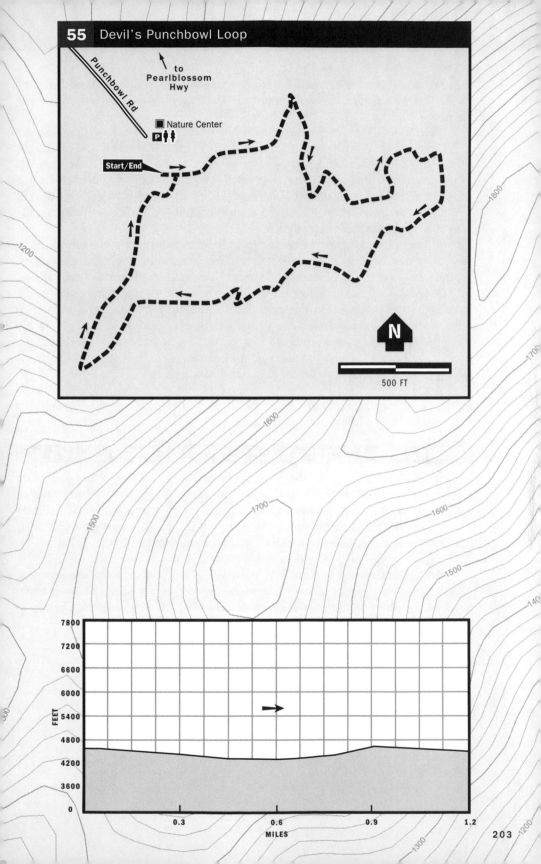

Punchbowl Rd

to
Pearlblossom
Hwy

■ Nature Center
P

Start/End

N

500 FT

7800
7200
6600
6000
5400
4800
4200
3600
0

FEET

0.3   0.6   0.9   1.2
MILES

to Devil's Chair, an overlook with 360-degree views of the rock formations. I encourage anyone who visits to allow enough time—at least three hours—to fully explore the park's offerings.

The loop trailhead begins behind the Nature Center. If you have time, stop by the center and speak with the ranger on duty to get the lowdown on trail conditions (the path is sometimes blanketed by snow in winter). The loop trail is well marked with signs, so it's difficult to lose your way, though the many boulders that cover parts of the trail can make it a little confusing. The Punchbowl is home to an array of desert plant and wildlife, including red manzanita, juniper, and piñon pines, Pacific rattlers, geckos, and great horned owls.

Almost immediately, you'll see the giant sculpted sandstone rocks for which the park is famous. At about half a mile, the trail loops around to the right; to your left you may hear the gurgle of a seasonal stream that lies at the bottom of the canyon. At 0.7 miles, you'll come to sign on the left marked CREEK that leads down to the stream. Continue straight on the loop trail to a small, level area, with wide-open views of the rock formations (this is a good photo opportunity). Soon you'll reach a stone bench and the path will start to ascend. You'll pass more stone benches and a sign for the Burkhart Trail on the left. Continue straight past a shady grove of picnic tables on the left toward the nature center and parking lot.

I only saw one couple on the trail when I did this hike on a weekday afternoon in March. Weekends tend to be busier, when the trails attract a mix of picnicking families and serious hikers and mountain bikers.

▶ NEARBY ACTIVITIES

The tiny town of Pearblossom, about 8 miles from Devil's Punchbowl, is a good place to stop for lunch or fresh produce. Valley Hungarian Sausage and Meat, a casual eatery along Route 138, is known among road-trip junkies for its housemade sausage and deli sandwiches. Charlie Brown Farms is another rest stop on Route 138 catering to tourists; it specializes in barbecue, shakes, candy, and all types of kitschy souvenirs. Its Web site can be found at www/charliebrownfarms.com.

Another interesting side trip is St. Andrew's Abbey, a Benedictine monastery in nearby Valyermo. There is a tiny church with services every Sunday, a meditation pond, and a shop selling religious-themed ceramics. For more information, go to www.valyermo.com.

HUMMINGBIRD TRAIL

▶ IN BRIEF

Despite its proximity to a busy highway, this trail can be quite beautiful, combining dramatic rocky outcroppings with delicate wildflowers. The consistent elevation gain of 500 feet makes for a good workout as well. This hike can also be extended by switchbacking another mile or so uphill to a junction with Rocky Peak Trail, a popular path leading to a viewpoint with an elevation of 2,700 feet and one of the highest points in Simi Valley.

▶ DESCRIPTION

Once the domain of the Chumash Indians, Simi Valley was discovered by eastern pioneers in the mid-nineteenth century as an ideal farming site for sheep and cattle. The name *Simi* allegedly came from the Chumash word *Shimiji*, which means little white clouds. Settlement began in earnest in the late 1880s. Today, the area has grown to a city of 110,000 people that's known for its affluent gated communities and record low crime rate, though the wide open spaces that attracted such residents as Ronald Reagan can still be found amid the suburban sprawl. This trail offers a window into both sides of the area—the dramatic rocky outcroppings that date back to the Chumash, and clear views of a major freeway and tightly packed residential developments with street names like Cowboy Court and Sasparilla Drive.

Don't let the nondescript trailhead and dreary brown landscape beyond stop you from exploring

▶ DIRECTIONS

From downtown Los Angeles, take the Golden State Freeway (I-5) north to the Ronald Reagan Freeway (118) in Simi Valley and head west. Exit at Kuehner Drive and turn right at the bottom of the ramp. Follow Kuehner 0.4 miles to a pullout parking area on the right side of the road. The trailhead begins at the opening in the chain-link fence. There is no sign marking the trail.

ⓘ KEY AT-A-GLANCE INFORMATION

LENGTH: 2.4 miles

CONFIGURATION: Out-and-back

DIFFICULTY: Strenuous

SCENERY: Simi Valley views, spring wildflowers, sandstone rock formations

EXPOSURE: Sunny

TRAFFIC: Light

TRAIL SURFACE: Dirt and gravel

HIKING TIME: 1.25 hours

ACCESS: Free; open daily sunrise–sunset

MAPS: USGS Simi Valley East

FACILITIES: None

SPECIAL COMMENTS: This trail is best hiked in the spring, when the wildflowers are in glorious bloom and the weather hasn't yet reached the triple digits. It can also be accessed from a connector trail in Corriganville Park, though it requires crossing the freeway by way of an unattractive tunnel

UTM Trailhead Coordinates for Hummingbird Trail

UTM Zone (WGS84)   11S

Easting   347032

Northing   3794488

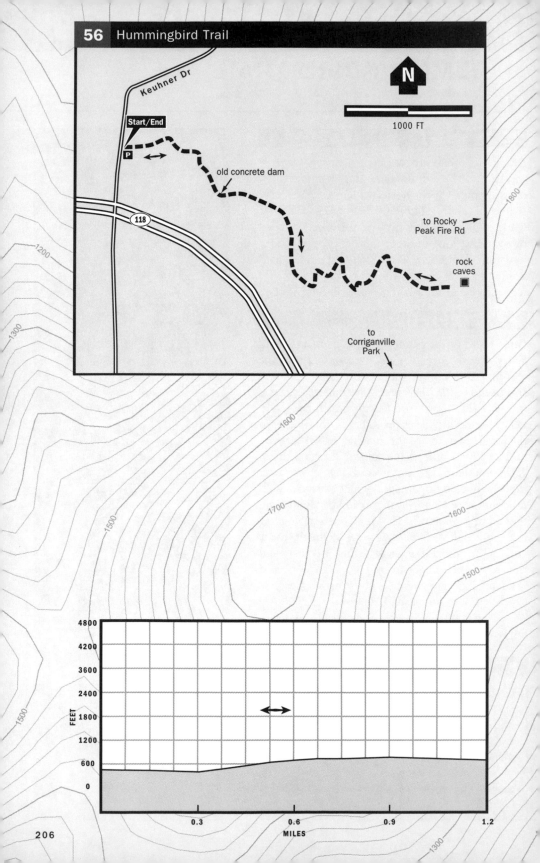

56 Hummingbird Trail

Keuhner Dr

Start/End

P

old concrete dam

N

1000 FT

118

to Rocky
Peak Fire Rd

rock
caves

to
Corriganville
Park

1800

1200

1300

1600

1700

1600

1500

1500

1500

1300

FEET

4800
4200
3600
2400
1800
1200
600
0

0.3   0.6   0.9   1.2

MILES

this trail. It's worth it to persevere, especially if you find yourself here in the spring. Yellow and purple wildflowers are in abundant bloom and the hovering little birds that give the trail its name are guaranteed to dominate your hike.

To get to the trailhead, pass through the open gate of a nondescript chain-link fence that sits just north of the 118 freeway. Follow the loose dirt path east as it heads downhill between a couple of oak trees, then take the first right back toward the highway. I had this trail all to myself on a weekday afternoon, though the freeway noise that accompanied most of the hike reminded me I was never completely alone. Don't be surprised if you cross paths with mountain bikers headed down the trail toward the parking lot. They tend to take this trail one-way downhill, accessing it from the north–south Rocky Peak fire road.

At about 0.4 miles the trail makes a steep descent, then crosses over a cement dam. At this point, the rocky outcroppings you will soon be scaling are straight ahead

A view of rock outcroppings from the bottom of the Hummingbird Trail

of you and the 118 freeway is to the right. After crossing the dam, bear to the left past a sign for Rancho Simi Recreation District. The single-track trail then begins a relentless ascent via switchbacks to the rock formations at the top of the canyon. There are several trails that branch off the main one along this route.

At about 0.75 miles, you will come to a signed trail marker and a plastic green fence. Continue straight up the hill. The path gets rocky here and a bit hard to navigate. Watch out for loose boulders. At this point you will find yourself in the middle of the rock formations visible from the trailhead and freeway. This is a good spot to stretch out on one of the smooth boulders and observe the mountain-fringed valley unfolded in front of you. From here, you can follow the path downhill and back to the trailhead or continue up the canyon another steep mile to Rocky Peak Fire Road.

▶ NEARBY ACTIVITIES

The Oak Tree Restaurant, at 1555 Kuehner Drive, south of the 118 freeway, is a good place to fuel up on breakfast or lunch after your hike. It has an all-but-the-kitchen-sink menu—burgers, tuna sandwiches, quesadillas, and pancakes are just a few of the items—and plenty of indoor and outdoor seating. There's even an extensive list of specialty coffee drinks.

PLACERITA CANYON: HERITAGE TRAIL AND BOTANY LOOP

KEY AT-A-GLANCE INFORMATION

LENGTH: 1 mile

CONFIGURATION: Balloon

DIFFICULTY: Easy

SCENERY: Native plants, remnants of ranch life, historic oak tree

EXPOSURE: Sunny

TRAFFIC: Heavy on weekends

TRAIL SURFACE: Paved sidewalk and dirt path

HIKING TIME: 30 minutes

ACCESS: Free; parking lot open 9 a.m.– 5 p.m.; trails open sunrise–sunset

MAPS: Available at Nature Center, open daily 9 a.m.–5 p.m.; USGS Mint Canyon

FACILITIES: Restrooms, water, picnic area; park is open from sunrise to sunset

SPECIAL COMMENTS: Wildfires swept through this park in 2003, wiping out much of the lush vegetation. Disaster struck again in early 2005, when the season's record rainfall caused the stream to overflow and left many of the trails impassable. Evidence of both natural disasters is still evident when you visit the park today, but all trails are open and in good condition.

UTM Trailhead Coordinates for Placerita Canyon: Heritage Trail and Botany Loop

UTM Zone (WGS84) 11S

Easting 365058

Northing 3805075

IN BRIEF

This easy hike highlights Placerita Canyon's natural and cultural history and is great for families with small kids who might find the other trails challenging. It ends at a century-old oak tree, reputed to be the site of one of California's first gold discoveries.

DESCRIPTION

Located at the western end of the San Gabriel Mountains, Placerita is an east–west canyon with a seasonal stream, chaparral- and manzanita-covered hills, and about 12 miles of hiking trails. Now run by the Los Angeles County Department of Parks and Recreation, much of the property once operated as a ranch belonging to a pioneer named Frank Walker and his family. Its picnic area and well-marked trails make it a popular weekend spot for families from the Antelope and Santa Clarita valleys. Be sure to stop in the nature center and pick up a map before setting off on the hike.

Look for the sign for the Botany Trail off the north side of the nature center parking lot. Head right along the shady trail lined with small boulders. You will pass sugar bush, wild rose, toyon (Christmas berry) bushes, black sage, and coast live oak trees. As the trail becomes more exposed, it winds past the entrance to a small hummingbird garden with a bench on the right.

As on other trails within the park, you will immediately see evidence of the 2003 wildfires that swept through this area—groves of charred oak

DIRECTIONS

From the Golden State Freeway (I-5), head north to the Antelope Valley Freeway (CA 14) and take the exit for Placerita Canyon Road. Turn right and drive about 2 miles to Placerita Canyon State Park. Entrance is on the right. There is plenty of parking in upper and lower lots. The Botany Loop begins on the north side of the nature center.

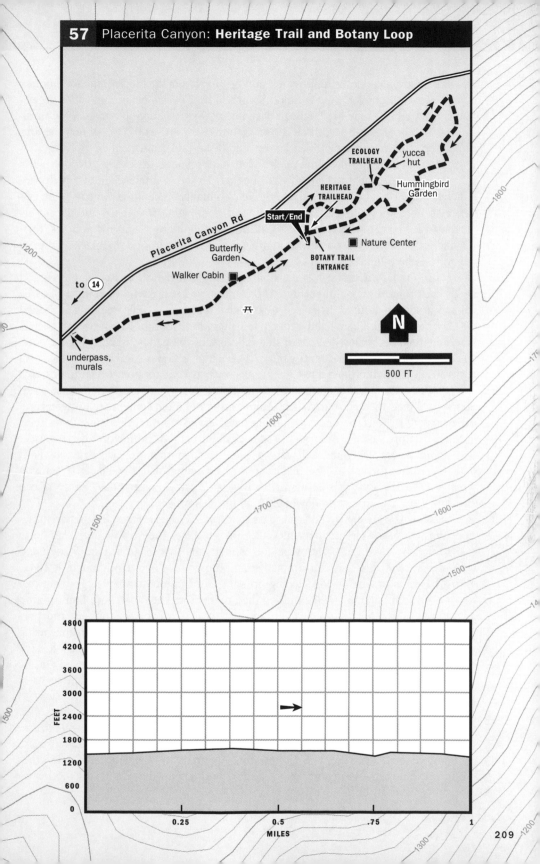

ECOLOGY
TRAILHEAD

yucca
hut

HERITAGE
TRAILHEAD

Hummingbird
Garden

Start/End

Placerita Canyon Rd

Butterfly
Garden

Nature Center

Walker Cabin

BOTANY TRAIL
ENTRANCE

to (14)

underpass,
murals

N

500 FT

trees and manzanita dot the hillside, resembling props from the movie *Haunted Mansion*. According to a posting at the nature center, it will be 15 years before the park's vegetation is restored to its pre-fire levels. In describing the devastation in a memo, the president of the not-for-profit Placerita Canyon Nature Associates said, "to say that the fires turned the park into an ashen wasteland would be an understatement."

After passing a small hut made from native yucca leaves on the right, the Botany Trail ends and the Ecology Trail begins. This is a single-track dirt path that parallels a dry streambed and loops past charred manzanita and oak trees—more evidence of the 2003 wildfires. It is easy (and sad) to imagine how shady and dense this area must have been before the fires. Wildflowers, including California poppies, thistle, and other native plants, were blooming in abundance around the blackened trees when I was here in late May.

At 0.3 miles the trail winds downhill and crosses a narrow creek, then levels and heads back toward the nature center. At 0.5 miles, you will pass a California lilac tree (there's a sign in front of it labeled *Ceanothus*), a coast live oak tree, and a shaded wooden bench. The Botany and Ecology trails end here and the Heritage Trail begins. Cross the road and follow the paved sidewalk toward the park entrance. You will soon pass a turnoff for a small butterfly garden. A rectangular flower garden framed by small rocks sits in the middle, and a few tree trunks serve as benches from which to observe.

Back on the path, continue following the trail as it parallels the entrance road. Soon you'll pass the dark-red Walker Cabin on the right and some rusted wagons and other materials from the ranch's working days. Peek into the cabin's windows for a glimpse of more history. After you pass the cabin, you will want to cross the street and continue following the sidewalk past a bench and more pieces of old farm machinery. On the left is the picnic area and beyond that the Placerita Canyon stream. Then the trail crosses a small bridge and passes sugar bush, an evergreen shrub that bursts with white flower clusters in the spring.

Soon you will come to an underpass that leads to the Heritage Trail's star attraction: the Oak of the Golden Dream. Walk through the tunnel to a white picket fence and a huge old oak tree. A nearby plaque explains the tree's significance—Jose Francisco de Garcia Lopez had a dream while napping under the tree on March 9, 1842. When he woke up, he decided to dig up some wild onions that were growing just north of the old oak tree. While pulling the onions from the fertile soil, Lopez found a handful of shiny gold nuggets caught in their roots. For two years miners, prospectors, Chinese laborers, and outlaws flocked to the canyon to seek their fortunes using panning, sluicing, and dry-washing methods. According to the sign, Lopez's discovery predated James Marshall's famous gold strike at Sutter's Mill by six years. On the way back, stop to look at the colorful murals of frontier life painted on the walls of the underpass. From here, you can retrace your steps to the nature center or head to the picnic area and hang out near the stream for a while.

This isn't as peaceful a hike as the Canyon Trail, thanks to its proximity to Placerita Canyon Road and the nature center's parking lot, but it's an easy way to acquaint yourself with the area's interesting history. I only encountered one other group on this path—two young boys who were dragging their reluctant mother to look at the Oak of the Golden Dream.

▶ NEARBY ACTIVITIES

The indoor-outdoor Placerita Canyon Nature Center includes exhibits on the area's natural history and displays of live animals such as rattlesnakes, turtles, and red-tailed hawks. The center is also the place to pick up info on the park's itinerary of guided hikes: a few recent themes included birding, junior rangers, and wildflowers. It's open daily from 9 a.m. to 5 pm. For more information, call (661) 259-7721.

The Shambala Preserve, a home for rescued exotic cats founded by actress Tippi Hedren, makes for an easy side trip from Placerita Canyon. It's open once a month for safari tours, which are led by Hedren herself. Among its residents are Bengal tigers, African lions, black leopards, and mountain lions. From the Nature Center, return to the Antelope Valley Freeway and head north to Soledad Canyon Road. Drive about 10 miles to the entrance gate on the left. For more information, go to www.shambala.org.

PLACERITA CANYON: WALKER RANCH TRAIL

KEY AT-A-GLANCE INFORMATION

LENGTH: 4.2 miles

CONFIGURATION: Out-and-back

DIFFICULTY: Moderate

SCENERY: Streambed, waterfalls; oak and sycamore groves

EXPOSURE: Mostly sun, some shade

TRAFFIC: Heavy on weekends

TRAIL SURFACE: Dirt and gravel

HIKING TIME: 2 hours

ACCESS: Free; daily, trails open sunrise to sunset

MAPS: Available at Nature Center, open daily 9 a.m.–5 p.m.; USGS Mint Canyon

FACILITIES: Restrooms, water, picnic area

SPECIAL COMMENTS: Wildfires swept through this park in 2003, wiping out much of the lush vegetation. Disaster struck again in early 2005, when the season's record rainfall caused the seasonal stream to overflow and leave many of the trails impassable. Evidence of both natural disasters is still evident when you visit the park today, but all trails are open and in good condition.

UTM Trailhead Coordinates for Placerita Canyon: Walker Ranch Trail

UTM Zone (WGS84) 11S

Easting 365089

Northing 3804984

▶ IN BRIEF

This flat trail near Santa Clarita follows a seasonal stream past wildflowers, coastal sage scrub, and scores of charred trees stripped by the wildfires that swept through the area in 2003.

▶ DESCRIPTION

Located at the western end of the San Gabriel Mountains, Placerita is an east–west canyon with a seasonal stream, chaparral- and manzanita-covered hills, and about 12 miles of hiking trails. Now run by the Los Angeles County Department of Parks and Recreation, much of the property once operated as a ranch belonging a pioneer named Frank Walker and his family. Its picnic area and well-marked trails make it a popular weekend spot for families from the Antelope and Santa Clarita valleys. Be sure to stop in the nature center and pick up a map before setting off on the hike. On my way back from Walker Ranch, I passed several groups of people who quizzed me on where the trail ended and how long it would take to reach the waterfall.

To get to Walker Ranch via the Canyon Trail, cross the stream at the south end of the parking lot and walk up the dirt path to a brown trail sign. The trail is lined with small boulders and parallels the stream to the left. Besides the ranch grounds, this trail also links up with the Waterfall Trail, a 0.5-mile trek to a 25-foot cascade, and Los Pinetos Trail, the park's toughest hike, with a 1,400-foot elevation gain.

▶ DIRECTIONS

From the Golden State Freeway (I-5), head north to the Antelope Valley Freeway (14) and take the exit for Placerita Canyon Road. Turn right and drive about 2 miles to Placerita Canyon State Park. Entrance is on the right. There is plenty of parking in upper and lower lots.

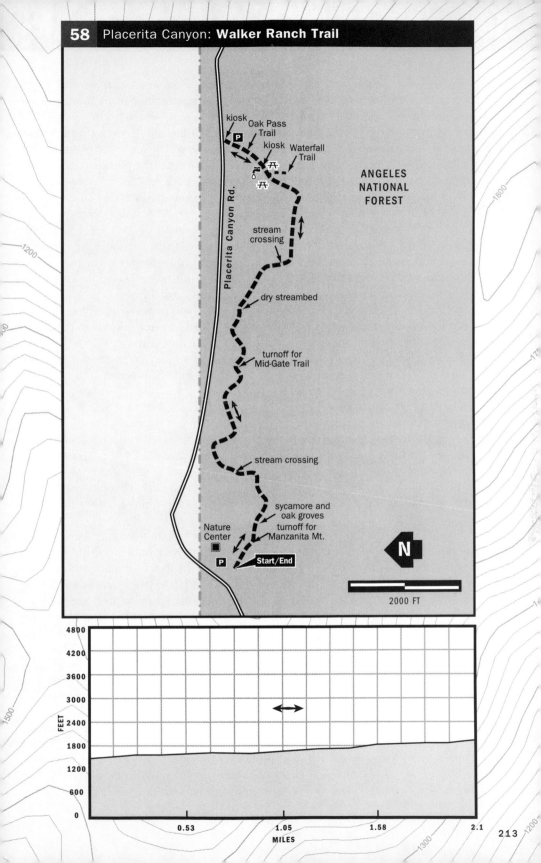

kiosk
Oak Pass Trail
kiosk
Waterfall Trail

ANGELES
NATIONAL
FOREST

Placerita Canyon Rd.

stream crossing

dry streambed

turnoff for
Mid-Gate Trail

stream crossing

sycamore and
oak groves
turnoff for
Manzanita Mt.

Nature Center

Start/End

N

2000 FT

Soon after setting out, you will see evidence of the 2003 wildfires that swept through this area—groves of charred oak trees and manzanita dot the hillside to the left. Morning glories, wild cucumber, buckwheat, sage scrub, and other plants have grown in around the burned trees, but it's still a startling sight. According to a posting at the nature center, it will be 15 years before the park's vegetation is restored to its pre-fire levels. In describing the devastation in a memo, the president of the not-for-profit profit Placerita Canyon Nature Associates wrote, "to say that the fires turned the park into an ashen wasteland would be an understatement."

Shortly after hitting this trail, you will pass a turnoff for Manzanita Mountain Trail, a mile-long uphill trek to a lookout at an elevation of 2,063 feet. Continue straight on the Canyon Trail. After about 0.4 miles, you will pass beneath a grove of coast live oak and sycamore trees that weren't damaged by the fires. The path is also lined with wooden signs that identify some of the park's native plants, including poison oak, hollyleaf, yerba santa, California buckwheat, and chemise.

The gurgling sound of the stream makes a pleasant companion as you meander along this easy stretch of the trail. At the half-mile marker, you will come to the first of several stream crossings and another brown sign that tells you Walker Ranch is another 1.5 miles. Those with small kids or those looking for an easy jaunt may want to turn around here. The path narrows at this point and gets full sun exposure as it continues back and forth along the stream for about 0.5 miles. It was also mildly washed out in some spots from the recent rains when I hiked it in late May. I saw a couple of dogs cooling off in the stream as their owners stood on boulders and watched.

At 0.75 miles, the trail briefly hugs the canyon wall, then turns shady before passing a series of small seasonal waterfalls on the left. Look to the right for more striking views of charred trees. Placerita Canyon is also home to plenty of wild animals, including coyotes, skunks, the ornate shrew, the California pocket mouse, the great horned owl, and 16 kinds of bats—though I only saw butterflies and hummingbirds on my visit.

After crossing a dry streambed, the trail turns away from the stream briefly and is surrounded by shrubs and tall weeds. The path starts to get a little overgrown here, but it's easy to forgive this given the park's recent troubles. At about 1.8 miles, you will pass a rattlesnake warning sign on the left, then a cluster of picnic tables, trash cans, and an open fire pit. After passing beneath a big old California sycamore tree, the full-scale Walker Ranch picnic area comes into view. It's very shady here with a handful of picnic tables, a water fountain, and a trail kiosk with big maps of the park and the entire Angeles National Forest. This was one of the few areas untouched by the 2003 wildfires.

Just past the picnic area you will come to the turnoffs for a couple of other trails—Waterfall and Los Pinetos. It's another 0.6 miles and 300-foot elevation gain to a 25-foot waterfall and 2.3 miles to a fire road with scenic views of the San Fernando Valley.

From this intersection, the Walker Ranch Trail crosses another small streambed, then winds uphill past a grassy meadow on the right and the remains of Walker Ranch—a water cistern and a cluster of old wooden fences. The path ends at a small parking lot off Placerita Canyon Road. From here, you can follow the shady Oak Pass Trail back to the picnic area and retrace your steps back to the nature center.

▶ NEARBY ACTIVITIES

The indoor-outdoor Placerita Canyon Nature Center includes exhibits on the area's natural history and displays of live animals such as rattlesnakes, turtles, and red-tailed hawks. The center is also the place to pick up info on the park's itinerary of guided hikes: a few recent themes included birding, junior rangers, and wildflowers. It's open daily from 9 a.m. to 5 p.m. For more information, call (661) 259-7721.

The Shambala Preserve, a home for rescued exotic cats founded by actress Tippi Hedren, makes for an easy side trip from Placerita Canyon. It's open once a month for safari tours, which are led by Hedren herself. Among its residents are Bengal tigers, African lions, black leopards, and mountain lions. From the Nature Center, return to the Antelope Valley Freeway and head north to the exit for Soledad Canyon Road. Turn right and drive about 10 miles to the entrance gate on the left. For more information, go to www.shambala.org.

TOWSLEY CANYON LOOP TRAIL

KEY AT-A-GLANCE INFORMATION

LENGTH: 2.2 miles

CONFIGURATION: Loop

DIFFICULTY: Strenuous

SCENERY: Rugged mountains, coastal sage scrub, wildflowers (lupine, wild rose, monkey flower)

EXPOSURE: Sunny

TRAFFIC: Light

TRAIL SURFACE: Packed and loose dirt

HIKING TIME: 1.5 hours

ACCESS: Daily, sunrise to sunset; free parking in lower lot; $5 fee at self-pay kiosk in upper lot

MAPS: Posted at kiosk in lower parking lot; also available at ranger office; USGS Oat Mountain

FACILITIES: Picnic area

SPECIAL COMMENTS: There are several good trails within Santa Clarita Woodlands Park. The East and Rice Canyon trails, in the park's southern region, are also worth checking out for their views, diverse vegetation, and wildlife. Portions of these trails were washed out by 2005's record rainfall, but they reopened to hikers in late spring 2005.

UTM Trailhead Coordinates for Towsley Canyon Loop Trail

UTM Zone (WGS84) 11S

Easting 356021

Northing 3802903

IN BRIEF

This hike begins with a gradual ascent past chaparral, coastal sage scrub, and seasonal wildflowers; peaks at a viewpoint with spectacular mountain and valley views; then descends into a canyon past a small creek that still seeps natural oil from the park's days as an oil production facility. An arduous 200-yard uphill detour to a viewpoint with panoramic vistas of the Santa Clarita Valley puts this is in the strenuous category.

DESCRIPTION

Towsley Canyon is part of the 4,000-acre Santa Clarita Woodlands Park, just east of Santa Clarita. Fifteen million years ago this area was covered by deep ocean. Marine organisms built up in thick beds on the ocean floor, gradually covered with sand and gravel as the waters became shallow and receded. Subsequent uplift of the area caused the presence of oil- and gas-bearing fields on the land.

The Tataviam Indians, whose name means "dwellers of the sunny hill," were the first inhabitants of this 4,000-acre park. They used the area's naturally occurring asphalt for medicinal purposes and as a sealant for their baskets, according to a park brochure. Next came Darius Towsley, who arrived here at the end of the Civil War and began skimming and drilling for oil by way of a primitive spring pole method. Towsley eventually sold the property to Chevron (then called Pacific Coast Oil), which used the land for oil production for 120 years. It was later used for horse shows and film production, until the Santa Monica

DIRECTIONS

Follow the Golden State Freeway (I-5) north to the Calgrove exit in Newhall. Turn left (west) and drive back under the freeway to The Old Road and head south 0.5 miles to the entrance for Towsley Canyon and Ed Davis Park on the right.

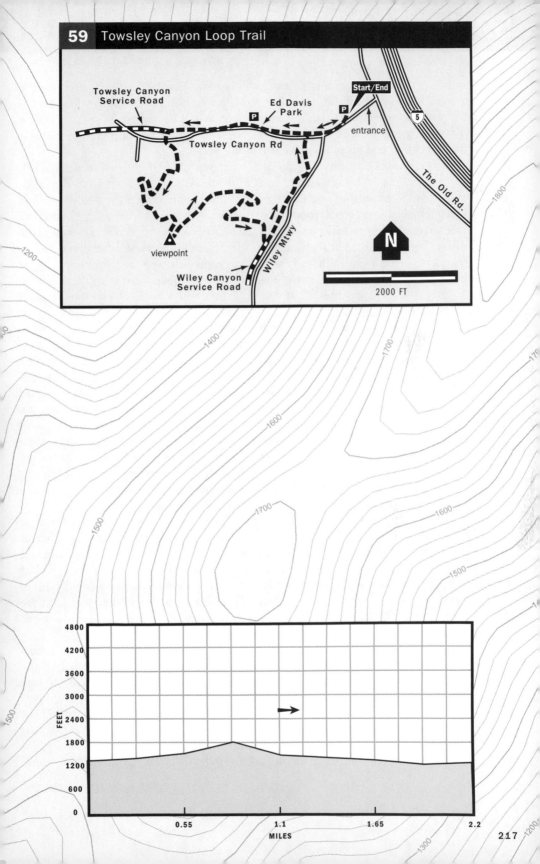

Towsley Canyon
Service Road

Ed Davis
Park

Start/End

entrance

5

Towsley Canyon Rd

The Old Rd.

1800

1200

viewpoint

Wiley Canyon
Service Road

Wiley Mtwy

N

2000 FT

1400

1700

1600

1700

1600

1500

1500

1500

4800

4200

3600

3000

2400

1800

1200

600

0

FEET

0.55   1.1   1.65   2.2

MILES

Mountains Conservancy turned it into public parkland in 1995. It is home to a wide variety of plants and wildlife, including red-tailed hawks, mule deer, coyotes, mountain quails, scrub jay, and California thrashers. When I was here in spring 2005, a park ranger warned me to avoid the trails in the early morning and evening because a mountain lion had taken up residence in the hills.

To get to the Canyon View Loop Trail, park in the first lot off The Old Road, if you want to avoid the $5 fee required to park in the second (westernmost) lot. Turn right (west) from the parking lot and follow the paved road about 0.4 miles past the second parking lot and a small creek. Soon you will come to a bridge and see a large house and picnic area ahead of you to the left. This is the location of the ranger office, as well as the Towsley Canyon Lodge, a facility available for rent for meetings and other events.

The Canyon View trailhead is past a small grassy area to the left of the lodge. If you follow Towsley Canyon Service Road, which continues west, it will take you to the Towsley View Loop trail, a strenuous 5.5-mile hike with an elevation gain of about 1,000 feet.

The single-track Canyon View path immediately begins climbing uphill past tall grass, coastal sage scrub, wildflowers, and skeletal-looking oak trees that were burned in the 2003 wildfires that swept the area. The dirt path continues to switchback up a ridge for the next half-mile or so, giving way to stellar views of chaparral-cloaked mountains on the right and the Santa Clarita Valley on the left. At 0.5 miles you will come to a turnoff for a steep single-track path that leads to a viewpoint. It's a strenuous 200-yard climb to the top, but it's well worth the exertion for the 360-degree mountain and valley views. There is no place to sit, save for a single large rock, but you won't be able to keep yourself from staying a moment to revel in the fantastic views. Santa Clarita is home to many residential developments, and you can see their closely spaced orange rooftops from here, but the dramatic Santa Susana Mountains are by far the dominant scenery from this vantage point.

Once back on the main trail, the path levels and follows the mountain crest briefly, then begins its gradual descent into the canyon. Soon the parking lots and Golden State Freeway come into view, though they are far enough away that you still feel as if you are in the wilderness. At about 1.2 miles, the trail passes under an old canyon oak tree—one of the few patches of shade—then levels again at the bottom of a canyon. To the left you will see the hillside from which you descended. To the right is a fire-road gate that leads to Wiley Canyon Service Road. This takes you to the Towsley View Loop Trail.

To continue on the Canyon View Trail, turn left at the old oak tree and follow the dirt trail north. You will cross what looks like a small stream, identified on the map as a ponded oil seep, then continue past seasonal wildflowers and low-lying sage scrub. I passed a couple of parents with kids in tow on this stretch of the path, perhaps looking for the bubbling tar that still allegedly seeps from the stream. These were the only signs of life I encountered on the entire hike, not counting the dozens of lizards and butterflies that crossed my path.

From the stream crossing, it's an easy half-mile walk back to the first parking lot.

WILDWOOD PARK: LIZARD ROCK TRAIL

▶ IN BRIEF

This hike begins as a straightforward stroll past grassy meadows and spring wildflowers, then gets steep as it climbs to Lizard Rock and panoramic views of the Conejo Valley and the Santa Susana Mountains. It is used by hikers, mountain bikers, joggers, dog walkers, and the occasional equestrian.

▶ DESCRIPTION

Like many of today's southern California trail systems, Wildwood Park was once used by film crews as a substitute for the Old West. Films that shot scenes here include *The Grapes of Wrath, Spartacus,* and *Duel in the Sun.* Most of the cameras stopped rolling in the early 1970s, when bulldozers showed up to make room for tract home developments and a water treatment plant, though the park is still used for commercials and the occasional TV show. Today, the park is a 1,300-acre oasis amid urban sprawl and run by the Conejo Recreation and Park District. You can read about its history at the trailhead kiosk. There is also information about the park's wildlife, which includes mountain lions, rattlesnakes, and rabbits. Located in the city of Thousand Oaks, the park is bordered to the north by Mountclef Ridge,

▶ DIRECTIONS

From the 101 Freeway headed north, take the Moorpark Freeway (CA 23) north about 2.5 miles to Avenida de los Arboles. Turn left and follow the road until it ends at Big Sky Drive. Turn left into the parking lot and look for the trailhead beyond the kiosk.

Alternate Directions: From the Ronald Reagan Freeway (CA 118) in Simi Valley, take the Moorpark Freeway (23) south to Avenida de los Arboles. Turn right and follow it for 2.5 miles until it ends at Big Sky Drive. Turn left into the parking lot and look for the trailhead beyond the kiosk.

ⓘ KEY AT-A-GLANCE INFORMATION

LENGTH: 3 miles

CONFIGURATION: Balloon

DIFFICULTY: Moderate

SCENERY: Grasslands, rocky outcroppings, panoramic views of Simi Valley

EXPOSURE: Sunny

TRAFFIC: Light

TRAIL SURFACE: Dirt and gravel

HIKING TIME: 1 hour

ACCESS: Free, park gate is open daily until sunset

MAPS: At trailhead kiosk; USGS Newbury Park

FACILITIES: None

SPECIAL COMMENTS: There isn't a stitch of shade on this hike, so plan it for early or late in the day, and be sure to bring hats and sunscreen. During the summer months, it can get scorching hot. During the rainy season, the park tends to close after heavy storms. Call the Conejo Recreation and Park District to check conditions: (805) 495-6471.

UTM Trailhead Coordinates for Wildwood Park: Lizard Rock Trail

UTM Zone (WGS84) **11S**

Easting **324699**

Northing **3788164**

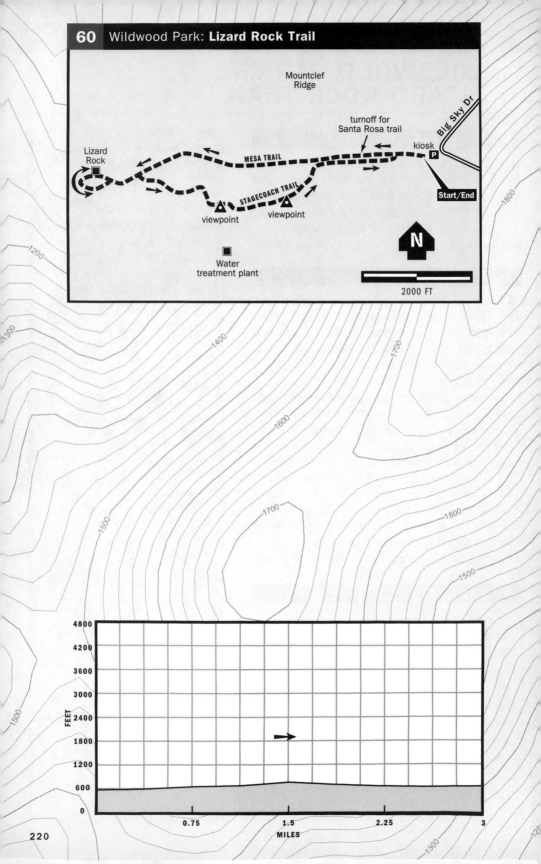

Mountclef
Ridge

turnoff for
Santa Rosa trail

Big Sky Dr

kiosk

P

MESA TRAIL

Lizard
Rock

STAGECOACH TRAIL

Start/End

viewpoint   viewpoint

Water
treatment plant

N

2000 FT

FEET

4800
4200
3600
3000
2400
1800
1200
600
0

0.75   1.5   2.25   3
MILES

The trail is named for this rock formation, which resembles a lizard.

a volcanic-rock outcropping and wildlife corridor that can be seen from the Mesa Trail. The area is also home to Conejo dudleya, a rare and endangered yellow-flower succulent that grows in a 10-mile radius around Mountclef Ridge, and yerba mansa, a white coneflower also known as lizard root, which thrives in moist soil.

Lizard Rock is a nice introduction to the park, but there are other well-marked trails from which to choose. The Santa Rosa Trail is a 5-mile loop that leads to Mountclef Ridge. The Paradise Falls Trail is a family-friendly 3-mile downhill jaunt to a 70-foot waterfall and picnic area. Moonridge Trail skirts a pretty creek and leads to a serene overlook marked by a large tepee. I followed Mesa Trail to Lizard Rock, then looped back on the Stagecoach Bluffs Trail, which is a little more difficult than the Mesa Trail.

To get to Lizard Rock, take the uphill path behind the trailhead kiosk and follow the signs for Mesa/Box Canyon. The first leg of this hike is pancake-flat and heads due west past grassy meadows and prickly pear cactus, with views of your final destination—Lizard Rock—in the distance. At about 0.3 miles, you will pass the turnoff for the Santa Rosa Trail on the left, marked by a small sign. On the day I was here, the trail was closed due to disrepair.

The Mesa Trail continues for about three-quarters of a mile, then meets up again with the Stagecoach Bluffs Trail. To get to Lizard Rock, head straight as the path starts a gradual climb up toward the rock formation that is now looming over the trail. At the top, take a moment to drink in the breathtaking views of valleys and mountains. I saw a handful of hikers along the Mesa and Stagecoach Bluffs Trail, but there wasn't a soul lingering at Lizard Rock.

To get back, follow the trail along the back of the rock formation and take it downhill to the right-hand turnoff for Stagecoach Bluffs. This trail is rockier and will give you more of an uphill/downhill workout (the elevation gain is 100 feet) as you head back to the parking lot. It also has views of the park's southern side, which includes the Hill Canyon water treatment plant and the tepee overlook that marks the end of the Moonridge Trail. After about 2.5 miles, the trail rejoins the Mesa trail. Turn right and retrace your steps back to the parking lot.

▶ NEARBY ACTIVITIES

Wildwood Park isn't part of the Santa Monica Mountains Recreation Area, but its headquarters and visitor center is a short drive away. It's a good place to stock up on maps, check trail conditions, and check out rotating art and wildlife exhibits. Also featured is *Mountains, Movies & Magic,* a film co-produced by the Discovery Channel that highlights the history and resources of the Santa Monica Mountains. To get there from Wildwood Park, turn right from the parking lot onto Avenida de los Arboles and follow about 1 mile to Lynn Road. Turn right on Lynn and drive 2.2 miles to Hillcrest Drive. Turn left and follow 0.7 miles to the visitor center. For more information, call (805) 370-2301.

60 Hikes within 60 MILES

LOS ANGELES
INCLUDING SAN GABRIEL, VENTURA, AND ORANGE COUNTIES

APPENDIXES
& INDEX

APPENDIX A:
OUTDOOR SHOPS

▶ **LOCATION/CITY**

Adventure 16 Outdoor & Travel Outfitters
www.adventure16.com

5425 Reseda Boulevard
Tarzana, CA
(818) 345-4266

11161 Pico Boulevard
Los Angeles, CA
(310) 473-4574

REI
www.rei.com

214 N. Santa Anita Avenue
Arcadia, CA
(626) 447-1062

18605 Devonshire Street
Northridge, CA
(818) 831-5555

1800 Rosecrans Avenue
Manhattan Beach, CA
(310) 727-0728

7777 Edinger Avenue
Huntington Beach, CA

Sport Chalet
www.sportchalet.com

400 S. Baldwin Avenue
Arcadia, CA
(626) 446-8955

201 E. Magnolia Boulevard
Burbank, CA
(818) 558-3500

100 N. La Cienega Boulevard
Los Angeles, CA
(310) 657-3210

920 Foothill Boulevard
La Cañada, CA
(818) 790-9800

16242 Beach Boulevard
Huntington Beach, CA
(714) 848-0988

Sportmart
www.sportmart.com

1919 S. Sepulveda Boulevard
Los Angeles, CA
(310) 312-9600

1900 Empire Avenue
Burbank, CA
(818) 260-0504

21301 Victory Boulevard
Canoga Park, CA
(818) 715-1400

13702 Jamboree Road
Irvine, CA
(714) 669-5150

The Plaza at West Covina
837 Plaza Drive
West Covina, CA
(626) 813-7566

APPENDIX B:
HIKING CLUBS & ORGANIZATIONS

▶ LOCATION/CITY

Altadena Trails
www.altadenatrails.org

La Cañada-Flintridge Trails Council
P.O. Box 852
La Cañada Flintridge, CA 91011
www.lacanadaflintridgetrailscouncil.org

Santa Monica Mountains Conservancy
(310) 589-3200
http://smmc.ca.gov

Sierra Club Los Angeles
3435 Wilshire Boulevard #320
Los Angeles, CA 90010-1904
(213) 387-4287
www.angeles.sierraclub.org

Sierra Club Orange County
P. O. Box 26757
Santa Ana, CA 92799-6757
www.angeles.sierraclub.org/orange

INDEX

INDEX

INDEX

INDEX

INDEX

INDEX

INDEX

NOTES

NOTES

NOTES

NOTES